Paul Einzig follows up his first volume on London's money markets with a volume covering overseas money markets of the five continents. His book is divided into four parts: Part I deals with the money markets of the United States; Part II with those of Canada; Part III with those of the European continent; and Part IV with those of the other four continents.

This is the first attempt to produce such a comprehensive survey of the world's money markets. A number of the markets, especially those of the United States and Canada, are new markets. While they are well known in their respective countries, little has been said about their recent developments in British financial literature.

In addition to these institutional innovations, Dr Einzig also covers a multitude of more conventional money markets which came into existence recently, or comparatively recently, in a number of advanced countries and in some less advanced countries. It is not widely realised that during the last two decades or so quite a number of countries have created money markets. Their description is presented here within the covers of one book.

This material gives an idea about the world-wide trend towards the creation of local facilities ev for borrowers and lenders. I

describes the official attitude towards these new countries and the use made of the new facilities for the application of monetary policy devices, especially open-market operations.

A postscript brings Volume One up to date by dealing with the effects of the new Bank of England regulations on the London money markets.

Paul Einzig was born in Transylvania in 1897 and educated at the Oriental Academy of Budapest and the University of Paris, where he gained his doctor's degree in Political and Economic Sciences. He held various posts on leading London financial newspapers between 1921 and 1956, including long periods as Foreign Editor and Political Correspondent. He is also London Correspondent of the *Commercial and Financial Chronicle*, New York. He is the author of over fifty books, mainly on foreign exchange and related problems.

PARALLEL MONEY MARKETS

PAUL EINZIG

VOLUME TWO
OVERSEAS MARKETS

MACMILLAN
ST MARTIN'S PRESS

First published 1972 by
THE MACMILLAN PRESS LTD
London and Basingstoke
Associated companies in New York Toronto
Dublin Melbourne Johannesburg and Madras

SBN 333 11807 3 (hard cover)

Library of Congress catalog card no. 75-143999

Printed in Great Britain by
R. & R. CLARK LTD
Edinburgh

Contents

Preface

THE collection of the factual material on London's parallel money markets, published in Volume 1 of this book in May 1971, was a comparatively easy task. Sources of information on these markets were within easy reach, and I was able to consult hundreds of people who possessed first-hand experience in their functioning. Had I tried to follow the same procedure of field research to accumulate the material contained in the present volume, dealing as it does with overseas money markets on the five continents, it would have been the task of a lifetime and would have required the resources of some well-endowed research organisation.

Fortunately I was able to consult, without leaving London, a large number of experts with first-hand experience in the operation of the overseas markets described in this book. For, thanks to the presence of a large number of foreign bank branches and brokers specialising in foreign business is London, there are now in the City a great many practical experts who had many years' experience in their respective local money markets overseas before settling here. Most of them have retained close contact with the money markets of their countries and therefore have been able to supply me with up-to-date information about these markets. I am greatly indebted to them, and to many British bankers and brokers with contacts abroad, for their invaluable assistance.

I also owe a debt of gratitude to a number of bankers and Central Bankers abroad with whom I carried on correspondence on the subject of their respective money markets. In addition to answering my inquiries, many of them sent me up-to-date publications describing those markets. Even though the number of my sources of information on any one of the overseas markets was necessarily much smaller than the number of those who had helped me with material on the London market, between them they provided me with material that gave me a fair idea about each market.

For background information I had to rely on the published literature which was plentiful on some markets but scant on some others. Annual reports, quarterly or monthly bulletins and other publications by Central Banks and other banks and brokers were particularly helpful. In the Bibliography I quote a selection of private publications in addition to official material.

I am greatly indebted to all these sources of information. Admittedly, the chapters relating to the overseas money markets are not as detailed as the material in Volume 1 on London. This could not be helped. To meet criticism on the ground that I ought to have spent enough time to be able to produce equally detailed information on the overseas markets, I should like to point out that there is urgent need for a single volume which covers a wide range of money markets situated all over the world. Rightly or wrongly I considered it more important to produce the relatively easily accessible material without delay than to defer the publication of this book for the sake of being able to collect less easily accessible additional material.

I trust to be able to amplify my material on overseas markets, if and when I should have an opportunity to revise this book for a new edition. Alternatively, it might inspire others who had sufficient time and opportunity to investigate on the spot the various overseas markets and to bring my information up to date, at the same time as enlarging more thoroughly on its broader implications.

In order to avoid having to delay the publication of this book I had to deal summarily with some of the financial centres and had to omit some which are on the borderline of becoming markets. There is therefore ample scope for further research, especially as all markets are subject to frequent structural changes as well as changes in practices.

While the detailed description of London's new markets breaks much new ground, much of the material in the present volume has been dealt with in monographs, in books on comparative banking and in articles. My main task, in addition to bringing such material up to date, is to produce it in an easily accessible form within the covers of the same book. I hope that students of money and banking as well as practical bankers and businessmen concerned with short-term credits will find it useful for reference purposes.

120 CLIFFORD'S INN,   P. E.
   LONDON, E.C.4
     July, 1971.

CHAPTER ONE

Introduction

(1) MARKETS OF THE FIVE CONTINENTS

VOLUME I of this book dealt in detail with the new money markets that emerged in London during the last decade or two – the inter-bank deposit market, the markets in sterling and dollar Certificates of Deposit, the markets in Local Authorities and finance house deposits, the Euro-dollar market and other Euro-currency markets, the market in inter-company deposits and the market in dollar commercial paper. To complete the picture it also devoted, to begin with, brief chapters to the traditional markets of London.

The task of the present volume is to cover money markets of overseas financial centres. As far as the United States and Canada are concerned, the same plan is applied as in respect of the London markets – stress is laid on the new parallel markets but the traditional markets are also covered briefly. In respect of the Western European markets and the markets in Asia, Africa and Australia, however, the chapters covering them are concerned mainly if not exclusively with the traditional markets, for the simple reason that outside London and North America there are very few markets corresponding to our new parallel markets.

(2) MANY RECENTLY CREATED 'TRADITIONAL' MARKETS

Notwithstanding this, I deemed it necessary to include in this book also financial centres which possess traditional markets only. Most of them are of relatively recent origin. On the face of it it may sound a contradiction in terms to describe a recently created market as 'traditional'. What is meant is not that it has traditions in the country concerned but that the system or device recently applied in that country has long traditions in London or in some other old-established money market. They are hardly known abroad, and ought to be known better.

Another reason why it was necessary to include such markets in a book dealing with parallel money markets is that because quite possibly, indeed in some instances probably, these traditional markets will prepare the way for the creation of parallel money markets in the course of time.

While at the present stage none of these markets are as sophisticated as the British, American and Canadian markets, their progress since the Second World War, and especially during the 'sixties, has been truly remarkable. It justifies the assumption that the development of markets corresponding to at least some of our parallel markets in the recently created money markets is only a question of time. Indeed some of them actually already possess some parallel markets, such as the well-developed inter-company deposit markets in Australia and South Africa, dealing in deposits in terms of their local currencies, the Asian dollar market in Singapore and the beginnings of other markets in deposits in other countries, on lines similar to those of the Euro-currency markets which already exist in many financial centres, albeit on a much smaller scale than in London.

A survey of the overseas money markets, traditional or new, discloses remarkable world-wide progress achieved within a short time in this sphere. Although London still claims to hold the lead in some money markets, New York has more or less caught up with it in many respects and has even cut ahead of London in some respects. The progress of the money markets in Toronto and Montreal within a brief space of time was truly spectacular. On the other hand, having regard to the increased importance of the Deutschemark, the French franc, the Swiss franc and the yen, the progress of the German, French, Swiss and Japanese money markets has not been too impressive. Nevertheless the first two have made appreciable headway in recent years, and the possibility of escalation is distinctly there.

In a number of financial centres with less prominent currencies, local call money markets have developed or are beginning to develop, and the governments concerned aim at encouraging them by issuing Treasury bills, and by applying other devices. Most of them have been unable so far to create a market in commercial bills, because banks prefer to keep them in their own portfolios or, if necessary, to re-discount them with the Central Bank rather than sell them to other banks. But there has been unquestionably an all-round progress in the evolution of money markets in most economically advanced countries.

(3) END OF LONDON'S MONOPOLY

As a result, London no longer possesses anything like its former extent of monopoly in money market facilities. Even so, its money market mechanism has remained in some respects superior to all other money markets. It is easily the most important market in foreign currency deposits. Considering the short-sighted hostility of the Labour Government towards the City during 1964–1970, and the equally short-sighted policy of Mr Heath's Conservative Government, eager to satisfy the French Government's demand to discontinue London's role as an international financial centre, it is indeed remarkable that the London money market has held its ground to the extent to which it has. The City still provides a selection of excellent short-term lending and borrowing facilities, some of which few, if any, other financial centres are able to equal. It has proved its adaptability to ever-changing requirements, and in spheres where rival money markets took the initiative – for example in respect of the issue of Certificates of Deposits – it followed the lead in due course. The fact that the number of foreign bank branches and affiliates, and that of international banks with British participation, greatly increased during the 'sixties and early 'seventies speaks for itself.

However it would be idle to deny that a large number of foreign countries no longer depend on London's money market facilities to the same extent as they did until recently. The universal progress in advanced countries towards the creation of new money markets has weakened London's monopoly, and also the London–New York duopoly that existed in more recent times.

(4) EFFECT OF HIGH INTEREST RATES

The improvement of the money market facilities of many other financial centres has been due to the coincidence of several circumstances.

Ever since the war London has been handicapped by frequently recurrent sterling crises and by the need for defending sterling with the aid of exchange control and credit control measures, and it had abnormally high interest rates before most other centres. This has provided opportunities for foreign financial centres to develop and expand their own money markets. The establishment of many foreign branches in London and of many British branches abroad enabled local banks of foreign centres to acquire the knowhow through the experience of their London staffs in money market operations, and through their direct contact with British bankers in their own centres.

The sharp increase in interest rates all over the world, especially during the late 'sixties, made it necessary and advantageous everywhere to provide additional local facilities for lucrative employment of liquid resources. Many firms and individuals have come to be induced by high interest rates to employ more profitably their reserves which had been left to lie more or less idle and unproductive during the prolonged period of cheap or relatively cheap money. From the point of view of borrowers, the high interest rates made it more important to look round in quest of cheaper facilities nearer home than London.

Above all, the imposition of credit restrictions in most countries made it imperative for borrowers and lenders alike to resort to devices by which lawfully to circumvent the credit ceilings. Hence the instant popularity of the newly introduced unconventional devices for short-term credits.

It has become more important for banks, both in their capacity of holders of deposits and of lenders, to have at their disposal improved facilities for adjusting their liquidity positions without depending exclusively or excessively on their Central Banks or on foreign credits. The development of a wider variety of lending and borrowing facilities has enabled banks and non-banking institutional investors of short-term funds to diversify their risks. It has enabled both borrowers and lenders of such funds to gain access to a wider variety of sources of funds and of outlets for funds.

(5) OFFICIAL ENCOURAGEMENT OF MONEY MARKETS

The monetary authorities in most countries – with some notable exceptions such as Switzerland – came to the conclusion during the 'fifties or 'sixties that it was to their advantage to encourage the development of local money markets. Their aim was partly to facilitate the satisfaction of the governments' requirements of short-term funds and partly to create markets in which Central Banks could pursue their monetary policies by means of open market operations instead of depending on Bank rate changes and other conventional devices to regulate the volume of credit. Open market operations were considered for a long time an essentially

Anglo-Saxon device, so much so that in France and other countries which have come to adopt them the English term is used wherever reference is made to official intervention in the markets for the purpose of regulating the volume of credit.

(6) PROGRESS NOT CONFINED TO ADVANCED COUNTRIES

The world-wide trend towards the emergence and expansion of new money markets has not been confined to financially advanced countries. Even in some developing countries such as India there have been signs of progress towards the expansion of the modern money market that co-exists with the primitive indigenous money market of the bazaars. A number of additional countries have created markets corresponding in character, if not in size, to the traditional markets in advanced countries. Although these markets cannot be classed as being 'parallel' in the sense in which that term has come to be applied in London, New York and one or two other advanced countries, their description in the present volume is justified, because from the point of view of providing an alternative to lending or borrowing in money markets of advanced countries they do constitute parallel markets. In any case, as already observed, in some countries at any rate the progress of traditional markets is likely to be followed in due course by the creation of parallel markets.

All this is in accordance with the secular trend of progress towards the achievement of an increasingly efficient and more sophisticated monetary mechanism. There has also been a tendency lately towards breaking down the rigidity of the banking system by the operation of money markets that induce banks to become more adaptable in meeting the requirements of their depositors and their borrowers. They themselves have stood to benefit in many ways by a higher degree of flexibility and by the establishment of closer relationships in dealing with each other. For one thing, it has greatly facilitated the adjustment of their liquidity positions.

(7) EFFECT OF INCREASE IN CONFIDENCE

Having regard to the experience of the last decade or two, it seems perplexing in retrospect that it should have taken so long for banks and other dealers in short-term credits in most overseas countries to learn from the practices of the London market. Why was London allowed to retain for so long its quasi-monopolistic position as a money market? It had attracted foreign funds not only because sterling had inspired confidence abroad – in fact, more often than not short-term investments in London were covered against exchange risk by means of swap transactions – but also because for a long time no other market was able to provide comparable facilities. Possibly one of its advantages was that, thanks to its large turnover, it was able to operate on a narrow profit margin, while other financial centres, having been accustomed to work with wider profit margins, did not deem it worth while to offer rival facilities at the cost of acquiring the specialised skill needed for operating a money market success-fully.

Another reason was the confidence inspired by the London banks and discount houses. The complete absence of any bank failures in Britain during the troubled inter-war period – even during the world-wide banking crises of the early 'thirties – and for a long time after the Second World War induced many possessors of liquid capital to employ at least part of their re-sources in the London market, even during periods when sterling was under a cloud, if only in order to spread their risk. Although the dollar, and later the Deutschemark and other currencies, inspired more confidence than sterling during most of the period after the war, British banks continued to inspire the high degree of confidence that is one of the basic conditions of the existence and successful operation of a money market.

But the prolonged absence of major banking crises in many other countries since the war, due largely to the absence of major slumps and of prolonged business depressions that are liable to inflict crippling losses on banks through a series of business failures, has come to inspire increasing confidence in many over-seas banks. First-class banks in many countries enjoy now the same degree of confidence as first-class British banks have enjoyed for a long time. The monopoly of London, and the subsequent London–New York duopoly came to an end largely because of the confidence inspired by many leading banks on the five continents.

(8) CHANGE IN OFFICIAL ATTITUDE

As a result it has become possible in a number of centres to develop inter-bank markets in unsecured credits. Finance Ministries came to realise the advantages of issuing short-term paper and Central Banks made arrangements to enable banks and other holders to re-sell them in secondary markets or use them as collateral for short-term credits, whether from Central Banks or from other banks. The use of commercial bills has also been encouraged, but in this sphere progress has been remarkably slow in most centres. There are still very few good markets in commercial bills and London is still the best amongst them, in spite of the decline in the use of sterling acceptances.

It is only comparatively recently that Central Banks in a number of countries came to realise the advantages of possessing local money markets. Until the 'fifties little or nothing was done in official quarters of most countries to encourage and actively assist the emergence and growth of such markets. But now it is the official policy in many countries to assist in their creation and expansion.

(9) COMPENSATORY ADVANTAGES ENTAILED BY LONDON'S LOSS

It would be idle to deny that from a British point of view the cessation of the quasi-monopolistic position of London's money market constitutes a loss. But the change is not without its compensatory advantages. The existence of money markets in foreign centres gives rise to additional opportunities for arbitrage from which London, being still the best foreign exchange market and Euro-dollar market, stands to benefit greatly. Of course the new money market facilities in the majority of centres have not yet become sufficiently developed to provide much opportunity for international arbitrage. But the relative inadequacy of their facilities tends to direct attention to the superiority of London's facilities.

To the extent to which the development of rival money markets tends to divert short-term funds from London, it satisfies the wishes of those in Britain and in other countries who consider London's role as an international monetary centre disadvantageous because of the de-stabilising effect of capital movements.

This is not the place to argue about the merits or demerits of the arguments put forward by this school of thought. I merely want to point out that, for better or for worse, the emergence and expansion of money markets in an increasing number of countries might *tend* to reduce London's role as an international monetary centrè. But the reduction operates in a relative sense only. For, owing to a variety of other considerations, the London banking centre has become increasingly international, so that the development of money markets abroad has not reversed or halted but merely slowed down to some extent the overall progress of London's money market.

(10) LIMITATIONS OF OUR SCOPE

As pointed out in the Preface, this volume does not aim at dealing in great detail with all money markets that are in existence at the time of writing, for it would be a task well beyond the capacity of a single human being to collect reasonably up-to-date information about more than a limited number of markets. In any case, in a great many instances it is a matter of degree whether the volume of transactions in short-term credits at rates fluctuating according to changes in supply-demand relationship is sufficiently large, and dealings are sufficiently systematic, to come within the definition of a money market. Almost invariably markets originate through a limited number of transactions, and it is very much a matter of opinion at what stage the turnover becomes sufficiently extensive to justify the application of the term 'market'.

In allocating the space of this volume I devoted a great deal of attention to the money markets in New York and in Canada, because they are by far the most highly developed money markets besides London. Frankfurt and Paris are next in importance to Canada, not necessarily from the point of view of their turnover – which does not always surpass the turnover of the Canadian markets fed from the United States on a large scale – but from the point of view of the relatively advanced stage of evolution attained by their money market mechanism. They are described in several chapters. Amsterdam, Zurich, Brussels, Luxembourg, Milan and Vienna are dealt with in one chapter each. Dealing with centres outside Europe and North America – the latter includes the Nassau money market – the book contains chapters on India, Singapore, Hong Kong, Tokyo, Australia, New Zealand, South

Africa and Rhodesia. There are some other minor markets or near-markets, but the above selection gives a reasonable all-round picture of the world's money markets at their various stages of evolution.

(11) MATERIAL FOR FURTHER RESEARCH

This volume aims at providing both information for practical purposes and raw material for those who want to investigate broader aspects of the way in which money markets are organised and operated. Some of the information is available, at any rate for a more limited number of markets and in a less detailed form, in books on comparative banking, such as those by J. S. G. Wilson, R. S. Sayers, and others. But that literature treats money markets as an aspect of banking, while my aim is to deal exclusively with money markets and to treat them as the focus of my study. Differences between the various markets described here are as instructive from a broader point of view as the many points of similarity that exist between them.

To forestall criticism that this book is repetitive, because it re-states in a number of chapters many points in quite identical terms, I must point out that such repetitions are necessary because many readers are likely to use the book for reference purposes. They might only want to read the chapter or chapters relating to the markets in which they have a special interest. To meet such limited requirements I arrived at producing independent and largely self-supporting essays on each market, ensuring the continuity of the book by making cross-references to practices in other markets. By pursuing this plan I could not avoid being repetitive, and much of the description and comment was bound to overlap. In any case, even those who read the book from cover to cover for the sake of gaining an overall picture, stand to benefit by comparisons between the markets.

PART I

MONEY MARKETS OF THE UNITED STATES

CHAPTER TWO

New York *v.* London

(1) NEW YORK'S POSITION IN THE U.S.

WHEN we talk about the New York money market what we really
have in mind is the market of the whole of the United States. This
is not a matter to be taken for granted. For while London is the
sole money market of the United Kingdom, New York is by no
means the only money market in the United States, even though
it is by far the most important money market, towering well above
the other American money centres. Nevertheless when we discuss
the American money market in general it simplifies matters if we
talk about the New York market, just as it simplifies matters if we
talk about the Zurich market when we discuss the Swiss money
market, even though Switzerland has important money centres
also in Basle and in Geneva.

In both countries the de-centralisation of the money market is
due to some extent to their political system of Federation, though
as far as the United States is concerned discrepancies between
business hours in the three time zones and the nature of the
Federal Reserve System also contributed towards the development of secondary monetary centres with markets of their own.
Indeed, given the political and geographical circumstances of the
United States, and the jealousy with which member States of the
Federation seek to safeguard their high degrees of autonomy,
strictly defined and limited as it is by the Constitution, the extent
to which the New York money market has achieved and retained
its supremacy over the other money markets is indeed remarkable.

(2) SUPREMACY OF THE DOLLAR

What was perhaps even more remarkable was the slow pace of the
evolution of the New York money market long after the dollar
succeeded in achieving supremacy over sterling as a result of the
First World War and its economic and financial consequences.
Early in 1915 sterling came to be overshadowed by the dollar and,

apart from some relatively brief intervals in the 'thirties when the dollar came under a cloud because of major crises, it remained superior to sterling right until 1971. Notwithstanding this, during the inter-war period the efforts made by the New York money market to capture the lead from Lombard Street met only with partial success.

Admittedly, during the boom of the 'twenties the New York market in loans to Wall Street overshadowed in importance any London market in short-term credits. But its supremacy came to an abrupt end in 1929 as a result of the Wall Street slump and the ensuing long depression. The New York market in bank accept-ances made good progress in the 'twenties, because New York banks were competing fiercely for customers in Central Europe and elsewhere. But the setback in the bill markets resulting from the series of currency and banking crises affected New York to a higher degree than London, because the latter retained its accept-ance business with Sterling Area countries, and because there were no bank failures in Britain while in the United States banks closed down by the thousand.

(3) SLOW DEVELOPMENT OF BILL MARKET

Treasury bills were not very prominent in New York before the war and the market in them was not so good as that of the British Treasury bills in London. In any case the mechanism of Lombard Street was superior to the rival mechanism of Wall Street. After the War the New York market in Treasury Bills made consider-able progress and in due course surpassed the London market. But it took longer for the market in dollar bank acceptances to get into their stride after the setback of the early 'thirties.

Both money markets branched out in new lines in addition to the conventional lines and New York developed and greatly expanded its commercial paper market and its market in Federal Funds. Later it also created a big market in Certificates of De-posits. On its part, London increased its international importance through the development of a gigantic market in Euro-dollars and also smaller markets in other Euro-currencies. Later the London market in inter-bank deposits came into being. London also re-vived its market in fine trade bills which eclipsed in the inter-war period, and it managed to emulate the United States in creating markets in dollar CDs and later also in sterling CDs. Both centres have markets in various forms of credits to Local Authorities and to instalment selling finance companies. The experiment in London to emulate the New York market in commercial paper made an unimpressive start.

(4) FIGHT FOR SUPREMACY WITH LONDON

Considering the difficulties of Britain and of sterling, London's success in maintaining a money market comparable in importance with the New York money market was indeed remarkable. Had it not been for the balance of payment difficulties of the United States during the second half of the 'sixties and in the early 'seventies, the relative importance of the London money market would have declined very considerably below that of the New York money market, in spite of the longer experience of the former. As it is, they may be said to be running more or less neck-and-neck in the race. While in some markets New York easily surpasses London in importance, this is often offset, and from time to time more than offset, by the overwhelming importance of the London Euro-dollar market. The significance of London's victory in this sphere came to be mitigated, however, towards the end of the 'sixties when New York's influence in that market increased to such an extent that it became for some time virtually a branch of the New York money market.

One of the reasons why New York has not been able to benefit fully from its prolonged advantage over London was the insistence of American banks on the maintenance of excessive minimum balances on foreign banks' accounts with them. As such balances bear no interest the cost of their maintenance deters many small and medium-sized banks from opening accounts in New York for the sake of operating in its parallel money markets. Differentials in their favour would have to be fairly wide to make it worth their while to keep large non-interest bearing current account balances in New York.

(5) SUPERIOR CAPITAL RESOURCES

The conquest for supremacy between the London and New York financial centres was not confined to the sphere of the domestic market in short-term credits. The superior financial resources of the United States ensured a decisive lead for New York in the sphere of long-term capital lending, but in the 'sixties London became a very important Euro-bond market, when New York came to be handicapped by exchange control and by a series of dollar scares. These aspects of the financial centres are, however, outside the scope of this book, apart from the extent to which they necessitated the maintenance of balances in both centres, the financing of Euro-bonds in parallel money markets and the opening of branches and affiliates by foreign banks. Once these banks are here, and even once foreign banks have opened accounts in London for the sake of facilitating foreign exchange operations in the London market, opportunity and incentive are provided for operating also in the parallel money markets. Likewise the overwhelming international importance of the dollar has made it necessary for many thousands of non-resident banks and other institutions to maintain balances in New York, and their existence provides opportunity and incentive for their owners to take an active interest in the parallel money markets of New York for the sake of taking advantage of the higher yields they offer.

CHAPTER THREE

Federal Funds

(1) THE MOST IMPORTANT MONEY MARKET

THE market in Federal Funds – that is, in sight deposits with Federal Reserve Banks – is the most important and the most interesting money market in the United States as far as loans overnight are concerned. The advantage for American banks of holding Federal Funds compared with holding balances or deposits with other American banks lies only to a ngeligible extent in the fact that deposits with Federal Reserve Banks, which have the privilege to issue notes and the means to create credit, are a 100 per cent safe. After all, in spite of the memories of major bank failures in the United States during the world crises of the 'thirties, the leading American banks are trusted and trust each other implicitly.

A much more important reason why it is an advantage to hold liquid assets in Federal Funds is that they can be converted into cash without any delay. Of course ordinary current account balances and sight deposits can be withdrawn at any time in cash. But it would be cumbersome and risky for banks and business firms to make large payments to each other in that primitive form instead of making them in the form of cheques. Moreover banks are under statutory obligation to report to the Revenue Authorities any large withdrawals of notes. Yet since cheques drawn on commercial banks or on any banks other than Federal Reserve Banks represent clearing house funds, they have to go through the process of clearing before their recipients can actually obtain payment. For payments within New York City this entails a delay of one day, but for payments to other financial centres of the United States it may take two days and even longer.

(2) MAINTAINING RESERVE RATIO

For this reason, only Federal Funds are suitable for purposes for which immediate cash payment is required. What is even more important, National Banks – member banks of the Federal Reserve System – have to comply with the statutory reserve requirements which compel them to keep a certain officially fixed percentage of the amount of their sight and short-term liabilities in cash or in deposits with the Federal Reserve Bank. At the time of writing that reserve ratio is $17\frac{1}{2}$ per cent for sight liabilities and 5 per cent for time deposits and for commercial paper issues.

The original purpose of the market in Federal Funds – which came into being soon after the creation of the Federal Reserve System in the early 'twenties – was to facilitate the task of member banks to maintain the proportion of their reserves in the close vicinity of the minimum reserve ratio, which in practice means holding reserves a shade above the prescribed figure. The development of the market in Federal Funds enabled banks with excess reserves to sell the surplus to banks with inadequate reserves, and it enabled banks with a deficiency of reserves to meet the deficiency by buying Federal Funds from banks with an excess reserve. In practice sellers of Federal Funds are not always necessarily banks with excess reserves and purchasers are not always necessarily banks with reserve deficiencies. In given circumstances banks may deliberately acquire or increase excess reserves, or they incur an increase of deficiencies in the hope of being able to reverse their positions profitably before the end of the 'reserve period' when their average reserve ratio is reckoned.

(3) EFFECT OF WALL STREET SLUMP

In the early 'twenties New York was virtually the only market in Federal Funds. Within a few years markets came to develop in several other important cities. By the second half of the 'twenties there were markets in the centres of all Federal Reserve districts and in other big cities. Inter-communication between the regional markets and New York, and also between each other, has now developed sufficiently to create a truly nation-wide market with New York as its main centre and with several important local centres serving the different regions.

The market in Federal Funds had a checkered career. During the advanced phase of the Wall Street boom in the 'twenties the Federal Funds market became temporarily overshadowed by the spectacular expansion of the market in call money loaned to brokers. Most banks adopted the practice of adjusting their reserve positions mainly by means of increasing or reducing their call money loans to Wall Street, as these were more profitable than lending Federal Funds. But immediately after the great slump of 1929 the market in Federal Funds came into its own again, partly because the volume of loans to brokers fell sharply to a fraction of its pre-slump maximum, and partly because money was flowing back to New York from every direction, in order to meet demands by brokers and banks for additional margins on depreciating stocks of their clients that had been financed with borrowed money.

Throughout the ensuing long depression, Federal Funds were in ample supply, and demand was slack, so that their rate declined to $\frac{1}{4}$ per cent and for a time even to $\frac{1}{2}$ per cent. There was a revival of demand in the late 'thirties. During the Second World War the turnover in the Federal Funds market was fairly high, mainly in connection with transactions in Government securities. There was also an increasing participation in the market by country banks, helped by the decline in the relative importance of the markets in acceptances and in commercial paper. The wartime expansion in the volume of Federal Funds transactions connected with transactions in Government securities continued for some time.

(4) RIVAL MONEY MARKETS

In the early 'sixties a big market developed in Certificates of Deposits described in Chapter 7 – which became to some extent a rival to the Federal Funds market. Another market which was, in a sense, also a rival, but was at the same time complementary to the Federal Funds market, was the highly expanded Euro-dollar market in London and other centres, providing alternative opprotunities for banks to equalise their excesses and deficiencies in Federal Funds. On the other hand, the relative importance of the reserve equalising functions of the markets in call money to brokers, acceptances and commercial paper, and even of Treasury bills, declined.

In the late 'sixties the importance of the Federal Funds market's function of helping banks handicapped by credit restrictions to meet the credit requirements of their customers increased considerably. Even so the basic function of the market remained to assist banks in their task of complying with reserve requirements.

(5) FEDERAL FUNDS PREFERABLE TO CASH

In recent years banks were authorised to include their holdings of cash in their vaults for the purpose of reckoning their reserve ratio. But it is not convenient for banks to keep in their vaults much more cash than the amounts they expect to need for meeting current withdrawals in the form of cash. In modern times most withdrawals are not effected in actual notes. Banks therefore keep the bulk of their cash reserves in the form of deposits with the Federal Reserve Banks of their district. But since no interest is allowed on such deposits, they aim at keeping no more than is considered necessary for complying with reserve requirements. They prefer to hold secondary liquid reserves in the form of various market papers yielding the highest interest compatible with the required degree of liquidity and with considerations of security.

Any excess of deposits with Federal Reserve Banks over reserve requirements entails unnecessary loss of interest. On the other hand, if a bank's reserve ratio falls short of the legal minimum it becomes subject to penalising provisions under Regulation A. It is therefore to the banks' advantage to keep their reserves very slightly above the prescribed minimum. In actual practice the average reserve ratio of big commercial banks seldom exceeds 18 per cent, which means that their excess is a mere $\frac{1}{2}$ per cent or less over legal requirements.

In this respect practice differed quite appreciably until recently between banks in New York and other Eastern districts on the one hand, and those further west on the other. The latter remained open for one or two hours after the closing of the New York market, and during those hours they found it at times difficult to meet large unexpected requirements. They deemed it expedient therefore to carry excess reserves in order to avoid being caught short, especially at the end of reserve periods. But in more recent years the Federal Funds markets – other than New York – in Chicago, San Francisco and Los Angeles, and also in St Louis, New Orleans, Kansas City, Dallas, Boston and Philadelphia, expanded to such an extent that banks west of the New York time zone are now able to depend on meeting their requirements even while New York is closed.

(6) PROBLEMS OF MAINTAINING RESERVE RATIO

The ratio of reserves to sight liabilities is reckoned on the basis of the closing figures on each day during the reserve reckoning period which is subject to changes. It is fixed at the time of writing at a fortnight ending at closing time on alternate Wednesdays. Every day during that period the banks have to report their figures to their Federal Reserve Bank, but it does not matter if their reserve ratios decline on particular days below the minimum, so long as their increase above the minimum on other days offsets the temporary deficiencies, ensuring that the average over the entire period is not under the statutory minimum.

One of the differences between the British system and the American system is that under the former the only figures that matter are those at closing time of the day for which the returns are submitted to the Bank of England, while under the American system it is the average of closing figures over the entire reserve period that counts. Another difference is that under the British system the minimum ratio is, at the time of writing, merely conventional and not statutory. It is therefore not observed as rigidly as the minimum reserve ratio in the United States. As we saw in Chapter 2, Volume I, the Bank seldom deemed it necessary to take a serious view of occasional moderate and temporary declines below the conventional ratio, though it does indicate its disapproval it if occurs too frequently or if it is prolonged, or if its extent is substantial. It is prepared to accept a reasonable explanation of departures from the self-imposed rule and to let off 'offenders' with a warning. On the other hand, member banks of the Federal Reserve system are penalised by their Federal Reserve Bank for deficiency of their reserves if it exceeds the permitted 2 per cent which can be carried forward to the next reserve period, provided that it is offset during that period.

This difference in which the letter and spirit of the rules on the reserve requirements is applied is largely due to the basic difference between the two banking systems. Owing to the very large number of banks in the United States it would be difficult to operate the quasi-voluntary system of self-restraint that is working quite satisfactorily in Britain where the number of banks is small and where the Central Bank's wish is regarded as a command.

(7) INCALCULABLE RESERVE REQUIREMENTS

One of the most important and most difficult tasks of American banks is to perform perpetual tightrope walking, maintaining a strict balance between excess and deficiency of reserves. This is difficult because the banks are seldom in a position to know in advance the exact or even approximate amounts of the inflow and outflow of funds which are liable to affect their reserves during the reckoning period. They have to base their decisions whether to buy or sell Federal Funds not only on the actual amount of their relevant assets and liabilities at any given moment – which itself is no simple matter owing to the complexity of bank transactions and to the ever-changing situation – but also on estimates of likely changes in those figures before the end of the reserve period. While some items of the inflow and outflow, such as the banks' maturing claims and liabilities, are known in advance, and others may be estimated on the basis of the banks' knowledge of the more or less regularly recurrent transactions of their clients, such as tax payments or dividend payments, a large proportion of the movements of funds is quite unpredictable.

Banks are therefore usually unable to calculate in advance the approximate extent of their future gains and losses of deposits. Their estimates can only be well-informed guesses based on past experience which need not necessarily repeat itself. Admittedly, large commercial banks with a great many small accounts may rely to some extent on the operation of the law of averages – or, as it is sometimes called, the law of big figures – for in ordinary circumstances the multitude of small withdrawals and of new small deposits tend to offset each other to a fairly high degree.

(8) UNEXPECTED LOSSES OF DEPOSITS

But large banks have also a number of big deposits belonging to correspondent banks or to big business corporations. Such deposits are liable to become subject to very sharp unexpected changes. The balance of such changes is purely fortuitous and is unaffected by the law of averages.

It must be borne in mind that under the American system the withdrawal of a short-term deposit – i.e. deposits under thirty days – of $100,000,000 reduces the bank's cash and Federal Fund holdings by that amount, but it only reduces its minimum reserve requirements by $17,500,000, so that the net result of such a with-drawal is a decline of the bank's reserve by $82,500,000. Unless the bank concerned has a sufficient reserve during the whole reserve period the deficiency has to be made good before the end of the reserve period in order to prevent the average ratio from declining below 17½ per cent. This is easy if the unexpected loss occurs during the early part of the reserve period but not quite so easy if it occurs shortly before closing time on the last day. Hence the concession under which deficiences up to 2 per cent can be carried forward to the next reserve period, though not beyond it.

(9) HOW RESERVES CAN BE ADJUSTED

To avoid such situations the banks have to manage their opera-tions in such a way as to safeguard themselves against surprise withdrawals without applying an overdose of 'safety first' by keeping unnecessarily large amounts of non-interest bearing reserves. They can choose between a variety of means by which to adjust their reserves. The following are the most important amongst them:

(1) Buy (borrow) or sell (lend) Federal Funds.

(2) Borrow Euro-dollars from their London branch or other foreign branch or a foreign bank, or repay amounts previously borrowed.

(3) Buy or sell Treasury bills.

(4) Buy or sell other Government securities, or Government Agency securities.

(5) Buy or sell acceptances.

(6) Increase or reduce their issues or holdings of Certificates of Deposits.

(7) Buy or sell commercial paper.

(8) Increase or reduce their holdings of call money (loans to brokers or dealers).

(9) Reduce or increase their balances with correspondent banks.

(10) Reduce or increase their loans to customers.

(11) Borrow from the Federal Reserve Bank or reduce the amount borrowed.

Methods of adjusting reserves through operations in domestic money markets other than the Federal Funds market – the market in Treasury bills, securities of Government Agencies, acceptances, CDs, call money and loans to dealers, and commercial paper – are discussed in Chapters 5 to 9. Adjustment of reserves through operations in Euro-dollars was already discussed in Chapter 11 of Volume 1, but further reference will be made to it later in this chapter when reference is made to the international aspects of the market in Federal Funds. It is outside our scope to deal with operations in medium- and long-term Government and other securities or with adjustments of reserves through operations arising from changes in inter-bank correspondent balances or with adjustments through increases or reductions of credits to customers other than operations in Federal Funds on their account.

(10) FEDERAL FUND OPERATIONS PREFERABLE

In most circumstances the most convenient method of adjusting reserves is by buying or selling Federal Funds. Although strictly speaking these are loan transactions, amounting to lending and borrowing deposits, it is customary among banks and in the American technical literature on the subject to refer to them as 'selling' and 'purchasing'. The special significance of this terminological point in the United States lies in the fact that amounts *lent* or *borrowed* by individual banks or to individual banks are in some States of the Federation subject to official limitations between State banks – though not between National banks. If the transactions are treated not as loans but as sales and purchases the rule does not apply. The Comptroller of the Currency gave his blessing to circumvention of the limitations when giving his official approval to the use of the term 'selling' and 'purchasing' to transactions in Federal Funds.

(11) THE NEW YORK MARKET IN FEDERAL FUNDS

Federal Funds have a highly developed market in New York and fairly substantial markets in the other important cities previously referred to. There are markets in the centres of all Federal Reserve Districts – though some of them are rather limited – and in addition there are local markets between country banks (i.e. banks located in towns without a Federal Reserve Bank) in smaller centres. Country banks often deal with banks in the centres of their Federal Reserve districts and there is an increasing trend for the bigger amongst them to have direct contact with New York banks. The bigger banks in the centres of Federal Reserve Districts are of course in close touch with New York – which acts as a clearing house for Federal Funds for the whole of the United States – and also with each other. Owing to keen competition of banks in New York and in other leading cities, an increasing number of smaller country banks now have accounts with them and transact Federal Funds with or through them. Country banks are mostly sellers of funds.

The market is not exclusively an inter-bank market. The normal proportion of transactions with non-banking buyers and sellers is estimated at 10 per cent, but in given circumstances it is known to have risen temporarily to something like 25 per cent. Nevertheless it may reasonably be described as an inter-bank deposit market. It bears much similarity with the inter-bank market in London which was described in detail in Chapter 6 of Volume 1. Because of its basic function of equalising bank reserves it is to some extent also comparable with the London money market and discount market, described in Chapters 2 and 3 of Volume 1, with some essential differences.

(12) DIFFERENCE BETWEEN BRITISH AND U.S. SYSTEMS

(1) British clearing banks do not borrow from or lend to each other but adjust their liquidity positions largely through the intermediary of discount houses, and they do so not through buying and selling deposits but through increasing and reducing their loans to discount houses. But transactions in the inter-bank sterling market, as in the Federal Funds markets, are in bank deposits, though deposits dealt in London are with private banks, not with the Central Bank. To a very large extent they serve identical purposes. There are some essential differences between the two systems in addition to those referred to above, and it is important to make them clear already at this early stage.

(2) While in the United States national banks have the option of adjusting their reserves by borrowing from the Federal Reserve Banks and reducing their debt to them, British banks have no direct access to credit facilities from the Bank of England, even though they can adjust their reserves in operations in the bill market or in the market in Government loans, in addition to

B

changing the amounts of their loans to discount houses which, in turn, have access to the Bank of England. On balance such measures may result in changes in the amounts borrowed by the discount houses from the Bank of England. The difference is, therefore, to some extent one of form rather than one of substance.

(3) While in the United States the instruments of the transactions in the inter-bank market are non-interest-bearing deposits with Federal Reserve Banks or cheques drawn on such deposits, in the London market there are no transactions in balances of banks with the Bank of England, even though the settlements of transactions in inter-bank deposit deals may result in changes in those balances. Deposits that are transacted in London are interest-bearing deposits held by non-clearing banks.

(4) While in New York the big commercial banks are the principal operators, their opposite numbers in London, the clearing banks, do not operate at all in the inter-bank deposit market, though they are concerned indirectly through operations by their wholly-owned affiliates.

(5) Inter-bank deposits lent in London are unsecured, while deposits transacted in the Federal Funds market, since they are held with Federal Reserve Banks, are of course 100 per cent secure. There is of course a risk that the buyers of Federal Funds might not be able to repay them on the following day or on whatever day the deposit is due to be repaid.

(6) While in London operations in inter-bank deposits are almost exclusively for the sake of profit, in the United States many banks buy and sell Federal funds at the same rate, with no spread between the buying and selling rate, for the sake of securing other business from their correspondents or customers. Brokers, too, transact much of their business free of the customary $\frac{1}{16}$ per cent commission, for the sake of obtaining Stock Exchange business from their customers.

(7) While for reasons to be described below the Federal Funds market provides substantial profit possibilities in respect of operations over weekends or holidays, there are no comparable regularly and frequently recurrent special opportunities in the London inter-bank deposit market.

(8) Likewise there are no systematic profit possibilities in London on operations connected with the various phases of the interval between return dates comparable with the operations in

the market in Federal Funds during various phases of the reserve period.

(9) While a relatively high proportion of London inter-bank deposits is for medium-term and some transactions are for long-term, the bulk of Federal Funds transactions is for overnight and the rest for very short maturities, hardly any of them ever exceeding the current reserve period.

(10) While Federal Funds sold are delivered to the purchaser immediately, London inter-bank deposits are only due to be delivered after a lapse of two clear business days in the absence of a specific provision to the contrary.

(11) Owing to the operation of the unit banking system in the United States in contrast with the British branch banking system, the number of banks participating in the Federal Funds market is much larger than those participating in the inter-bank sterling market. But the number of big operators is larger in London than in New York, and so is the number of brokers.

(12) While in Britain London is for all practical purposes the only market, we saw above that there are several major Federal Funds markets in the United States besides that of New York, and that there are many minor markets. The relative importance of New York as the centre of the Federal Funds market is also reduced by the difference in time between the zones of the East, the Mid West and the West. The markets of Chicago, Denver, San Francisco and Los Angeles become important after New York and the other Eastern markets are closed.

(13) ADJUSTING BANKS AND ACCOMMODATING BANKS

There are only about half a dozen major commercial banks which operate in Federal Funds on a really large scale. Three brokers – two members of the New York Stock Exchange and a money-broker – and one bank, the Irving Trust Co., act as intermediaries. The Irving Trust Co. combines the role of broker with that of principal, buying and selling both on its own behalf and on behalf its customers.

Banks participating in the market are divided into two categories, adjusting banks and accommodating banks. The former, as their description implies, use the market solely for adjusting their own reserve positions, buying whenever they expect that their average reserve ratio for the current reserve period might turn out to be under the official minimum and selling whenever they reckon that their reserve ratios are likely to be found to have been higher than necessary for attaining the official minimum. Accommodating banks, as their description implies, use the market, in addition to adjusting their own reserve positions, for accommodating other banks by assisting the latter to adjust their reserve positions. While adjusting banks only deal in Federal Funds when they want to cover an anticipated reserve deficiency or unload an anticipated reserve excess, accommodating banks very often operate independently of their own immediate reserve requirements. They do so on the assumption that before the end of the current reserve period they would be able to cover any deficiency or unload any excess resulting from the multitude of their accommodating transactions during that period.

It is of course difficult to draw a rigid borderline between the two types of banks. Adjusting banks, too, have a number of correspondents' accounts and therefore have to operate in the market not only to meet their own requirements but also to carry out instructions by their correspondents. To some extent the difference is merely one of degree. Adjusting banks are apt to be more prompt than accommodating banks to cover any anticipated long or short positions in Federal Funds resulting from transactions undertaken on behalf of their correspondents. But it is difficult to imagine that their positions can be more or less permanently balanced. In view of the complexity of the pattern of their operation there are bound to be time lags between unbalancing and balancing operations, and from time to time they are bound to have substantial surpluses or deficiencies.

(14) COMMERCIAL BANKS THE MAIN OPERATORS

In addition to commercial banks, other types of banks and other financial institutions are also interested in the market in Federal Funds, and so are Government agencies, large business corporations and foreign banks, Central Banks and Treasuries. But over 70 per cent of the transactions is estimated to be between commercial banks. Cheques on Federal Funds may also be issued, in addition to those of national banks, by the U.S. Treasury, by certain clearing non-member banks and by foreign official bodies if they have an account with a Federal Reserve Bank. Under a regulation issued by the Comptroller of the Currency in February

1970 the definition of 'banks' that may operate in Federal Funds was revised to include domestic and foreign banks, savings banks, savings and loan associations and the Export-Import Bank of the United States.

As mentioned above, the Federal Funds market was originally confined to New York, but in the course of a few years it spread geographically to all parts of the United States. At the same time the circle of participating banks tended to expand everywhere and a large and increasing number of smaller banks came to use the market. Their number is still increasing, so for that reason alone the turn-over tends to increase not only in New York but also in other centres.

(15) USE OF FEDERAL FUNDS FOR CREDIT EXPANSION

In addition to serving the purpose of adjusting reserves, the market in Federal Funds may serve the following other purposes:

(1) Buyers may use the additional Federal Funds to expand or at any rate maintain the amount of their credits to customers.

(2) Sellers may use the market for acquiring a short-term investment which combines the highest grade of liquidity with the highest grade of security, giving at the same time yields which, allowing for normal differentials, bear comparison with those of other short-term market investments.

(3) The market provides opportunities for speculation on basic changes in the trend of interest rates.

(4) It also provides opportunities for what amounts to time arbitrage anticipating technical changes in rates during the various phases of the reserve period.

The role of Federal Funds acquired to serve as a basis for expanding or at least maintaining credits to customers, increased very considerably during the concluding years of the 'sixties as a result of the escalation of the credit squeeze in the United States. According to some commentators, having regard to the tightening of credit conditions, a large number of banks came to aim at securing large amounts of Federal Funds, just as they came to aim at securing large amounts of Euro-dollars, mainly for the purpose of being able to meet the credit requirements of their clients without having to depend on the discount window of the Federal Reserve Banks.

Needless to say, the grand total of Federal Funds available in the market cannot be increased by such operations against a determined opposition of the authorities who are in a position to mop up any unwanted excess Federal Funds. What happens is that banks which attract Federal Funds by offering higher rates divert them from other banks which are not prepared to attract or retain them at such a high cost. The high interest rates do attract money to the Federal Funds market from various alternative employment, also from new banks which did not participate in the market until then. This means a decline of the secondary liquid reserves of some banks hitherto held in the form of correspondent deposits, or bills, or CDs, or promissory notes, etc. The outstanding total of various market papers is liable to fall. Unlike such assets, Federal Funds can serve as a basis of credit expansion. But the Federal Reserve authorities are in a position to counteract any unwanted expansion. Even so, it is possible for individual banks to achieve expansion with the aid of borrowed Federal Funds, although it does not necessarily or even probably mean an expansion of the grand total of bank credits.

On the other hand, in recent years many banks were willing sellers of the Federal Funds that exceeded their reserve ratio requirements, for the sake of the high yield that was obtainable on lending them. Since most of the loans are overnight the selling banks maintain a maximum of liquidity even if they temporarily relinquish the actual possession of the Federal Funds. So long as they take care that their average reserve ratio does not decline below the prescribed minimum they stand to benefit by increasing their earnings through the investment of their surpluses in an absolutely liquid form. Hence the flow of funds from small country banks to the Federal Funds market.

(16) SPECULATION AND ARBITRAGE

The Federal Funds market, like all short-term money markets, provides opportunities for capital gains through speculating on changes in the trend of interest rates. In particular in situations when the rise in Federal Fund rates is not limited by the prevailing discount rates, the scope for speculation on anticipating movements in Federal Fund rates is much wider. It is of course restricted by the fact that most Federal Funds can only be bought overnight, so that they do not provide facilities for medium-term or long-term speculation. But amidst the unsettled conditions in the money market that prevailed much of the time during recent years there were fair possibilities for making speculative profits, even on Federal Funds bought overnight and reinvested in market papers that could be sold against payment in Federal Funds at a profit next day as a result of a change in their interest rates.

The market also provides opportunities for interest arbitrage containing a speculative element. In adjusting their reserve positions, dealers rely on regularly recurrent changes in rates in various phases of the reserve period or at the beginning of the next reserve period. The range of fluctuations on the last day or the first day of a reserve period can be as wide as 8 to 10 per cent. Operations to take advantage of such movements are not free of a certain degree of speculative risk, for the extent of the changes – and even their direction, however regularly they may recur during the various phases of reserve periods – is subject to unpredictable supply-demand influences.

Banks have no means to know even their own last-minute requirements, let alone those of all their correspondent banks. The extent to which banks have to buy Federal Funds at the end of the reserve period may or may not be guessed correctly by treasurers. In addition, basic influences are liable to distort the extent and even the direction of the changes. Normally recurrent movements might be more than counteracted by unexpected changes in the basic trend in the opposite directions. Such changes might easily wipe out, and more than wipe out, the accumulated fractional profits earned over a long period through playing on the recurrence of technical changes during phases of reserve periods.

(17) HOW THE MARKET OPERATES

The market opens between 10 and 10.30 a.m. local time, after the banks have ascertained their positions resulting from the morning clearing. On the basis of the net gains or losses, and of their known incoming and outgoing payments expected during the day, they try to estimate their requirements of Federal Funds, having regard to their closing figures on the previous days of the reserve period, and try to anticipate any foreseeable changes during the remaining days of the reserve period. The trend at closing time on the previous day influences the tentative opening quotations, but they are affected by the trend of interest rates in general and by the Euro-dollar rate in particular that develops in London and to a much less extent in other European markets before the opening of the New York market. In the course of the day they usually have to repeatedly adjust their initial estimates of their requirements.

At the opening of the market brokers quote tentative rates solely for the purpose of testing the response of the banks. In normal conditions, prior to the development of the strong upward trend of interest rates in the 'sixties, the tentative opening rate was usually the discount rate of the local Federal Reserve Bank. Thereafter it is influenced by supply-demand relationship and by tendencies in other money markets.

(18) IMPACT ON DISCOUNT RATES

The Federal Fund rate tends to be uniform throughout the United States, owing to the perfection attained by the system of inter-centre dealing. The spread is usually narrower in the New York market than in dealings with out-of-town banks or within second-ary centres. There are minor discrepancies represented by the cost of transfers which is negligible for large amounts, especially because the Federal Reserve Banks do not charge for transfers of large round amounts through their own wire system. When Federal Reserve discount rates are not uniform in all Federal Reserve districts, the difference between them does not create discrepancies between Federal Fund rates. What it does is to influence supply-demand relationship in Federal Funds in the various districts. If the official discount rate is higher in Chicago than in New York, fewer banks in the Chicago district avail them-selves of their discounting facilities with the Federal Reserve Bank of Chicago in preference to purchasing Federal Funds. The increase of local demand over local supply overflows to New York or to other centres where the discount rate is lower. With the decline in borrowing from the Federal Reserve by the Chicago banks the grand total of the demand for Federal Funds over the entire United States increases and the rate tends to rise, especially if banks widely anticipate that other Federal Reserve Banks are liable to follow the example of the Federal Reserve Bank of Chicago and raise their discount rates.

Likewise any Federal Reserve Bank which takes the initiative for lowering its discount rates influences movements of Federal Funds between its districts and other districts. For instance, if the Federal Reserve Bank of Boston reduces its discount rate the result will be a fall in demand for Federal Funds by banks in the Boston district, because in many marginal cases it becomes more profitable to borrow from the Federal Reserve Bank in preference to purchasing Federal Funds at the prevailing rate. To that extent reductions in individual discount rates are liable to affect the Federal Fund rate throughout the country-wide market, in additional to any psychological effect of such changes.

The regional markets are now so closely inter-connected that any local deviations due to local changes in supply-demand relationship are apt to become absorbed by the vast nation-wide market in a matter of minutes. Since the New York market is by far the largest, a change in the discount rate of the Federal Reserve Bank of New York influences Federal Fund rates to the highest degree.

(19) MARKET PRACTICES

The standard unit of individual transactions is $1 m., but very often much larger amounts change hands in single transactions. Items of $25 m. are not unusual, and I have heard of individual deals of up to $50 m. As the old rule, limiting the amount that a bank is entitled to lend to any other bank to 10 per cent of its capital and open reserves, no longer applies to member banks there is nothing to prevent even larger transactions – unless the selling bank itself is reluctant to place too many eggs in the same basket and prefers to divide up between several banks the large amounts it wants to sell.

On the other hand it is possible to deal in much smaller amounts than the standard figure of $1 m. Transactions with smaller banks may be in amounts of $500,000 or $250,000 or even $100,000. Some banks which are anxious to secure the accounts of small country banks are quite willing to deal in $25,000, and the smallest transactions between banks I have heard of was $10,000. With the increase of the turnover and with the gradual depreciation of the currency, manifesting itself in an all-round increase of amounts, the maximum limit for individual transactions tends to increase. At the same time, owing to the eagerness of city banks and of large country banks to obtain new correspondent accounts, the minimum limit has declined. But the clerical work involved in handling a large number of small transactions sets a limit to the decline of the minimum amount of individual deals.

Transactions in Federal Funds are very easy-going and informal, comparable in their informality with transactions in the foreign exchange market rather than with those in other money markets. All deals are concluded verbally by telephone within the same market and either by telephone, teleprinter or telegraph between different markets. The transactions are confirmed subsequently by an exchange of notes. There is a network of private telephone lines between the leading banks and dealers and brokers. Most inter-bank transactions within New York or within some other large centres are direct between banks. The role of brokers is confined mainly to acting as intermediaries between various markets, or between large banks and small banks or with non-banking clients, either within the same centre or with other centres.

(20) EFFECT OF INTEREST RATE TRENDS

The policy of individual banks towards Federal Funds for reserve purposes differs at any given moment and is liable to change over a period of time. Some banks like to err on the safe side at the beginning of the reserve period, in case of some unexpected drain on their deposits at a later stage. Should there be no such drain they reduce their excess reserves later. Thanks to possessing excess reserves during the early part of the period they are in a position to incur a deliberate deficiency before the end of the period. Other banks prefer to go short at the beginning of the reserve period on the assumption that they would be in a position to acquire an offsetting surplus on advantageous terms towards the close of the period.

During periods of rising interest rates there is a tendency for Federal Fund rates to fall on alternate Wednesdays, because at early stages of the reserve periods most banks are inclined to be on the safe side and secure excess reserve to insure themselves against the expected rise in the rate, until they know how they stand. Towards the close of the period they can then afford to sell their surpluses. Indeed they have strong inducement to do so before the period is concluded, because only 2 per cent of the excess reserve can be carried forward, and only to the next reserve period, for the purpose of calculating the average ratio, so that their surplus in excess of 2 per cent or carried to another reserve period would cause an unnecessary loss of interest.

During periods of falling interest rates banks are tempted to allow their ratios to decline below the minimum at the beginning of the reserve period, in the hope that they would be able to cover their deficiency towards the end of the reserve period at lower rates. When interest rates have a distinct trend the turnover increases towards the end of the reserve period if the trend is expected to continue. The covering transactions – whether buying or selling – are liable to be reversed after the opening of the new reserve period.

(2) ANTICIPATION OF REGULAR CHANGES

If changes of rates during various phases of the reserve periods tend to recur again and again in the same sense, even if not necessarily to the same extent, a number of treasurers get into the habit of anticipating them, and their operations tend to smoothe out the fluctuations at the end of the period and at the beginning of the next period. There is a great deal of such interest arbitrage by banks playing the regularly recurrent rate curve towards the beginning and the end of reserve periods.

On Fridays and on the eve of holidays there is a regularly recurrent technical rise in the rate because, for the purpose of calculating the average reserve ratio, the figure of reserves at the closing of the last day is applied for the days when the market is closed. This means that if the ratio is raised through purchases of Federal Funds on a Friday the closing figure of reserves is applied also for Saturday and Sunday. It is therefore worth while for banks to pay a higher rate on Fridays for the sake of raising their average for the whole reserve period. This enables holders of surpluses to lend larger amounts at profitable rates between Mondays and Thursdays, without thereby reducing their reserve ratio below the minimum. The popularity of Federal Funds for week-ends and on eves of holidays has important international effects at the time of writing. But arrangements which were under consideration at the time of writing and which are expected to become operative by the time this book appears are expected to change the situation by making all foreign exchange transactions and Euro-dollar transactions payable in Federal Funds instead of clearing funds.

A minor technical influence that tends to raise Federal Fund rates on Fridays is that it saves paperwork and telephone calls if three days' requirements can be covered by one transaction instead of having to renew the position twice. Although it is usually possible to transact Federal Funds for three days, it is not such a good market as the market overnight which on Fridays means deposits over weekends.

In the absence of a pronounced upward trend of interest rates the discount rate is supposed to be, in theory, the maximum limit for the Federal Fund rate, because national banks are in a position to borrow from their Federal Reserve Bank in preference to paying higher rates for Federal Funds.

(22) WHY BANKS PREFER FEDERAL FUNDS

In practice even during periods of steady interest rates there may be many situations in which banks prefer to buy, or have to buy, Federal Funds at rates somewhat higher than the rate at which they could borrow at the discount window. The following are some of these situation:

(1) It is simpler to borrow in the Federal Funds market.

(2) If a bank already owes a substantial amount to the Federal Reserve Bank it may prefer to buy Federal Funds rather than borrow more.

(3) Even if a bank does not owe the Federal Reserve Bank too much, indeed if it has not borrowed from it anything at all, it might prefer to treat the Federal Reserve Bank as lender of last resort, in the sense that it is to be used only if it is impossible or unduly costly to cover its requirements in other ways.

(4) Borrowing from the Federal Reserve means submitting to supervision under Regulation A, and banks prefer to avoid it.

(5) If a bank assumes that the Federal Reserve Bank does not approve of the purpose for which it requires the money it may prefer to buy Federal Funds.

(6) It may be the Federal Reserve Bank's policy to discourage credit expansion in general, in which case it is reluctant to lend and tends to discourage borrowing.

For these and other reasons, Federal Fund rates are apt to rise at times above discount rates, even in normal conditions. The discrepancy is only fractional amidst conditions of stable interest rates, but it is apt to rise to 1 per cent or more above the discount rate during periods of credit restraint and rising interest rates. On the other hand, during slack periods Federal Fund rates are apt to decline considerably below the discount rate.

(23) FEDERAL FUNDS AND CREDIT SQUEEZE

Foremost among the conditions in which Federal Fund rates are apt to rise substantially above the discount rate, is the official policy aiming at discouraging credit expansion and even aiming at credit contraction. During the advanced phases of the Stock Exchange boom of 1928–1929 the Federal Reserve authorities discouraged banks from borrowing at the discount window for the purpose of lending at much higher rates in the market for call money. Federal Fund rates rose well above the discount rate, but it was still profitable to buy Federal Funds and lend the money in Wall Street.

During the late 'sixties the credit squeeze restricted the use of the discount window, and open market operations tended to mop up excess reserves. Banks were therefore willing to pay for Federal Fund rates above the discount rate if they needed more Federal Funds to keep their reserve ratios above the minimum while expanding, or at least maintaining, their loans to customers.

The increased borrowing of Euro-dollars by American banks, largely through their London branches, during the same periods, also led to demand for Federal Funds by banks which had lost deposits as a result of such Euro-dollar transactions by other banks because the borrowed dollars had to be transferred from the lender's bank to the borrower's bank. This was one of the causes of the increase of the turnover in Federal Funds simultaneously with the boom in Euro-dollars. During the 'sixties the average daily turnover increased something like fivefold and towards the end of the decade it ranged between $13 billion and $16 billion.

(24) REPURCHASE AGREEMENTS

A high proportion of Federal Funds is sold to brokers dealing in Government securities, because payment for such securities is in

Federal Funds. Such transactions are secured by the securities they finance. They very often assume the form of repurchase arrangements under which lenders buy securities from a dealer and re-sell them to him for the following day at a fixed price. The difference between the two prices represents the interest on the transaction. This system of financing is also applied in the commercial paper market, and in the market for Certificates of Deposits. Adjustments of reserves with the aid of buying or selling Treasury bills or other market paper is usually more expensive than their adjustment by means of Federal Fund operations, because brokers always charge a commission and there is a spread between buying and selling rates. It also involves more clerical labour, because all those transactions are more complicated. Moreover, except in the case of transactions in market paper maturing on the next day, there is always some slight risk resulting from fluctuations of the market rates. Admittedly there is a corollary to it in the form of profit possibilities.

(25) EURO-DOLLAR RATES AND OTHER INFLUENCES

There are almost invariably differentials between Federal Fund rates and other market paper rates, and these differentials are apt to fluctuate. But generally speaking all rates tend to be affected in the same sense, if not necessarily to the same extent, by basic trends of interest rates. They are all liable to be influenced by Euro-dollar rates which, in turn, are apt to react to their movements.

Interest rates outside the markets fixed by banks in their dealings with customers, first and foremost prime rates, are liable to affect Federal Fund rates. The latter are a very sensitive barometer indicating money market trends, owing to their large turnover and their homogeneity. They are only representative, however, for the tendency of overnight rates, because the volume of turnover for longer maturities is much larger in other money markets.

But in this respect, too, as in so many other respects, there are no hard and fast rules. In the late 'sixties Federal Funds came to be used increasingly for financing not only overnight requirements but also transactions for longer terms. Proceeds of Federal Funds sold overnight came to be employed in transactions which tied them down for weeks and even months, on the reasonably safe assumption that the buyer was in a position to purchase an identical amount of funds again and again at current market rates every day. Even if the original seller did not want to renew the arrangement, there was usually no difficulty in finding immediately some other bank willing to sell at the current rate.

Such an assumption might not have been considered absolutely sound banking even ten years ago, but in the meantime the Federal Funds market has expanded to such an extent that banks of good standing may now safely rely on being able to renew their purchases without running the risk that their operations would move the rate against themselves to an undue extent. There are now many large banks, especially in New York and in the big centres, which are more or less permanent holders of borrowed Federal Funds. The counterpart is provided mostly by Federal Funds sold by smaller banks, especially country banks which are more or less permanent sellers.

(26) CHANGES IN OFFICIAL POLICIES

Changes in the rules concerning reserve requirements tend to considerably influence the volume of Federal Funds available in the market. Any reduction in the reserve ratio automatically increases the amount of the banks' deposits with the Federal Reserve Banks that they are in a position to sell, and it reduces the amount they have to purchase in order to meet deficiencies. On the other hand, any increase in the reserve ratio automatically reduces the amount of excess reserve which is available for sale, and it increases the banks' reserve requirements which they have to cover through purchases in the Federal Funds market or through some other means.

Another way in which the authorities are able to influence the volume of Federal Funds available in the market is by changing the sphere of application of reserve ratio. For instance, in August 1970, the volume of Federal Funds was increased by a reduction of the reserve ratio for time deposits from 6 to 5 per cent, although the effect of this measure was more than offset by a simultaneous application of the same ratio to commercial paper issues which were until then not subject to any reserve requirements.

Yet another device at the disposal of the authorities is to extend or reduce the list of the types of institutions which are in a position to operate in Federal Funds. In February 1970 foreign commercial banks were included in the list, though it is doubtful whether this made much difference in practice, because foreign commercial banks with correspondent accounts in banks in the United States have always been able to operate in Federal Funds through the intermediary of American correspondents acting on their behalf. In any case, any effect of changes in the list of institutions eligible for operations on the supply or demand of Federal Funds may be purely incidental, and the changes may have been made for some other purpose.

(27) BORROWING FROM FEDERAL RESERVE BANKS

The extent of borrowing from the Federal Reserve Banks by member banks obviously affects the volume of Federal Funds. Banks may prefer to borrow from the Federal Reserve Banks rather than pay the current market rate for Federal Funds in which case they will increase their holdings of balances with the Federal Reserve Banks without having to reduce the balances of other member banks, so that the grand total is increased. Accommodating banks may borrow at the discount window for the purpose of meeting the requirements of their clients in preference to raising the necessary amount through purchases of Federal Funds in the market. Member banks may increase their lendings to their non-banking customers without having to buy Federal Funds, by borrowing an additional amount from the Federal Reserve Banks. They may increase the amounts of their holdings of market paper with the aid of loans from the Federal Reserve Banks as an alternative to buying Federal Funds. And they may be able to increase the amount of their sight liabilities by about 470 per cent of the additional Federal Funds (on the basis of the prevailing reserve ratio of $17\frac{1}{2}$ per cent) by borrowing from the Federal Reserve Banks or by purchasing Federal Funds.

(28) AUTHORITIES DETERMINE GRAND TOTAL

The Federal Reserve Authorities are in a position to influence the volume of Federal Funds through the various monetary policy devices at their disposal. Indeed, such is their power in this sphere that, while transactions in the Federal Funds market change the allocation of Federal Funds or their velocity – the frequency with

which they change hands – it is really the Authorities that determine their grand total. To be quite accurate, in practice the
volume of Federal Funds cannot be changed materially by the
banks if the change is contrary to the policy of the authorities and
if the latter feel sufficiently strongly against it to deem it necessary
to prevent or reverse it. The simplest and most direct way to that
end is the device of open market operations by which the Federal
Reserve Authorities can increase the volume of Federal Funds or
can mop up excess reserves by buying or selling securities.

Even though transactions in Federal Funds are unable to alter
the total of excess reserves of the entire banking system, their re-
allocation amongst various types of banks and, within the types,
amongst individual banks, is liable to influence the monetary
trend. Since different banks are apt to pursue different policies,
it is not a matter of indifference from the point of view of the
general trend if excess reserves are transferred to other banks.
Some banks are more inclined than others to use their excess
reserves as a basis for credit expansion. For this reason, whenever
Federal Funds change hands, and even whenever holders of
excess reserves change their policies – which they are apt to do –
the resulting change in the allocation of reserves is liable to affect
the volume of credits to some extent, even in the absence of any
change in the grand total of Federal Funds. Alternatively it is
liable to change the velocity of circulation of credits.

CHAPTER FOUR

Call Money

(1) EFFECT OF WALL STREET SLUMP

FOR a long time the call money market was an open market in which demand for call money was matched either by supply offered by lenders, through money brokers or by the money desk of the New York Stock Exchange. At the time of writing money at call in the old sense of loans to Wall Street is not a market in the real sense but largely a banker-to-customer loan. The customer is entitled to repay it at any time. It is not lent for any definite period, although by common consent it may be carried on for very long periods, even indefinitely. Another essential change in the character of the market is that since the early 'thirties banks are not permitted to act as agents for lending call money on behalf of correspondents or customers, only on their own account.

In the 'twenties, and indeed during the century that preceded the Wall Street crash of 1929, call money was used mainly for financing speculation or investment in equities, but since the war it has been lent almost entirely for financing holdings of Government securities, mainly to houses specialising in dealing in such securities.

Even though the market in Wall Street loans, which played such an important part in the Wall Street boom in the 'twenties, now plays a subordinate part, a brief description of the old system in a chapter dealing with call money is necessary. Apart from its historical interest, a revival of that market on a large scale in case of a removal or relaxation of official restrictions imposed on it cannot be ruled out. It is conceivable that, as a result of some prolonged decline in Wall Street, the authorities might deem it expedient to encourage speculative demand by rescinding the measures which were adopted in the 'thirties in order to prevent a recurrence of the speculative boom of the 'twenties. In any case, even in the 'sixties the market for brokers' loans was far from being negligible. As a result of prolonged periods of rise in Wall Street and the expansion in the volume of

securities, the amount of bank loans to brokers expanded considerably, although the high margin requirements were aimed at discouraging its expansion.

(2) EARLY HISTORY

The market in call loans emerged in New York in the 1830s. Bank
loans on securities which could be recalled at any moment constituted useful secondary reserves for the banks. They provided the
medium for adjusting their liquidity positions in the absence of
markets in Treasury bills, bank bills or commercial bills other
than promissory notes. All these loans to brokers were fully
secured by collateral, with a reasonable margin to safeguard
lenders against the risk of a depreciation of the securities.

Until the 1930s, when an official minimum margin was fixed,
banks were at liberty to fix their margins in excess of the value of
collateral at any figure they deemed to be expedient. It depended
largely on their opinion of the likelihood and extent of a fall in the
securities, either because of the speculative character of the stock
or owing to the chances of a general decline in Wall Street. The
standing of the borrowing broker was also taken into consideration. Banks reserved the right to ask borrowers of call money to
provide additional collateral if the original margin was no longer
sufficient as a result of a fall in the value of the stocks.

Although the market had originated in New York, Chicago
and other major centres followed its lead, and country banks lent
their surplus cash to New York and other City banks engaged in
call money operations, and even directly to brokers or dealers. At
a later stage corporations, foreign banks and various types of non-
banking investors also became interested in the market as lenders.
For a long time banks continued to use the market for brokers'
loans for the adjustment of their liquidity positions, lending their
surpluses and recalling their loans whenever they wanted to
increase their liquidity. The establishment of the Federal Reserve
System in 1914 discouraged this use of call money, because
Federal Reserve Banks, while willing to finance short-term
commercial loans, were not prepared to finance call money loans.

The extensive use of call money for speculative purposes greatly
accentuated the instability of interest rates and also of prices in
Wall Street. Call loans stimulated speculative buying during
booms and aggravated selling during slumps, because demands

by banks for additional collateral forced holders to sell, and banks themselves had the right to sell their customers' securities whenever the value of collaterals declined to such an extent that they ceased to provide the prescribed minimum margins. Thus the behaviour of the call money market greatly aggravated the panics of 1884, 1893, 1903 and 1907, and especially the slump of 1929, the latter being preceded by a spectacular increase in the amount of call loans to a maximum of $9½ billion – an astronomic figure for those days.

(3) RULES OF THE MARKET

As a rule call loans need not be negotiated individually but are based on general agreements with banks, under which dealers in Government securities or brokers may borrow up to the stipulated limits against depositing the necessary amounts of securities. Banks have usually a list of eligible securities which they are prepared to accept as collaterals, and they prefer it if the securities are diversified. In order to be considered eligible, securities must be stocks of firms of high standing, actively traded on the Stock Exchange so that banks should find no difficulty in disposing of them in a hurry if borrowers failed to provide the additional margins required. One of the reasons why 'blue chip' equities are liable to rise faster than the average in Wall Street is because they are more acceptable as collateral for brokers' loans.

Borrowers are entitled to change the securities during the duration of the loan provided that the new securities are considered eligible if they or their customers want to sell the securities which were originally used or if they find a more convenient way of securing new holdings.

Separate rates are quoted for new loans and for renewals. Since banks are entitled to recall their loans any day, the rates they charge on loans which are not recalled vary from day to day according to the changes in the current rates. Renewal rates are usually fixed for the whole day. In the old days the initial rates for brokers' loans were fixed by the money desk of the New York Stock Exchange, on the basis of the requirements communicated to it by brokers and of the available funds communicated to it by the banks. Any party dissatisfied with the rate had the remedy in its own hand by calling or repaying the call loan.

Normally loans are called by 12.15 p.m. and are repayable by

14.15 p.m., but banks are entitled to call them up to 3 p.m., borrowers having to repay the loans on the same day before closing times. Payments are made through the Stock Exchange Clearing Corporation, through which body the securities are returned to the borrowers.

(4) RATES OF BROKERS' LOANS

Call money may be borrowed to finance the borrowers' own portfolio or customers' holdings. As pointed out above, under the Securities Exchange Act of 1934 bankers are forbidden to lend call money on account of non-banks, but before the slump the high interest rates for Wall Street loans attracted large amounts of money for investment from all quarters within and outside the United States.

The rate for brokers' loans was very sensitive and was subject to very wide fluctuations even within the same market day. During booms and crises it rose to very high levels. It reached 30 per cent in 1920 and nearly 20 per cent in 1929. The demand fluctuated according to the Stock Exchange trend and the volume of specula- tive and investment operations. The supply was less flexible, because banks had to reserve a high proportion of their resources for their regular customers' business requirements, no matter how tempting the call money rate became. Besides, the amount of liquid banking funds available for lending was subject to the policy of the Federal Reserve. After the great slump the Federal Reserve reinforced discipline over bank lendings of call money by laying down the rule that any bank that overlent would be denied access to the discount window. At the same time the ban on brokers' loans by non-banking corporations was also im- posed.

As a result of these restrictions the market for brokers' loans ceased to be an open market. The amount of such loans slumped to a fraction of its maximum attained in 1929. Another measure to safeguard against the recurrence of the panic of 1929 was the fixing of an official minimum limit to margins. The Federal Reserve was authorised to change the limit according to changing requirements, and for some time in the 'sixties it was fixed at 100 per cent, which meant that all stocks had to be paid for by buyers in cash in full out of their own resources or those of their clients. Although the margin requirements were reduced from time to time, they were always sufficiently high to discourage large-scale speculative purchases of securities financed with the aid of call money.

(5) CALL MONEY TO FINANCE GOVERNMENT STOCKS

Nevertheless an active market in call money continues to exist. But, as already said, it now assumes the role of financing dealers in Government securities, instead of financing brokers dealing in equities. The volume of such securities has increased very considerably since the war, and from time to time the market has to absorb very considerable new Government issues. It is therefore essential for the authorities to give dealers a chance to finance the stocks they have to acquire and carry on their own behalf or on behalf of their customers. The moribund call money market has come to be revived for the benefit of dealers and brokers in the market for Government loans of all maturities. Some of the same houses use the market also for financing the markets in Federal Agency Notes and in Certificates of Deposits. But the main task of the call money market is now the financing of the immense market in Government securities.

The dealer who acquires Government securities transfers them to the lender of call money or to the latter's agent for the duration of the loan. In practice banks usually allow these loans to continue until the borrower chooses to repay them, either because he has sold the securities or because he has chosen an alternative method of financing his investment.

(6) ORGANISATION OF THE MARKET

At the beginning of the 'seventies there are about twenty dealers in Government securities, most of them in New York. Some of these dealers are the securities departments of big banks. Other banks, brokers and other firms also operate in Government securities, though most of them are not specialised dealers but operate through one of the specialised dealers. Such dealers keep a large portfolio of various Government securities out of which they are able to meet their customers' requirements, or which can absorb sales by customers when it appears inopportune to operate in the market pending an anticipated change in prices. This function provides a stabilising influence on the market in Government securities and increases its absorbing capacity. It also increases the safety of dealers' loans secured by Government issues. It facilitates the matching of buying and selling orders, so that even large amounts can be dealt in without unduly affecting the prices of Government securities. But for the call money market it would be more difficult in given circumstances to issue large amounts of new Government securities or to re-finance maturing issues.

The average financial requirements of dealers in Government securities was estimated at over $3 billion a day during the 'sixties. At the end of 1969 it was nearly $4 billion. While corporations are not permitted to lend for financing equities through banks, they are at liberty to lend to dealers for financing Government securities, and in 1969 their share in dealers' loans was over one-third, compared with the New York banks' share of a little over one quarter. Banks outside New York usually charge a slightly lower rate. Owing to the difference in time it is possible to borrow in the West after the New York banks are closed. Nevertheless most New York dealers find it more convenient to borrow in New York in spite of the slightly higher rates. New York banks and banks in centres with Federal Funds markets are willing to lend to dealers even if there is a possibility that they might have to meet deficiency of reserves through purchases of deral Funds.

(7) HOW THE MARKET WORKS

Country banks lend to New York dealers through New York banks which charge them a commission of $\frac{1}{2}$ per cent per annum, though New York banks are prepared to repay the loan at any time, so that country banks are in a position to regard their call loans, lent through New York banks, as part of their secondary reserves.

The banks that are active in the call loan market announce each morning their initial lending rates for renewals and for new loans. These rates are not uniform; they depend on the reserve position, commitments and intentions of each individual bank. If they are not anxious to lend they price themselves out of the market. Some banks change their rates for new loans during the day but others try to gain goodwill by maintaining the rate announced in the morning throughout the day in normal conditions, allowing their customers to benefit by being able to borrow at the initial rate, in spite of any subsequent increase in interest rates, or by being able to repay outstanding loans at the initial rate in spite of a subsequent fall in interest rates.

As observed earlier, in theory either side could terminate the arrangement at any time, but in present-day practice banks hardly ever call their dealers' loans. The market has long ceased to be a medium through which banks adjust their reserve positions. They can now do so with the greatest ease either in the Federal Funds market or in the markets for acceptances, commercial paper or Treasury bills. The discount window of their Federal Reserve Bank is also at their disposal. Normally they prefer to resort to any of these channels rather than disturb their arrangements with dealers.

(8) HOW LIQUID ARE CALL LOANS?

Although call loans to dealers are secured, there are two opinions about the degree of their liquidity. It is true, banks are not bound either legally or morally to observe the well-established, self-imposed rule described in the last paragraph not to call these loans; they seldom make use of their right to depart from the practice. One of the rare instances, quoted in textbooks, occurred in 1955 when one of the New York banks made what is known as 'sharp' calls – i.e. calls without warning for immediate repayment – just to remind dealers that it is the banks' right to do so even if they choose to refrain from exercising that right. But since all dealers have accounts with several banks such action by one bank need not embarrass them.

Nevertheless in situations of tight money it is conceivable that all banks might feel impelled to avail themselves of their rights, in which case dealers would have to sell out their securities, regardless of losses, in order to meet such calls. Even so, owing to the present wide margins which have to be maintained, it is difficult to imagine situations in which dealers in Government loans would be unable to meet their liabilities as a result of any conceivable sudden depreciation of their securities.

Dealers in Government securities may borrow from banks not only on Federal securities but also on State securities or Municipal securities. Interest rates on such loans are somewhat higher than those granted on the security of Federal Government loans. Perhaps it is not forgotten altogether that some of the pre-Civil War State loans are still in default, and that more recently other failures occurred in Municipal loans.

In addition to loans by banks to dealers based on general agreements, it is possible to borrow for definite maturities on specific securities, in amounts that are multiples of $100,000. Rates charged on such loans are usually the banks' prime lending rates.

The official minimum margin requirements relate only to the original purchase prices and banks are under no legal obligation to raise margins if the market value of the securities depreciates. Nevertheless it was a widespread practice among banks when the margin was 20 per cent to raise their margin requirements above that minimum in order to safeguard their interests.

Call loans have no secondary markets, as indeed they have no need for one, since either party is in a position to terminate the transaction at a few hours' notice and re-lend or re-borrow the amount, either in the call money market or in some other form. The market, which was an open market until the early 'thirties, is no longer one, and the money desk of the New York Stock Exchange, which for many years provided the mechanism for the market, was discontinued soon after the Second World War, having greatly declined in significance some fifteen years earlier. In the market in Government securities, which is largely an over-the-counter market, dealers find it necessary on many occasions to resort to borrowing day loans – the American equivalent of the British 'daylight overdrafts' – for a few hours, to bridge them over temporary shortages of cash, or they borrow overnight loans which are definitely repayable on the following day, having served the purpose of bridging a time-gap between two transactions.

(9) RE-PURCHASE AGREEMENTS

Many systematic lenders and borrowers of call money prefer to resort to the alternative method of lending and borrowing by means of re-purchase agreements. The dealer sells Government securities to the lending bank and undertakes to re-purchase them at the same price plus interest at an agreed rate. Such agreements may be for definite periods or they may be subject to termination without any advance notice. Corporations as well as banks lend on such a basis. The yield on such transactions is usually $\frac{1}{8}$ to $\frac{1}{2}$ per cent below the interest on call loans proper quoted by New York banks. They involve a certain amount of extra trouble, because while the securities serving as collateral for call loans are merely deposited with the lenders the ownership of those involved in purchase agreement is actually transferred to the purchaser, but many borrowers prefer this to straight loans and only arrange the latter in the last resort. Re-purchase transactions are unprofitable unless they are for a minimum period of at least three days, owing to the additional work and expense involved. Some of these agreements are for fixed periods of several months.

The Federal Reserve Bank of New York may itself engage in such re-purchase agreements with non-bank corporations. It usually takes the initiative for such operations and the yield on the transaction is usually the discount rate. The authorities apply this practice as an alternative to regulating the volume of liquid funds by means of outright purchases and sales of Government securities by them, when they want to ease tight money conditions without thereby unduly lowering the level of interest rates, or when they want to tighten money conditions without raising interest rates. The device may operate both ways. While during the first half of the 'sixties this practice was applied mainly to increase the banks' liquid resources, from 1966 it came to be applied for mopping up temporary excess reserves by means of reverse re-purchase agreements. The Federal Reserve sold Government securities to dealers, undertaking to re-purchase them at a date fixed in the contract. It is assumed that such operations affect interest rates to a more moderate extent than outright sales of securities by the authorities.

(10) COMPARISON WITH LOMBARD STREET

The American call money market differs in some essential respects from the equivalent market operating in London, described in Chapters 2 and 3 of Volume 1. Although both markets deal in loans which are liable to be discontinued at any time by either party, they serve a totally different purpose. Their superficial similarity conceals some important differences which must be borne in mind by those comparing the two markets, whether for theoretical or for practical purposes.

The main purpose of loans of money at call in Lombard Street made by clearing banks and other banks to discount houses is to adjust their cash reserve positions. They unload unwanted cash surpluses by lending to discount houses, and it is fully understood that they may replenish their cash resources by calling in at any moment the amounts thus lent. In this respect the New York call money market did serve a similar purpose – that of adjusting banks' liquid reserves – until the beginning of the 'thirties. But, as already observed, American banks no longer use that market for that purpose. The initiative for terminating call loans on Government securities is now left almost entirely to borrowers, at any rate as far as loans obtained from banks are concerned. This being so, call loans are no longer considered to be available in practice as a matter of course for improving reserve ratios, even though they can be used for lowering reserve ratios. While in the United Kingdom call loans are considered part of the secondary reserves of banks, in the United States the reluctance of banks to take the initiative for the termination of the call loans to dealers disqualifies such loans, in fact if not in law, from serving that purpose.

While the London call money market occupies a crucial position in the British monetary system, the New York call money market is no longer of a comparable importance, even though it was undoubtedly the most important section of the New York money market during the 'twenties. But, as we saw in Volume 1, the relative importance of the London market for call money also declined during the 'sixties as a result of the development of other parallel money markets.

CHAPTER FIVE

Bankers' Acceptances

(1) OFFICIAL ENCOURAGEMENT

THE New York market in bankers' acceptances – the American equivalent to the London market in fine bank bills – is of comparatively recent origin. Although acceptance credits existed in the United States since about the middle of the 19th century, until the establishment of the Federal Reserve System this activity was mostly confined to a small number of private banks. National banks were not authorised to accept bills, and no bill market in the proper sense of the term existed. The Federal Reserve Act of 1913, by authorising National Banks to engage in acceptance business, made the creation of such a market possible as from 1915. But it took some years after the end of the First World War before a market in acceptances actually developed in New York.

The Federal Reserve Authorities were, from the very outset, in favour of the development of such a market, as a means of securing for New York the position of the world's leading financial centre. For, in spite of the change in the financial balance of power between Britain and the United States which resulted from the First World War—it was not until 1925 that 'the pound was able to look the dollar in the face', and even then its position was from time to time precarious—London continued to perform its traditional role of financing world trade by means of sterling acceptance credits. For the sake of strengthening New York's prestige as an international financial centre, the Federal Reserve Authorities actively encouraged the expansion of the market for bank acceptances in the early and middle 'twenties by buying dollar acceptances regularly in the market, in addition to their readiness to discount such bills. Their intervention in pursuit of their open market policy assumed largely the form of buying or selling dollar acceptances.

(2) U.S. COMPETITION RESISTED BY LONDON

Notwithstanding this, and in spite of the periodic weakness of sterling, London was able, in many areas all over the world, to uphold until recently its traditional leading role of financing international trade with the aid of sterling acceptance credits. Competition of American banks with their London rivals in the inter-war period assumed largely the form of granting acceptance credits liberally to German and other central European banks and other borrowers and cutting commissions to a minimum. Even though British banks followed their example, by 1929 the amount of American acceptances rose to $1·7 billion. This amount was well above London's total of acceptance credits on the eve of the slump.

As a result of the slump of 1929 and the ensuing American banking difficulties, and even more of the losses and immobilisations of acceptance credits resulting from the financial crises in Central Europe in 1931, the volume of American acceptance business – not counting the outstanding 'Standstill' credits which were 'frozen' – came to decline to about $100 m. during the early 'thirties. Before the setback there was a certain amount of arbitrage in bills between New York and London, also with other smaller acceptance centres. All this came to a halt from the 'thirties when international acceptance business came to a standstill in every centre.

(3) REVIVAL OF ACCEPTANCE MARKET

After an interval of some two decades, interest in bankers' acceptances was revived in the United States. A market developed once more in bankers' acceptances – the bulk of the business was transacted in New York – and, like other money markets, it expanded rapidly during the second half of the 'fifties and throughout the 'sixties. Its expansion was assisted not only by the increase in the volume of American foreign trade but also by the increasing use of dollar acceptances instead of sterling acceptances for financing international trade, owing to the decline in the use of sterling in trade outside the sterling Area, and to credit restrictions adopted in Britain from time to time. A large proportion of the dollar acceptances financed trade between third countries which was formerly financed by sterling acceptances.

By August 1970 the amount of acceptances granted by Ameri-

can banks rose to $5·4 billion. This was more than twice the size
of the amount of sterling acceptances, in spite of the fact that by
then the latter included a high proportion of domestic acceptances, while dollar acceptances consisted almost entirely of bills
financing foreign trade. Even so, the New York market in acceptances remained a bare fraction of several other New York money
markets. Its *relative* importance in New York was smaller than the
relative importance of the corresponding market in London.

The Federal Reserve Bank of New York sought to encourage
the growth of the New York acceptance market both before and
after the war, not only with the aid of operations arising from the
open market policy of the Federal Reserve System, but also by
buying and selling dollar bills on account of foreign Central
Banks. Most dollar acceptances bought on official account were
held to maturity unless a reversal of open market operations led
to their re-sale in the market.

(4) DOLLAR ACCEPTANCES CONFINED TO FOREIGN TRADE

While the revival of the London bill market in the 'fifties and
'sixties was largely due to the revival of the 19th-century practice
of granting domestic acceptance credits, American acceptance
business conformed to the inter-war practice of financing almost
exclusively foreign trade. Yet American member banks are
authorised to grant acceptance credits not only for financing
American exports and imports and trade between non-American
countries, but also for financing the transport and storage of
easily marketable domestic goods within the United States as well
as abroad. In spite of this the extent to which American acceptance
credits are used for domestic financing is quite negligible, except
in the cotton trade. As we saw in Chapter 4 of Volume 1, this
type of financing is now done on a large scale in London. British
banks even grant acceptance credits for financing the domestic
production of goods.

Another difference between British and American practices is
that since the war American accepting banks usually expect that
their clients should produce the relevant documents – bills of
lading, warehouse receipts, insurance policies, etc. – while in
London this practice, having been abandoned before the war, has
not been resumed to anything like the extent to which it has been

resumed in New York. This means that to finance goods with acceptance credits in New York is more cumbersome and involves more clerical labour and complications than to finance them by other means such as by borrowing Euro-dollars in London. If in spite of this the volume of dollar acceptance credits has increased appreciably if not spectacularly, it has been largely due to the world-wide expansion of credit requirements and to the replacement of sterling by the dollar as the main vehicle currency for international trade. Euro-dollar credits do not necessarily compete with dollar acceptances very actively, because they are only available for large borrowers.

The Federal Reserve Act empowers National banks to accept bills up to the total of their capital and reserves. Loans by State banks to any individual borrower must not exceed 10 per cent of these resources, but this does not apply to acceptance credits. Nor is it subject to the legal provisions concerning reserve requirements. Acceptances are eligible for discount by Federal Reserve Banks and have therefore the status of secondary reserve. Because of their eligibility, and also because they are generally welcome by banks as collaterals and have a good secondary market, they are considered an essentially liquid asset, especially if, in addition to the signature of the issuing firm and the acceptor, they also bear the endorsement of another bank or a dealer. But since the secondary market is not quite as good as that of Treasury bills they rank somewhat behind the latter.

(5) ORGANISATION OF THE MARKET

The number of active dealers in the secondary market for acceptances is much smaller than that of dealers in Treasury bills. Only some half dozen dealers specialise in bank acceptances. Most of them are also dealers in Government securities. The number of American banks and foreign agencies which submit to the Federal Reserve Authorities returns on the amount of their acceptances was about 170 in 1970.

Accepting banks often retain in their own portfolios the bills accepted by them, or they may swap them through a dealer in return for bills accepted by other banks. The object of such swaps is that it results in the addition of a third signature on the bill, as a result of which it becomes more eligible for discounting with the Federal Reserve Bank or for use as collateral, or for selling in the secondary market. Banks buy and sell acceptances also for account of correspondent banks or of non-banking customers.

The technique of the market is substantially the same as that of the market in Treasury bills, described in Chapter 8. Acceptances may be bought or sold outright, or they may be bought or sold temporarily through re-purchase agreements. As in the Treasury bill market. the majority of the transactions assumes that form rather than outright purchases or sales.

One of the disadvantages of the acceptance market – and also of the commercial paper market – is that many individual trans-actions with customers are too small to be covered by dealers in the interbank market. While Treasury bills and CDs are usually transacted in sufficiently large individual amounts to find a counterpart in the market, banks are often not in a position to cover individual acceptances immediately or even after the ac-cumulation of several items in the market, because their amounts maturing on the same date are too small. This necessitates 'maturity grouping' – to wait till they have a sufficiently large amount of bills maturing on the same date, which entails delay and risk. Together with the additional clerical labour involved in dealing in a number of small individual items, this makes it necessary for dealers to charge a higher commission or less favourable discount rates to small customers on transactions which are smaller than the customary minimum items in which business is transacted in the market. It is to facilitate 'maturity grouping' that maturities for acceptances, as for commercial paper, tend to be standardised for small customers, though big customers, dealing in terms of millions, may fix maturities that suit them. Small customers, too, are accommodated for broken dates and broken amounts to suit their requirements, but the rate quoted is less favourable.

Acceptance credits are also arranged for foreign banks to enable the latter to acquire dollars, especially during the 'lean season' of the year. This practice is now much less prevalent than it was before, owing to the rival facilities provided by the Euro-dollar market, and to the 'guidelines discouraging such operations.

(6) HOLDERS OF DOLLAR ACCEPTANCES

Holders of bank acceptances are mainly banks. Owing to their practice of retaining in their own portfolios a high proportion of their acceptances – or of swapping them for the acceptances of other banks – the turnover in the secondary market is relatively small compared with the size of the primary market. Foreign banks, and Central Banks too, buy and hold acceptances. Many private foreign holders prefer them to holding Treasury bills, not only because their yield is slightly higher, but also because their yield is not subject to Federal withholding tax, provided that the United States has an agreement on double taxation and tax evasion with the country concerned. As such agreement exists with Britain and with most important countries, this consideration is of some importance.

Apart from amounts acquired temporarily through open market operations, the Federal Reserve System usually holds a small amount of acceptances. Other holders include savings banks, insurance companies, pension funds, trusts, etc.

Most bills drawn on American acceptance credits mature between thirty and 180 days, the most common maturity being ninety days. But customers can be accommodated by their bankers if they require credits for odd dates to correspond with the date of the payments for which they require the credits.

The standard rate of commission charged by accepting banks is now $1\frac{1}{2}$ per cent p.a. – three times the pre-war rate – but firms whose credit ratings are not high enough may have to pay higher rates. On the other hand, first-class foreign banks may be charged a somewhat lower rate. Discount rates on the primary market – that is, rates at which the acceptors discount their own acceptances or at which they sell the bills to dealers – are usually determined by the current quotations in the secondary market for the corresponding maturities.

(7) COST OF ACCEPTANCE CREDITS

When comparing the cost of acceptance credits and other forms of bank loans it is necessary to bear in mind that the rule concerning the compensating balances of 20 per cent which borrowers of bank loans have to leave on current account does not apply to acceptance credits. With interest rates at a high level the loss of interest on these sterile and unnecessary balances might well exceed the commission on acceptance credits. The balance of advantage depends on the level of interest rates in general and on

C

the degree to which banks adapt their prime rates to changes in market trends.

Any firm whose standing is high enough to issue commercial paper can meet its requirements by that means at a lower cost than through obtaining acceptance credits. But, as we shall see in Chapter 6, only firms of very high credit ratings are in a fortunate position to be able to take advantage of the relatively low cost of borrowing in the commercial paper market. Hence the low rates.

(8) FINANCING OF DEALERS

Dealers specialising in acceptances maintain a secondary market largely by their willingness to buy acceptances on their own account and to keep them in their portfolios. They post their 'bid' and 'offered' rates every morning and these rates do not necessarily follow very closely the fluctuations of other market rates during the rest of the day. For this reason the spread between bid and offered rates is somewhat wider than for other market papers, so as to safeguard dealers against minor adverse movements. In the late 'sixties dealers had to quote more flexible rates, owing to the wide fluctuations of interest rates during the course of a day, and to their persistent upward trend. When borrowers or investors compare yields they have to bear in mind that, because of the wider spread and owing to the smaller size of the market, they are liable to lose more on the turn if they have to operate in the acceptance market than in other markets.

Holdings of acceptances by dealers are financed either through re-purchase agreements or by borrowing call money from banks. The latter seldom if ever avail themselves of their right to call their loans from dealers. Because fine bank acceptances serve as collaterals the rates paid by dealers are usually between $\frac{3}{4}$ to $\frac{7}{8}$ per cent below prime lending rates. The rate for 90-day bills is normally slightly below the official discount rate, but amidst tight money conditions it is liable to rise above it. Because acceptance rates are more adaptable to changing trends than prime lending rates, during periods of slack money their decline tends to divert borrowing from straight loans, and this is liable to induce banks to lower their prime rates. Conversely, during periods of tight money the rise in acceptance rates is apt to induce borrowers to make use of loans rather than acceptance credits, and the resulting demand for loans is apt to induce banks to raise their prime rates.

(9) ADDITIONAL CREDIT FACILITIES

Cost differentials are not the only consideration which borrowers bear in mind when deciding whether to borrow by means of acceptance credits. Very often, especially during periods of credit squeeze, they are able to obtain additional credit facilities by resorting to acceptance credits. On the other hand, such credits are much more complicated than bank loans, so that, other things being equal, banks loans are considered preferable during periods of ample credit supplies.

From the banks' point of view too, acceptance credits involve more clerical labour than loans. On the other hand, they are much more liquid assets than loans to customers, because bank acceptances can be sold in the secondary market before maturity, or they can be discounted with the Federal Reserve Bank, while loans are usually tied down for a definite period and banks may even feel impelled to renew them on maturity.

Although dollar acceptances have largely replaced sterling bills as a means of payment in international trade and finance, even now they do not play such an important part as sterling bills did until recently. They have not such a good market and they have to compete not only with London acceptances – and to some extent with Deutschemark acceptances – but also with Euro-dollar credits. Nevertheless they are used extensively, especially for financing trade in staple products.

Within the limits of the relatively low volume of acceptance credits, the use of acceptance credits tends to cause an expansion of aggregate bank credits in the United States. As already stated, acceptance credits call for no reserve requirements, so that the amount granted by the acceptor is additional to the amount of loans it is in a position to grant, having regard to its reserve position. On the other hand, to the extent to which the accepting bank holds its own bills or the bills of other acceptors, its capacity to lend becomes reduced. But nearly two-thirds of the amount of outstanding acceptances is held by foreign holders, so that a relatively high proportion of acceptance credits must be regarded as additional to the credits American banks are in a position to grant.

Since the middle 'sixties the granting of acceptance credits by American banks has been subject to some degree of voluntary or statutory restrictions. For that reason the outstanding amount at the end of 1970 was no higher than it was five years earlier, while the volume of other market instruments expanded very considerably.

CHAPTER SIX

Commercial Paper and Financial Paper

(1) AN ESSENTIALLY AMERICAN INSTITUTION

THE market is commercial paper in an essentially American institution. Apart from Canada, no other country has such a market on a relative scale comparable with that of the American market, though there is of course much direct dealing in many countries in promissory notes between banks and their own customers. An attempt was made in 1970 to create a dollar commercial market in London, but it is as yet premature at the time of writing to form an opinion whether this institution suits London's requirements. It was unfortunately timed, having made its appearance shortly before the failure of the Penn Central. Nevertheless London's experience in trying to emulate American banks through creating a market in Certificates of Deposits might repeat itself sooner or later. Success of the London dollar commercial paper market might then be followed even by the creation of a sterling commercial paper market.

In the United States commercial paper existed ever since Colonial days and there is evidence that a market in commercial paper existed before the end of the 18th century. Like the London market for fine trade bills in the first half of the 19th century, it provided a substitute for a branch banking system as a channel for the re-allocation of credit resources between various parts of the country. But while in Britain an elaborate branch banking system developed during the second half of the 19th century, the system of unit banking was retained in the United States, so that the American economy still depends very largely on the commercial paper market for the re-allocation of credit.

(2) UPS AND DOWNS OF TURNOVER

The volume of turnover in the commercial paper market, apart from its secular trend of expansion, had its ups and downs. It was not until the late 'sixties that it came to assume really large dimensions and became able to exert considerable influence on the American money market and on the American economy. In spite of its present importance, very few people outside the United States are really familiar with it. In British banking circles it is widely regarded as the American equivalent to mere I.O.U.s, because commercial paper bears only one signature.

In reality, until the Penn Central crisis, commercial paper was universally looked upon in the United States as a highly secure short-term money market paper. After all, it had weathered the slump of 1907 and other major crises of this century remarkably well. Even in the middle of the great slump of the 'thirties, in 1932, the proportion of defaults to the outstanding total was less than 0·1 per cent, and there were no defaults whatsoever between 1936 and 1970. Unfortunately in June 1970 the failure of the Pennsylvania Central Transportation Company did blot the otherwise unblemished record of the commercial paper market. It remains to be seen how long it will take for the reputation of commercial paper to live down that incident. Considering, however, the large amount involved and the circumstances of that failure, the immediate reactions to it must be considered to have been relatively moderate. More will be said about this later in the chapter.

Because commercial paper is a one-name paper, it is all but generally regarded in London as being considerably inferior to the British fine trade bill which bears at least two signatures. This view is taken in spite of the fact that in the commercial paper market borrowers whose paper is eligible are selected with exceptionally great care. Many British firms whose trade bills are taken in the market would not be considered eligible in the American commercial paper market where a very much higher credit rating is expected. Moreover in the United States commercial paper, other than that issued by bank affiliates or bank holding companies, is usually secured by an open credit line. Admittedly, as we shall see later, the value of that security is very much open to question in given circumstances.

(3) DIRECT ISSUES TO INVESTORS

Commercial paper may be issued either directly to investors or to dealers specialising in it. Only concerns whose names are household words are in a position to issue notes directly, and even the number of firms whose paper is bought by dealers is very limited. If dealers are not absolutely satisfied that they would have no difficulty in re-selling the paper at short notice, they only undertake to act as brokers and charge a commission on the amount actually sold. But even the issuers of such bills must have a fairly high credit rating, for dealers are very careful not to risk their reputation by acting as brokers for dubious borrowers.

Although commercial paper is payable to bearer and is transferable it has no secondary market. It does change hands occasionally between dealers or between banks or other holders, but such transactions are not sufficiently frequent to be regarded as a proper secondary market. The main reason why there is no larger turnover is that a large number of issuing firms are willing to re-purchase their notes before maturity should the holders need the cash urgently. In some instances this arrangement is based on a firm undertaking, but much more frequently investors rely, even in the absence of a formal undertaking, on the keenness of the issuing firms to retain the goodwill of the lenders by redeeming the notes in case of need. They are under no moral obligation to do so and their willingness to redeem the notes before maturity is not supposed to be relied upon as a matter of course. What is important is that lenders should be able to depend on premature redemption in an emergency, and even in case of an unforeseen call on their resources, when they can satisfy the borrower that they do not want their money back just for the sake of being able to re-lend it on more favourable terms.

(4) LIQUID ASSETS FOR BANKS

The bulk of commercial paper was held originally by banks, but now they only hold a relatively small proportion. This in spite of the fact that banks consider commercial paper more liquid than the short-term credits they grant to customers. Even though bank credits are granted to customers for a limited period of, say, three months, the borrower is liable to ask for a renewal, or even for several renewals, in circumstances in which the bank might find it awkward to refuse to comply with this request. On the other hand, commercial paper is definitely non-renewable. If the issuer still needs the money when his note matures he has to issue new notes which may or may not be bought by the buyer of the original note. There is no question of automatic or even negotiated renewal of the old notes, It is because of this high degree of *de facto* liquidity, in addition to the *de jure* liquidity, that banks regard the notes as part of their secondary reserves, all the more since commercial paper is eligible for re-discount by the Federal Reserve Bank.

The importance of commercial paper increased considerably after the establishment of the Federal Reserve System in 1914, precisely because the notes were made eligible for re-discount from the very outset. Commercial paper was issued to dealers in New York, Baltimore, Boston, Chicago, San Francisco, Los Angeles and other leading financial centres. Dealers specialising in these notes usually combine that activity with Stock Exchange transactions, participation in underwriting syndicates and the marketing of bonds.

(5) FINANCE PAPER

After the First World War a new type of commercial paper made its appearance. It is referred to sometimes as finance paper, because it is issued by the American equivalents of British finance houses, mainly for the purpose of financing hire-purchase transactions by the parent company of the issuing firm or by other firms. The General Motors Acceptance Corporation initiated the issue of this type of paper and its example was followed by a number of other finance houses. These notes are usually quoted at slightly lower rates than ordinary commercial paper, and they may be regarded as a distinct market. But they are bracketed by the Federal Reserve Board with other commercial paper – referred to sometimes as 'industrial paper' – for statistical purposes. The volume of both types of paper increased considerably during the 'twenties, especially that of finance paper, owing to the popularisation of instalment selling. The market in finance paper is the American equivalent to finance house deposits in Britain, as neither instrument has a secondary market and both serve the same purpose.

But the Stock Exchange boom in the late 'twenties attracted funds from the commercial paper market to Wall Street, so that the turnover in the former market declined even before the slump of 1929. It fell sharply as a result of the slump and its consequences, even though, as already observed, there were very few defaults on commercial paper during that difficult period. During the period of economic recovery the volume of commercial paper expanded, especially owing to the institutional growth of hire-purchase business, which came to be financed extensively through the issue of commercial paper.

(6) EXPANSION OF THE MARKET

The decline in commercial paper issues during the Second World War was followed by an almost uninterrupted expansion from under $200 m. at the end of 1945 to over $13,000 m. at the end of 1966. Thereafter the expansion of the market assumed a truly spectacular character so that, by the middle of 1970, on the eve of the default by Penn Central the outstanding amount reached about $40 billion. Even so, its turnover remained considerably below that of other money market instruments which have secondary markets.

The main reason for the sudden escalation, in addition to the all-round growth of figures resulting from the increase in business activity and in prices, was the appearance of an entirely new type of paper. In the late 'sixties affiliates and holding companies of banks came to issue promissory notes in large and increasing amounts. While banks themselves were prevented by Federal Reserve regulations from expanding credit adequately to meet increasing requirements, those regulations did not apply to their affiliates – in the same way as the self-imposed rules of British clearing banks did not apply to their affiliates, as explained in Chapter 6 of Volume 1 – or to holding companies controlling them. Even though legally the banks were not responsible for the liabilities of their affiliates or of their holding companies, it was generally taken for granted that in practice they would assume full responsibility for the notes issued by those institutions, especially as it is largely to the benefit of the banks themselves and their customers that the notes were issued. As a result of their effort to get around the credit restraint, the amount of such notes issued in 1968 and 1969 ran into many billions of dollars. They came to overshadow in importance the conventional type of commercial paper, although the latter too expanded considerably because banks were unable to meet their customers' increased credit requirements in full.

(7) MECHANISM OF THE MARKET

The commercial paper is a promissory note, the text of which usually reads as follows:

$1,000,000   7 *February* 1971   No. 6478
On 7 *May* 1971 we promise to pay to the order of Bearer the amount of *One Million Dollars*. Payable at the *Wall Street Branch of the National Bank of New York*. Value received.
Industrial Company Inc.
(*signed*) *John Smith, Treasurer.*

Until the bank affiliates and holding companies entered the market, the amounts of individual notes varied from a minimum of $5,000 to several millions of dollars, the amounts being always in multiples of $5,000. The standard amounts were $100,000, $250,000, $500,000 and $1,000,000. But the amounts of individual notes issued by bank affiliates or holding companies were much higher. Single items of $100 m. and even higher amounts changed hands.

Maturities of the notes vary from a minimum of three days to a maximum of 270 days, beyond which it is necessary to submit the transaction to the approval of the Securities Exchange Commission. The standard maturities of notes issued to dealers are three, four, five and six months. Maturities issued direct to investors can be arranged to meet the lenders' requirements, as can the amount of the notes.

The notes do not bear a fixed interest but are discounted at current market rates. If sold to dealers the latter charge a commission that varies between $\frac{1}{8}$ per cent and $\frac{1}{4}$ per cent.

(8) ADVANTAGES OF BUYING THROUGH DEALERS

Dealers do not endorse the notes and are not legally responsible for them. But it is to their interests to avoid selling notes to investors unless they are fully satisfied that the issuers will honour them on maturity. They have to select borrowers with the utmost care, because a default on notes issued through them would damage their goodwill with investors. To minimise that risk, they only deal with firms whose Dun-Bradstreet credit rating is very high. Before buying the notes they study with the utmost care the issuer's past record, present position and future prospects, taking into consideration the position and prospects of the issuer's industry as a whole, as well as the relevant facts relating to the credit-worthiness of the individual firms concerned. They closely follow any change in the position and prospects of the firms or of their industries. This is one of the advantages of buying commercial paper through a dealer, since the latter has the necessary experience and facilities to familiarise himself with the issuer's credit-worthiness and to follow closely any changes in his standing or prospects. For this reason many investors deem it worth their while to pay a slightly higher price for notes issued through dealers.

As mentioned above, direct issues have the advantage of meeting the investors' requirements in respect of maturity, also in respect of the amount. But owing to the expansion of the turnover, dealers do not encounter any difficulty in supplying investors at short notice with the approximate amount of notes they require for standard maturities. They themselves hold a stock-in-trade of various denominations and maturing at various dates. If the notes they hold do not match the investors' requirements, they contact firms which issue notes regularly and are usually able to match supply and demand. Since they have to finance their holdings with bank credits which might cost more than the yield they earn on the notes while they are in their portfolio, they take care not to acquire notes in which the turnover is apt to be slow, either because the issuers' names are not generally accepted or because the amount of individual notes is too high or because the maturity is inconvenient.

All transactions, whether direct or through dealers, are conducted by telephone. Issuers generally receive immediate cash payment from investor or dealer. But, as we saw earlier, if the latter are not certain that they would place the notes without delay, they often only undertake to act as brokers, passing on to the issuer the rate they have been able to obtain, after deduction of their commission. In many such instances dealers pay a high proportion of the amount – say 80 per cent – immediately and the balance after they have actually sold the notes.

Although the standard rate of dealers' commission is $\frac{1}{4}$ per cent it may be subject to negotiation. If the differential between commercial paper rates and prime lending rates becomes too narrow dealers may have to be content with $\frac{1}{8}$ per cent, otherwise the cost of borrowing through issuing notes might exceed that of bank loans.

(9) DIFFERENTIALS BETWEEN COMMERCIAL PAPER RATES AND PRIME RATES

In order to compare the cost of borrowing from banks with that of borrowing through the commercial paper market it is not sufficient to compare commercial paper rates – which vary according to maturities and to some extent also according to the issuer's standing – with prime loan rates. The differential is slightly reduced by the fact that discount on commercial paper is deducted in advance, while interest on bank loans is payable on maturity only. It is also necessary to take into consideration the small commission on the credit line which the issuer of commercial paper has to arrange for the duration of the notes – unless his bank arranges it as a favour to a good customer. If the investor insists that it must be a guaranteed credit line – that is, the bank undertakes to keep it open until the note is paid – the commission it charges might be $\frac{1}{2}$ per cent per annum or more.

On the other hand, issuers of commercial paper save the loss of interest on the offsetting deposits – as a rule 20 per cent of bank loans have to be left on current account with the bank – because, while interest is charged on the entire loan, no interest is allowed on the offsetting deposit. None of these terms is absolutely rigid, much depends on the relative keenness of lender and borrower on the transaction, so the calculation of the differential is by no means always a matter of simple application of standard rules.

When differentials widen business firms tend to shift their borrowing from their banks to the commercial paper market. If this is done on a large scale the banks' earnings on loans to customers, which are their most profitable short-term assets, decline and their idle or less profitably employed liquid resources increase. If they re-invest these surplus resources in commercial paper the latter's rate tends to decline further and the differential widens further. The same effect is produced indirectly, though not to the same extent, if the banks invest in other money market paper. For a decline in the yield on these resulting from the additional demand tends to affect commercial paper rates in the same sense even though not necessarily to the same extent.

To recover the profitable business lost to the commercial paper market, banks have to reduce the differentials by lowering their prime lending rates. As far as the commercial paper market is concerned it is only the prime rates that matter, for firms who are in a position to issue commercial paper are also in a position to obtain bank loans on prime rates.

Conversely, when differentials between commercial paper rates and prime rates tend to narrow, demand for bank loans tend to increase while issues of commercial paper tend to decline. This might induce banks to raise their prime rates. When commercial paper rates approach, reach or exceed prime rates there is strong inducement for banks to take advantage of the situation by raising their prime rates.

(10) CONSIDERATIONS OF PRESTIGE

Comparative costs are not the only consideration that influences business firms' decisions whether to borrow through the commercial paper market. Once a firm has gained access to that market it is in a position to borrow from it as a matter of routine, with very little formality or delay. Every firm that is eligible to become a regular issuer of commercial ppaer likes to have this alternative source of credit handy, no matter how close and friendly its relation with its banker may be.

Considerations of prestige might tempt many firms to issue commercial paper as eligibility of their notes raises their status. As we saw above, only firms of good standing can issue commercial paper, so that the fact that dealers are willing to buy their notes is liable to improve their credit rating. To some extent and in given circumstances it might also help the sale of their products, partly because, other things being equal, corporations holding their notes are inclined to buy the goods of their debtors, and partly because the sale of their notes by dealers draws the attention of business executives to their products. This consideration is, however, of purely marginal importance.

A much more important advantage is the lower cost of borrowing, especially if the firms are of a sufficiently high standing to issue their notes directly to firms with surplus funds. This market between first-rate firms lending to each other their surplus funds bears some similarity with the inter-corporation deposit market. There is usually a fair differential even between prime rates and rates on commercial paper obtainable through dealers. The normal differential is between $\frac{1}{2}$ and $\frac{3}{4}$ per cent per annum, but in given circumstances this is apt to widen or narrow considerably. In June 1968, for instance, it widened to nearly $2\frac{1}{4}$ per cent, while a year later it disappeared altogether for a short time. During periods of slack demand for credit the differential is apt to widen, because of the reluctance of banks to adjust their prime rates to the downward market trend. For the same reason during periods of tight money the difference is apt to narrow until the banks decide to raise their prime rates. The policy in respect of adjusting their prime rates is of course the main determining factor. But the banks themselves are not always free to pursue the course they would like to pursue. They may be subject to official pressure.

(11) ADDITIONAL CREDIT FACILITIES

What is at times even more important than the relative cost of borrowing is the fact that facilities in the commercial paper market enable firms to borrow in excess of the amount of loans they are able to obtain from their banks. This consideration assumes decisive importance during periods of credit squeeze, when Federal Reserve policies prevent banks from meeting a large part of their customers' demand for loans.

The banks themselves came to realise in the late 'sixties the full advantages of the commercial paper market in enabling them to circumvent the credit restraint imposed on them by the authorities. As we saw above, they came to use the market extensively for replenishing their credit resources. Their affiliates or holding companies got into the habit of issuing commercial paper on a truly gigantic scale, thereby making it possible to exceed the official credit limits. Although the authorities were seriously considering the adoption of measures to stop this loophole through the application of Federal Reserve regulations to bank affiliates and holding companies, up to the time of writing no actual steps were taken.

Apart altogether from credit squeezes, in instances in which banks are not permitted to lend to any one borrower more than 10 per cent of their capital and published reserves, their large customers are enabled by the commercial paper market to raise additional funds.

(12) OTHER ADVANTAGES TO BORROWERS

Borrowers stand to benefit in more than one way by the competition of the commercial paper market with banks. We saw above that banks have to reduce their prime loan rates when these rates tend to lose contact with the declining commercial paper rates, because otherwise many of their customers would cover a larger proportion of their credit requirements by issuing commercial paper. Apart from this, banks might feel impelled in many instances to adopt a less rigid attitude towards their customers, for instance in respect of the proportion of offsetting balances retained on credits. Although the standard percentage of such balances which have to be left with banks by borrowers is 20 per cent of the amount lent, an exodus of customers from banks to the commercial paper market is liable to induce some banks to accept a lower percentage from customers whose accounts they are anxious to retain.

Having regard to the advantages listed above, it is no wonder that firms with good enough records to be eligible to issue commercial paper take advantage of these facilities. This consideration provides a more than marginal inducement for mergers between firms which are individually not important enough to be eligible but whose joint resources would raise them to the ranks of eligible firms. Given the level of interest rates and credit scarcities prevailing in the late 'sixties, the chances of saving on interest charges and of gaining access to an alternative source of credit must have played some part in inducing executives and stockholders of smaller firms to make takeover bids for the sake of expanding sufficiently to gain access to the commercial paper market.

Some firms are continuous borrowers in that market and the amounts raised through issuing commercial paper constitute part of their working capital. Maturing notes are met out of proceeds of new issues so long as the funds are needed. Other firms only appear in the market to meet seasonal or other intermittent requirements. But continuity of the flow of note issues by a firm is an advantage to borrowers, lenders and dealers alike. Issuers may find it to their advantage not to lose touch with the market, and if they are not keen on borrowing they simply quote prices for their notes at which investors or dealers do not consider it worth while to buy them, rather than inform them that they are not prepared to issue notes.

(13) THE CASE FOR BANK LOANS

All advantages are by no means on the side of borrowing by means of issuing commercial paper. Few business firms or finance houses could afford to depend entirely on the commercial paper market for covering their requirements. It is to their interests to maintain well-established relations with their banks. The latter are willing to go out of their way to accommodate good customers during periods of tight money conditions. Naturally enough they prefer to reserve their limited resources for their regular customers who use their facilities also during periods of easier money conditions, rather than accommodate firms which only want to make use of them when they find it difficult to be accommodated in the commercial paper market. Business firms have to balance the advantages of saving interest charges with the advantages of being able to depend on the goodwill of their banks.

Moreover it is easier to arrange the amount and maturity of bank loans in accordance with the borrowers' requirements. Although the spectacular expansion of the commercial paper market has made it easier than it had been before to find the right amounts for the right maturities, for odd dates or odd maturities it is even now easier to arrange a bank credit than to sell in the secondary market the commercial paper that suits exactly the holder's requirements.

In any case, loans exceeding 270 days are not obtainable in the commercial paper market without going through the cumbersome procedure of submitting the transaction for approval to the Securities Exchange Commission. Although bank credits are often a matter for negotiation even for shorter periods, good customers seldom find it difficult to arrange them for three months or six months and, if necessary, they may obtain a renewal on maturity.

(14) LIMITS FOR NAMES

There is also the question of limits for names in the commercial paper market. In practice there are virtually no limits for the upper two dozen firms which are important enough to be in a position to issue notes directly to investors. They may have many hundreds of millions of dollars outstanding at any given moment, and some of them may even exceed the billion dollar limit. But the failure of the Penn Central made all investors more cautious. In any case, their resources available for investment in commercial paper are not unlimited, especially when credit is scarce.

When it comes to firms which can only issue commercial paper through dealers, the latter take care not to encourage excessive issues by particular firms. They have lists of firms whose notes they are prepared to buy, together with limits to which each name is taken. They only exceed that limit if they have a definite customer willing to relieve them of the notes immediately instead of having to look round for investors. It is true, however, that the same firms are in a position to issue notes through several dealers, and in the absence of a secondary market it is not easy to ascertain whether an issuer has over-issued.

But investors, too, have their limits for all but the best names. Moreover during periods of rapidly rising interest rates they may prefer to employ their liquid funds in day-to-day loans rather than three-day commercial papers, while during periods when a decline of interest rates is anticipated they may prefer to invest all their available funds for periods of longer than 270 days.

(15) OPTION CLAUSES

When some investors are keen on buying commercial paper they are prepared to concede an escape clause under which they would raise the purchase price if within three days interest rates should change in favour of the borrowers. On the other hand, dealers are occasionally prepared to concede a trial period of up to ten days during which investors, having bought notes of comparatively unknown firms, might arrive at the conclusion that the names concerned are not, after all, up to their standards. The commercial paper market is virtually the only money market where such flexible terms are applied, amounting to options for the benefit of one party or the other.

Even if dealers are satisfied with the high standing of the issuer, they take good care not to buy on their own account notes of firms which are not sufficiently well known to ensure that their notes could be placed without undue difficulty or delay. The total holdings of all dealers at any given moment is estimated at 10 per cent of the outstanding grand total, and unless dealers expect an early fall of interest rates they are reluctant to go beyond that limit. During periods of rising interest rates dealers quote relatively high prices for notes to safeguard themselves against capital losses on their holdings, and against losses of interest on their holdings which have to be financed with bank loans. Such bank loans are secured with the notes, usually with a 5 per cent margin. In addition to the cost in the form of the interest differential between the yield on commercial paper and interest charged on bank loans, they run the risk of a capital loss as a result of a rise in interest rates.

It is true, this risk is offset in theory by the prospects of a capital gain as a result of a fall in interest rates. But in practice the odds are against the dealer in the long run because they have to keep a stock-in-trade regardless of whether the trend of interest rates is upward or downward, and they cannot run down their portfolio completely even if a rise of interest rate is considered certain. Dealers are also exposed to losses through defaults by issuers. While this risk was considered negligible until June 1970, the default of the Pennsylvania Central Transportation Company on $87 m. of promissory notes showed that the possibility of heavy losses is very real.

(16) MODERATE EFFECT OF DEFAULTS

Having regard to that disastrous experience and to the resulting atmosphere of uncertainty and distrust, the relatively moderate extent of the effect on the commercial paper market was really reassuring. From its maximum level of nearly $40 billion, the immediate decline of the amount of notes was a mere $5½ billion. The moderate extent of this reaction was partly due to the prompt intervention of the Federal Reserve Authorities to ease the monetary tension so as to avoid further defaults. Their action was contrary to the basic aim of the declared official policy which was at the time distinctly deflationary. But in face of the possibility of chain-reactions resulting from major defaults, that policy had to be relaxed. For this reason confidence in commercial paper was maintained to a reasonable degree.

The setback in the commercial paper market was perhaps a blessing in disguise. Its expansion had been too carefree and it was as well that dealers, lenders and borrowers should receive a forceful reminder that no compact had been made with Providence ensuring everlasting and ever-escalating prosperity. At the same time it was also useful to make prophets of doom and their disciples realise that the history of the Creditanstalt crisis of 1931, with all its prolonged chain-reactions, need not necessarily repeat itself.

Quite conceivably the experience of the commercial paper market in 1970, instead of repeating the history of 1931–1933, might prove to have repeated the experience of the Euro-dollar market in 1965, referred to in Chapter 1 of Volume 1. Several actual or narrowly-averted defaults caused then a setback in the expansion of the Euro-dollar market, but they failed to prevent a resumption of the expansion. And within a few years its expansion escalated on a spectacular scale. In the absence of fresh failures on commercial paper as a result of a liquidity crisis or a sharp recession, its volume might well surpass its previous record.

(17) INTEREST RATE DIFFERENTIALS

Commercial paper rates are higher than Treasury bill rates and bank acceptance rates but lower than rates on Certificates of Deposits, provided that the latter are not kept down artificially by Regulation Q. Because of this regulation, between 1968 and 1970 commercial paper rates rose above the authorised limits for time deposits, which accounted in part for the expansion of the commercial paper market, as many billions of dollars were transferred from CDs into commercial paper. When Regulation Q was removed for deposits exceeding $100,000 banks were able once more to compete with the commercial paper market for large deposits maturing between thirty and 180 days. Between them they were able to provide the degree of liquidity needed to offset the scare caused by the Penn Central default.

The differentials between these various sets of interest rates are subject to fluctuations due to sets of special influences affecting one market or another. But the basic trend is subject to the same sets of influences – supply-demand relationship of funds, future prospects, official policies, movements of Euro-dollars rate, movements of forward dollar rates, etc. Preferences of investors are apt to change and their changes are expressed in changes of the differentials. Above all, as noted above, changes in prime loan rates are liable to affect commercial paper rates to a somewhat higher degree than other short-term interest rates.

While the international role of commercial paper – apart from relationship between U.S. and Canadian issues – has been very limited so far, in more than one respect it played an all-important role within the domestic economy of the United States. As already pointed out at the beginning of this chapter, it provided channels through which funds were re-allocated from districts with surpluses to districts with deficiencies. In Britain and in most other advanced countries branch banking provided during the last hundred years or so such channels for re-allocation of funds. Owing to the continued operations of a system of unit banking in the United States, there is no similar automatic re-allocation of funds. As observed earlier in this chapter, this largely explains why an active commercial paper market developed during the 19th century and continued to expand in our century. Dealers in commercial paper are permitted to operate branches outside their districts and play a very important part in ensuring a more efficient use of credit by transferring money where it is in excess supply to other parts of the country where its supply is inadequate and where it can be put to more productive use.

(18) BROADER ECONOMIC IMPLICATIONS

Within the same centres of the same districts, too, the system fulfils a useful task in supplementing the role played by banks in the re-allocation of funds. In the United States this function is hampered by the rigidity of credit and deposit terms imposed on banks by official measures over prolonged periods, or by the inadequacy of the banks' own flexibility. The spread between deposit rates and loan rates is kept artificially wide for prolonged periods by Regulation Q. Through the operation of the commercial paper market first-rate borrowers of funds obtain loans at cheaper rates, while lenders of funds obtain higher interest than those paid on deposits by banks.

The part played by the commercial paper market in the frustration of the official American monetary policy of tight money is not due to any qualities inherent in the system, but to the omission of the American authorities to prevent a wholesale circumvention of the credit restraint it had tried to impose on the community. The U.S. Administration and the Federal Reserve system between them would have been able to keep the extent of such circumvention within relatively narrow limits. It was the omission of the authorities to do so, and not any inherently inflationary quality of the commercial paper market, that was to blame for the inadequacy of the half-heartedly applied hard money policy of the late 'sixties. In this respect the situation was the same as in respect of the wholesale misuse of the Euro-dollar market, described in Chapter 11 of Volume 1, for the mitigation of the effects of the official monetary policy.

CHAPTER SEVEN

Certificates of Deposits

(1) A COMPLICATED MARKET

BEYOND doubt, the American market in Certificates of Deposits is the most complicated of all money markets that exist in the United States, or, for that matter, anywhere else. It has all the complications of other money markets, arising from the standing and credit rating of the debtors and from other considerations affecting the degree of marketability of their papers; from the wide range of maturities; from the alternative methods of straight sales or resale agreements; from the inter-play between primary and secondary markets; from the competition of alternative methods of investing or borrowing; from the seasonal and other factors affecting the turnover and interest rates; and from the part played by the dealers.

But in addition to all that, the primary and secondary markets in CDs have a set of other complications from which the other money markets are free. They arise from the relationship between market rates and the ceilings imposed by Regulation Q on the rates in the primary market. Even though at the time of writing those additional complications have become greatly mitigated by the limitation of the application of Regulation Q to deposits up to $100,000 for a certain range of maturities, a resumption of its broader application remains an ever-present possibility and must be envisaged as one of the potential complicating factors affecting the system of CDs.

The market in CDs is one of the most recent American money markets. It deals in transferable and negotiable receipts for time deposits of fixed amounts and of fixed maturity dates, bearing a fixed rate of interest. Although such certificates existed for many years in the United States and elsewhere before they became a factor of importance, it was only since 1961 that a market in them emerged, first in New York, then in other American centres. Finally a market in Certificates of Deposits came into existence also in London, first in terms of dollars and later also in terms of sterling. These latter markets were discussed in Chapters 13 and 8 of Volume 1. In the present chapters we are concerned solely with the American market in dollar Certificates of Deposits.

(2) REVERSAL OF DECLINING TREND OF DEPOSITS

The main cause of the development of that market was the effort of leading New York banks to check and reverse the decline of their relative importance in the American banking system that was experienced during the early post-war period. Their share in total member bank deposits became reduced from about a quarter to over one-eighth in less than a decade and a half. Apart from a shift in the economic balance of power that reduced the relative predominant position of the eastern States after the war, the operation of Regulation Q limiting interest rates paid on time deposits and the increasing sophistication of corporation treasurers in seeking higher yields on their liquid reserve, was highly detrimental to deposits by banks in general and by New York banks in particular. To be correct, the banks failed to benefit adequately by the general expansion of assets because their largest clients became increasingly keen on employing their liquid resources more profitably in other forms. To that end they reduced to a minimum their non-interest-bearing balances on current account and their deposits up to thirty days. They invested such resources, and also deposits exceeding thirty days increasingly in money market instruments paying higher interest rates than those allowed on time deposits exceeding thirty days under Regulation Q. New York banks lost a particularly high proportion of their large interest-sensitive deposits.

(3) EFFECT OF REGULATION Q

To remedy this situation, the leading New York banks adopted in 1961 the practice of issuing negotiable Certificates of Deposits, issued to bearer. So long as they were in a position to pay on these deposits, under Regulation Q, interest rates which were competitive with those obtainable in rival money markets, they were able to reverse the flow of deposits towards those markets.

To ensure the marketability of the Certificate of Deposits arrangements were made for the development of a secondary market in them. A small number of dealers, mostly firms concerned also with dealing in Government securities, acceptances and other market instruments, have come to take an active part in this secondary market. They quote rates for CDs for various maturities and maintain portfolios in them, enabling them to find bankers or other investors providing a counterpart immediately, or at any rate at short notice, in the maturities for which their clients wanted to invest or borrow. To begin with, the secondary market consisted almost entirely of dealers in Government securities, but subsequently dealers of other types also took an active hand.

(4) EXPANSION OF THE MARKET

The primary market was first confined to a relatively small number of leading New York banks, mostly those with deposits exceeding $1 billion, but before very long banks in other large financial centres followed their example. The market in CDs expanded rapidly both geographically and in respect of the number of participating issuing banks. A high percentage of the outstanding CDs is now issued by smaller out-of-town banks. Nevertheless all issuing banks, in order that their certificates should be negotiable, have to be of high standing, either because of their size and national reputation or, in the case of smaller banks, because of their local reputation. Most out-of-town issuing banks have issuing agents and paying agents in New York, so as to have closer contact with the principal market in CDs instead of depending entirely on their own limited local markets.

Interest rates at which individual banks are able to issue CDs vary of course according to the banks' standing. Only between twenty and thirty banks of the highest standing can issue certificates at the prevailing standard rates for prime names. Banks of the second rank – and even first-rate banks if they over-issue – have to pay somewhat higher rates, and smaller banks – unless they have a high standing locally – even higher rates. The large majority of small banks are unable to issue marketable CDs, regardless of the high rates they are prepared to pay. Unless the issuers are of very high standing, in which case their CDs may be taken at prime rates, their certificates are less easily marketable, so that dealers or investors can only be tempted by high interest rates to take them and face the risk of finding it difficult to sell them at short notice at reasonably acceptable rates before maturity. After all, the whole point of CDs lies in the possibility of regaining, at any moment, possession of the amount deposited for a definite period before that period expires, whenever the holder needs the cash.

(5) INTEREST RATE DIFFERENTIALS

Differentials between rates on CDs of various classes are liable to change according to changes in general money market conditions. When money is tight a wider differential is necessary to induce investors to take CDs other than those issued by top-ranking banks. But when money is easy investors looking for higher yields are more willing to buy and hold CDs of banks which, without belonging to the upper twenty or thirty, have a good standing. They assume that amidst the prevailing conditions they are unlikely to need their money urgently and that, should they need it, they would be able to raise it without difficulty.

The amount of individual certificates varies mostly between $100,000 and $1,000,000. Most large banks are not prepared to issue units smaller than $1,000,000 or at any rate $500,000, for fear that the availability of smaller units might induce smaller corporations and other clients to transfer into CDs their liquid reserves from current account, ordinary time deposits or savings deposits. Smaller deposits are not nearly as interest-sensitive as large deposits of big corporations with sophisticated treasurers, and in the absence of facilities for being converted into CDs they are not likely to be converted into other kinds of money market investments.

When smaller banks came to issue CDs they were prepared to issue units of smaller amounts, anything down to $25,000. At the other extreme, with the expansion of the market, leading banks, in response to demand by big customers or dealers, came to issue certificates of $5,000,000 and occasionally even $10,000,000.

Certificates are usually issued on the initiative of the investor or the dealer, for amounts and maturities required by them. The issuing banks are in a position, however, to influence the amount of their issues and the maturities by their quotation of interest rates. If they are keen on issuing they reduce their rates in general or for some particular maturity or range of maturities. If they are less keen they price themselves out of the market by quoting too high rates in general or too high rates for maturities for which they are not keen on taking additional deposits. They always quote rates when asked, so as to avoid losing touch with the market. If banks repeatedly declined to quote rates to dealers the latter might get into the habit of asking other banks for quotations before asking them.

(6) TIME ARBITRAGE

As a general rule the proceeds of CD issues are added to the general pool of funds, though in the case of some deposits with long maturities they may possibly serve the purpose of meeting specific requirements in connection with some medium- or long-term transactions – to act as offsetting deposits for medium- or long-term credits. Or banks issuing CDs might re-invest the proceeds in some particular form, such as Municipal issues. Banks actively engaged in interest arbitrage between various maturities or between various money markets may issue CDs whenever they can secure a profit margin by investing the proceeds in another market, or for longer periods at a higher yield, or if they anticipate rising interest rates.

In normal market conditions big banks can afford to engage systematically in time arbitrage by issuing short-term CDs, to take advantage of the higher interest rates normally obtainable by re-investing in long-term CDs. They may rely on being able to renew their maturing short-term commitments as often as necessary, even though they always run the risk of changes in interest rates to their disadvantage. That risk is apt to increase during periods of rapidly rising interest rates to such extent that this type of time arbitrage ceases to appear to be profitable.

(7) FLUCTUATION OF OUTSTANDING ISSUES

The adoption of CDs succeeded in achieving the end of reversing the flow of deposits from banks in general and from New York banks in particular. Although the issue of CDs was handicapped from time to time by the operation of Regulation Q whenever market rates declined below the ceiling fixed for various maturities, on the whole the amount of outstanding CDs was increasing at an impressive rate as CDs were able to compete with alternative short-term investments. The trend came to be reversed, however, during the late 'sixties when the sharp rise in interest rates and the rigidity of the ceiling fixed under Regulation Q made it impossible for banks to issue more certificates. Funds deposited with banks against such certificates found their way back into the other markets as and when the deposits matured.

The trend became reversed once more in July 1970 when the Federal Reserve Board suspended the ceiling for deposits from $100,000 for certain maturities. There was a spectacular increase in the volume of CDs in a matter of months and the market regained its previous glamour.

Hitherto we have been dealing with the primary market. But there could be no really active primary market without an active secondary market. For in itself the issue of transferable certificates to depositors would not go a very long way towards assuring the latter that he would be able to convert their time deposits into cash before maturity if it should be necessary or advantageous for them to do so. To find a counterpart at short notice, some investor willing to take over a deposit for a particular amount and maturity, might be no easy matter, and if a depositor needed cash urgently he might have to accept an unfavourable price.

(8) NEED FOR SECONDARY MARKET

To assure holders of CDs that there was no risk of losses or delays if they wanted to realise their holdings at short notice, it was necessary for the issuing banks to make arrangements for the development of an active secondary market where CDs could be bought and sold easily as a matter of routine at rates corresponding to the market trend. It was the creation of a secondary market in CDs in 1961 in New York that ensured the success of the primary market. Thanks to the emergence of facilities enabling holders to unload their CDs when they deem it necessary to do so they may feel safe in depositing their money for some definite period – anything from thirty days to eighteen months, beyond which maturity the sale of CDs is usually a matter for negotiation and is subject to approval by the Securities Exchange Commission – in the certain knowledge that they are able to realise their investment at any time at very short notice.

Although usually smaller than some other markets, the secondary market in CDs is an efficient market, thanks largely to the willingness of the small number of dealers who operate actively in it to acquire and keep fair-sized portfolios in CDs of various maturities. Would-be buyers or sellers often need not wait until dealers can find a counterpart. Dealers add CDs offered for sale to their portfolios in anticipation of subsequent buying orders that would relieve them of any surplus holdings beyond the amount they wish to hold on their books. But dealers may find it difficult at times to sell CDs to customers if they do not hold the required maturities. They might have to cover open positions at short notice and buy at unfavourable rates if they want to find a counterpart for some odd maturity. It is because of the wide variety of possible maturities that dealers do not like going short in CDs. While they are always 'long' – having to keep CDs in their portfolios – they are reluctant to go short even for standard maturities (which cease to be standard in 24 hours or less), unless they take the view that interest rates are about to move in their favour. Nor can they always depend on issuing banks, many of whom do not like issuing CDs to dealers or to other banks, only to depositors.

(9) THE SECONDARY MARKET IN NEW YORK

The secondary market is confined almost entirely to New York, though transactions are also concluded through the network of private telephone lines with other financial centres. It is because of the important part played by the New York market that CDs issued by out-of-town banks are very often made repayable by their New York correspondents. The Hanover Manufacturers Trust Company acts as a clearing house for CDs bought and sold in the secondary market.

Another reason why the secondary market is concentrated in New York is that it has easily the best money market that enables dealers to finance their holdings. Their own capital covers only a small proportion of their portfolios. Dealers are able to borrow against the security of their CD holdings from banks other than the issuing banks of the CDs concerned, at rates slightly below prime rates. Although banks do not buy back their own CDs, they may buy CDs issued by other banks. They may lend against their own CDs, but they have to charge interest at least 2 per cent above the rate at which the CDs had been issued.

The reason why banks are discouraged from lending on their own CDs is that in doing so they would, for all practical purposes, redeem their CDs before maturity. Most banks charge higher rates on loans secured by CDs issued by other banks than on loans secured by Treasury bills or by other Government securities, though they charge lower rates than on loans secured by commercial paper.

(10) PRACTICES IN THE SECONDARY MARKET

CDs for maturities under thirty days are not issued, they are only obtainable in the secondary market. Some dealers specialise in creating short-term CDs by acquiring longer maturities and re-selling them on re-purchase agreements so as to regain possession when the CDs have only a short run left to their maturity. Or they hold CDs in their portfolios. financing them with borrowed money, awaiting the opportunity that is liable to arise to sell the CDs at favourable rates when they approach maturity.

Transactions in the secondary market are usually in units of $1 million and its multiples. Payment is usually in Federal Funds, though it is possible to stipulate payment in clearing funds. There is a great deal of speculative activity and interest arbitrage not only by dealers on their own accounts but also by banks and other firms.

In the secondary market, as in the primary market, there is a spread between the rates quoted for various classes of banks. The dealers announce their buying and selling rates every morning. There are discrepancies of between $\frac{1}{8}$ and $\frac{1}{2}$ per cent between CDs of the leading banks and those of less high standing 'prime', 'lesser prime' and 'off-prime' names. The spread fluctuates largely according to the basic trend, as in the primary market. But generally speaking dealers are not keen on keeping CDs of lesser-known banks in their portfolios, for fear that it might take some time before they can find buyers for them. Moreover, they are less readily accepted as security for loans – unless they form a small part of a package of CDs consisting mostly of those of first-rate names – or for re-purchase agreements, which method is often used by dealers to finance their holdings of CDs.

One of the reasons for the differentiation in respect of lesser-known names is that CDs, like other deposits, are not covered in full by the Federal Deposit Insurance Corporation. Following on bank failures in Texas, Colorado and California in 1964 and on rumours of other bank difficulties some years later, dealers found it more difficult to persuade their customers to take lesser-known names for the sake of their higher yield, unless they were willing to endorse the CDs or to cover them in full by deposit insurance. Limits for names outside the twenty or thirty biggest banks were reduced by dealers and by investors.

(11 IMPORTANCE OF NAMES

Some smaller dealers, who do not as a rule carry portfolios of DCs, act as brokers in the secondary market. Many banks too perform that service for their customers or for out-of-town banks. Dealers watch the market as far as possible and try to avoid acquiring CDs of banks which they suspect of having over-issued. There is, however, no pooling of information that would enable dealers and investors to secure prompt and reliable data about changes in the volume of CDs issued by any particular bank. They have to rely on rate differentials which indicate not only the market's assessment of the issuing bank's standing but also the general opinion whether the bank concerned has over-issued. While changes in rates in the primary market merely indicate the relative degree of keenness of the issuing banks to attract time deposits, fluctuations in the secondary market, which are at times inclined to diverge from those in the primary market, are followed with close attention because of the possibility that they might indicate over-issuing.

(12) A POPULAR INVESTMENT

Investors in CDs are mainly big corporations, and one of the reasons why the New York primary and secondary markets in CDs are so much larger than other markets is that a large number of the big corporations have their head offices there. Treasurers of corporations, as well as of banks and other institutional buyers of CDs, have their limits for the names of issuing banks. Changes in these limits are liable to affect the demand for CDs and their rates. Both supply and demand of CDs is liable to fluctuate relatively more widely than that of Treasury bills, commercial papers or acceptances.

The yield of CDs is usually attractive – unless it is kept down by the Regulation Q ceiling – since it is higher than that of Treasury bills, bank acceptances and commercial paper. The reason for this is that the Federal Reserve System does not intervene in the CD market and does not discount CDs or accept them for collateral. Many treasurers are attracted by CDs whenever their yield is higher than that of finance paper for corresponding maturities.

CDs soon became popular as investments among a wide range of investors besides corporations. Banks of all types hold CDs, though many of them are deterred by considerations of accountancy from holding large amounts. It might convey the misleading impression that they deem it necessary to keep a large proportion of their liquid assets in cash. This is because in balance sheets and returns cash in vault and balances and deposits with other banks are bracketed together in the item 'Cash and due from banks'. But some banks like holding CDs for that very reason, to reassure their depositors about the extent of their liquidity.

Some American banks often buy other banks' CDs, but others hold the view that in doing so they would assist their rivals in securing time deposits at a lower cost and in increasing the amount of their deposits. This consideration plays no part in influencing the choice of non-American banks, many of which – including some Central Banks – are willing buyers whenever CDs offer a reasonably higher yield. The extent of demand by unofficial foreign investors is of course limited by exchange controls operating in most countries, and at times by the terms of covering the exchange risk.

Other American financial institutions – insurance companies, mutual funds, trusts of various descriptions, savings banks and State banks – and various official authorities – State Governments and Municipalities – are among the regular buyers. Corporations often employ CDs for accumulating reserves for tax payments and for dividend payments, and the amount of their holdings declines sharply on the dates of such payments having increased gradually during the preceding weeks.

(13) RIDING THE YIELD CURVE

The interplay between CD rates and Regulation Q ceilings plays a very important part in determining the totals outstanding, the turnover, the amounts of CDs issued for various maturities and their interest rates. When different ceilings are fixed for different maturities the volume of issues of CDs for various maturities depends on whether the rate for the particular maturities is under the ceiling. It is of course always possible for dealers and investors to buy CDs on the secondary market, even if no new issues can be made owing to Regulation Q limitations until the CDs issued prior to the change in Regulation Q have matured. The attitude of issuing banks is by no means uniform when market rates tend to rise towards the official ceiling. Many of them make large issues while the going is good, preferably for long maturities, so as to ensure a high level of deposits during a period when they are not in a position to issue new CDs.

As already noted, in normal conditions yields on CDs tend to increase according to the length of maturities. This gives rise to 'riding the yield curve' – that is, banks acquire long CDs and finance their holdings by issuing short CDs with the intention of rolling them over again and again when they mature. Dealers and their customers, too, may engage in such operations, which are of course only profitable if the general trend of short-term interest rates is steady or declining or if its rise is less than the differential between long and short maturities.

The volume of demand for CDs by corporations depends of course to a very large degree on the volume of their business activities on the one hand and by the degree of their liquidity on the other. During busy seasons and when business is booming they use up their liquid resources to finance their expanding business, so that there are no reserves available for investment in CDs. During slack seasons and recessions their requirements for financing their business declines and, provided that CD rates are competitive with alternative short-term investment yields, they increase their holdings of CDs. If for reasons of monetary policy or other reasons official operations effect their liquidity, they tend to adjust the amounts of their CDs accordingly.

(14) CORPORATIONS TAKE CDS OF THEIR OWN BANKS

As a general rule most corporations do not shop around for the sake of fractional differences between the rates on CDs of various banks but acquire the CDs of their own banks, for the sake of strengthening the goodwill on which they may have to depend during periods of tight money.

The banks take great care not to issue CDs to customers who would otherwise hold current account balances or ordinary time deposits or savings deposits. The last thing they would want to do is to pay the current market rate of CDs for funds which they could obtain free of charge for deposits up to thirty days or on current account balances and at lower deposit rates for longer deposits. Moreover, in given circumstances they may have reason to assume that such deposits tend to be less volatile than funds obtained through issuing CDs.

The demand for CDs is affected by changes in the rules or policies of various kinds of investors, concerning their eligibility or the limits of their total holdings or those of individual issuers. Some treasurers make it a rule not to acquire CDs issued by banks the total deposits of which are less than certain limits – in many instances one billion dollars, in other instances half a billion dollars.

(15) THE LIQUIDITY OF TREASURY BILLS

Although the secondary market of CDs is very active its turnover bears no comparison with that of the market for Treasury bills or the market for Federal Funds. For this reason if treasurers find themselves in urgent need for securing large amounts of liquid funds they prefer to sell Treasury bills or Federal Funds rather than CDs, because any heavy selling of the latter is more likely to move the rate against them. According to Parker B. Willis, in a report on the secondary market, prepared for the Federal Reserve Board in 1967, the secondary market in CDs could usually absorb transactions of $5 m. to $10 m., and occasionally even $20 m. without any problem. Even so, treasurers of banks and of big corporations are inclined to prefer to sacrifice some yield for the sake of holding part of their assets in a form that is even more easily marketable in an emergency than CDs.

On the other hand, some dealers are inclined to hold larger amounts in CDs than Treasury bills or acceptances in relation to their turnover, for the sake of higher profit possibilities on riding the yield curve, always provided that they do not consider a rise in interest rates likely to occur.

When investors want a large amount of CDs for a particular maturity they acquire it from the primary market, because the issuing banks are usually prepared to meet their requirements. In the secondary market large amounts can only be easily obtainable for standard maturities such as tax payment or dividend dates or window dressing dates. For odd dates dealers can often only offer mixed packages which may contain some CDs of not top-ranking banks. Precisely because of this reason rates obtainable in the secondary market are usually a fraction above the corresponding rates in the primary market.

(16) ADVANTAGES OF LARGE BANKS

The operation of the system of CDs tends to increase the advantages of large banks over smaller banks. The latter are usually unable to issue CDs and, as a result, their deposits tend to become siphoned out by larger banks. Even those smaller banks which command sufficient local prestige to issue CDs to local corporations and other local investors are at a disadvantage, because for most of their clients the minimum of $100,000 fixed by Regulation Q is too high. Since smaller banks have to pay more than standard rates, their rates are liable to reach the official ceiling earlier than the rates of CDs issued by larger banks.

CDs of smaller banks are less well received in the secondary market. Smaller banks cannot depend on being able to replace their maturing CDs by new issues. It is essential for them, therefore, to match the maturities of their CDs with those of their claims or investments. Large banks, on the other hand, are reasonably certain to be able to roll forward their CD commitments even if the rate at which they will be able to do so must remain uncertain. They are safe in simply adding the proceeds of their CDs to their general pool of funds.

Larger banks are also at an advantage through their ability to issue large amounts of CDs because they can attract time deposits on which the reserve requirements are lower. For this reason they are better placed to expand credit than smaller banks – an important consideration during periods of credit squeeze or credit scarcity.

The view is widely held that the net result of issuing CDs is, to a very large extent, merely a re-allocation of deposits between banks. Those willing to pay higher interest rates and whose names are acceptable in the market siphon out the deposits of banks which are unwilling to pay high rates or unable to issue CDs. According to this view, even if CDs attract funds from other money markets the grand total of banking resources is not affected. For instance, if holders of Treasury bills or bank acceptances or commercial paper switch into newly-issued CDs, the gain of the

D

issuing banks in deposits is the loss of other banks whose depositors buy any of the market paper sold by their holders for the sake of acquiring CDs.

If CDs are acquired in the secondary market the buyers' deposits are simply transferred to the sellers' account, whether with the same bank or with some other bank. Federal Reserve Banks do not buy CDs, but various other institutions of the public sector might buy them. If so they increase the financial resources of the private sector.

(17) CDS' INCREASE OF CREDIT VOLUME

Another way in which the increase in the volume of CDs tends to increase the volume of credit is by increasing the total volume of time deposits and thereby replacing sight deposits. Since reserve requirements for the former are only 5 per cent, banks are able to expand credit to a large degree. But if such an expansion is contrary to the official policy the Federal Reserve is always in a position to offset it by open market operations or by other monetary policy devices. There are of course situations in which the Federal Reserve System is 'neutral' in face of an expansion resulting from the operation of the CD system.

Even though the total of deposits may not be affected by transactions in CDs they are liable to affect the average maturity of deposits. This again affects the banks' ability and willingness to grant credit for longer maturities. The importance of this consideration, during a period when there is an ever-increasing demand for longer credits for financing exports or the production of capital goods, cannot be stressed sufficiently.

CHAPTER EIGHT

Treasury Bills

(1) EXPANSION OF THE MARKET

THE market in United States Treasury bills has been for some time the largest market in short-term credits. Its increase has been truly remarkable. In July 1971 the outstanding amount was near $90 billion, compared with well under $3 billion thirty years earlier. Although a high proportion of this amount is held by the original holders to maturity, a very substantial though fluctuating proportion changes hands in the secondary market at least once, but possibly a number of times. The turnover in the secondary market is therefore very large, especially in maturities up to six months. Hence the possibility of buying or selling very large amounts without thereby moving the rate to any noteworthy extent.

There are five denominations of Treasury bills, ranging from $10,000 to $1 million. Like British Treasury bills, they have no fixed interest rates but change hands at a discount both in the primary market and in the secondary market. They mature in ninety-one days, 182 days, 270 days and 365 days. Originally only bills maturing in thirty, sixty and ninety days were issued, but it was decided later to issue bills with longer maturities at the request of banks which were in the habit of keeping a large permanent portfolio of Treasury bills and found it inconvenient to have to roll over their holdings in intervals of three months. From 1959 one-year bills came to be issued, first every quarter then every month. Since 1967 the monthly issues of one-year bills have been raised to $1 billion.

In the primary market the differences between the nominal amount of the bills and the price at which they are allotted represents the discount or the yield on the investment. In the secondary market the bills are discounted in the ordinary way. The discount rate is reckoned on a 360-day year basis.

(2) TWO DIFFERENT ISSUING METHODS

The method of issuing Treasury bills in the United States is substantially the same as in Britain – that is, they are issued by
tenders or, as it is usually termed in the United States, by auction.
Dealers in Treasury bills, banks and others wanting to invest in
newly issued bills, have to submit an application and offer a price
that would secure for them the discount they wish to receive. As
in London, there are in New York weekly auctions for maturities
of three months, but unlike in Britain, also for maturities of six
months.

An essential difference between the issuing methods of Treasury
bills in Britain and in the United States is that in New York there
are two kinds of bids – 'competitive' and 'non-competitive'. For
amounts exceeding $200,000 the method is similar to the one
employed in Britain as described in Chapter 5 of Volume 1. Large
investors tender for more or less substantial amounts and state the
price they are prepared to pay. Competition in the United States
is not regulated by any collective bidding by a syndicate of dealers.
They bid individually, and anyone may make several bids at
different prices. The average of the prices offered by competitive
bidders is computed, and non-competitive bidders – those who
bid for amounts between $10,000 and $200,000 – are allotted
the amounts of their applications on the basis of that price. What
is left over is allotted to competitive bidders, those bidding higher
prices taking precedence over those bidding lower prices. Non-
competitive bidders have the advantage of obtaining allocation in
full. On the other hand they run the risk of having to pay a higher
price than they had intended to pay.

(3) DEMAND FOR SMALL DENOMINATIONS

As and when interest rates were rising during the 'sixties, classes
of smaller investors came to take an increasingly active interest in
Treasury bill auctions. As a result the amount of non-competitive
bids increased. It was in order to discourage a multitude of small
bids that in 1970 the Treasury discontinued the issue of bills of
$1,000 and $5,000 denominations. The Treasury prefers to confine
its short-term borrowing largely to institutional investors, on the
assumption that they are likely to be steadier holders of bills. But
there is room for two opinions on this, partly because the opera-

tion of the law of averages in respect of small holdings is liable to make for a higher degree of steadiness, and partly because holders of small amounts, not being as sophisticated as institutional investors, are not likely to switch in and out of Treasury bills for the sake of fractional interest gains.

Normally tenders are invited on Thursdays. The Federal Reserve Banks act as agents for the Treasury and accept bids up to 1.30 p.m. (New York time) on the following Mondays. If Monday is a holiday tenders are invited on the preceding Friday and bids are accepted on the following Tuesday. The Federal Reserve Banks communicate the bids to the Treasury and the latter notifies the result on the following morning. Payments by those who receive allocations is due to be made on the following Thursday in Federal Funds or in maturing Treasury bills.

There is strictly speaking no American equivalent to the British device of debt management under which Treasury bills, in addition to being issued by tenders, are also 'on tap' at the Bank of England. Although the Federal Reserve Bank of New York is generally speaking much more active than the Bank of England as a seller (as well as a buyer) of Treasury bills in the secondary market, this is not done for the purpose of raising funds for the Treasury or for other Public Departments but in pursuit of ends of monetary policy – to influence the volume of bank reserves or the level of interest rates by means of open market operations. More will be said about this role of official open market operations in Treasury bills later in this chapter. Although such operations are carried out also by the Bank of England, their absolute volume and relative importance is as a rule smaller than that of open market operations in Treasury bills by the Federal Reserve.

(4) HISTORY OF THE MARKET

The system of Treasury bills is of comparatively recent origin in the United States. The first issue dates from December 1929. (Appearances notwithstanding, the timing of their appearance had no connection with the Wall Street slump of October 1929. Congress authorised the Administration in June 1929 to initiate the practice.)

Before the war Treasury bills were of relatively small significance. It was not until the spectacular expansion of the American public debt during and after the war that the Treasury came to deem it advantageous to issue a high proportion of its securities in the form of short-term bills, largely for the sake of saving interest cost which is normally higher on long-term loans. Problems of debt management, too, are easier to solve if a large proportion of the debt is issued and re-financed in relatively small amounts in weekly intervals than if large amounts have to be issued and re-financed in longer intervals, in the form of long-term issues which are liable to upset the Gilt-edged market if they are made at the wrong moment.

Certificates, notes and bonds bear a fixed interest and are issued at a fixed price. The advantage of issuing Bills by tenders is that the Treasury does not have to err on the safe side by being unduly generous when fixing terms for the sake of avoiding the risk that the loan might be under-subscribed and might open at a big discount. The system of tendering ensures that the cost of borrowing conforms exactly to supply-demand relationship prevailing in the market at the moment of issue. It saves the Treasury from paying unnecessarily high interest.

(5) POPULARITY OF TREASURY BILLS

American Treasury bills are a very popular form of short-term investment. They are a 100 per cent secure, because the United States Government has the power of raising revenue by taxation, and if there is a deficit it has the power of creating currency to meet its liabilities. Even such inflationary re-financing is preferable to defaulting on the public debt. Owing to the large size of the market, it is always possible to dispose of large Treasury bill holdings in a matter of minutes. Even amounts running into many hundreds of millions of dollars can be unloaded without unduly affecting the rates, though this depends on the mood of the market. Both in the primary market and even more in the secondary market maturities to suit all requirements are freely available in large amounts up to the limit of twelve months.

The market is organised very efficiently. There are some twenty big dealers – some of them banks in New York and other centres – and a number of secondary dealers operating in the market. They tender for new bills for their clients, or for themselves if they want to keep various maturities in their own portfolios, and they buy or sell in the secondary market either to execute an order for their clients or to adjust their own holdings. Their main source of profit is the turn between buying and selling prices, but they stand a chance of making a profit on their holdings if interest rates decline.

(6) A NARROW SPREAD

All dealing is through a network of private telephone lines. Dealers have such lines with each other, with the leading banks and with the Federal Reserve Bank. There is usually a very narrow spread between bid and offered prices. Nevertheless even a narrow spread, in addition to the minor transactional expenses, makes it sometimes unprofitable for banks to buy or sell bills maturing in a day or two as the cost, reckoned on an annual basis, represents relative high percentage per annum for such short periods. As in other markets, the longer the maturity of the bills at the time of their acquisition the smaller the cost in terms of percentage per annum.

The main attraction of Treasury bills for investors is that, owing to the ease with which they can be realised at very short notice, they are virtually as liquid as cash reserves. For this reason they are favoured by banks and other financial institutions, corporations, official bodies, foreign Central Banks, foreign banks and corporations, etc. The demand for them has increased in the 'sixties, owing to the sharp rise in the general level of interest rates as a result of which everybody seeks to keep cash holdings down to a minimum. In spite of the costs of the operations in Treasury bills, and in spite of the possibility of capital loss if interest rates should be higher when holders have to realise their holdings before maturity – which is offset to a varying degree by the possibility of making a capital profit if discount rates should be lower when the bills are realised than they were at the time of their acquisition – institutions and large individual investors deem it expedient to hold in Treasury bills much of what they were in the habit of holding in cash or in current account balances when interest rates were low. Investors need not concern themselves with the risk of losses resulting from higher interest rates if they have good reason to assume that they would be able to hold the bills till maturity. If they acquire the bills by tenders and if they hold them to maturity the costs are negligible.

(7) DECLINE IN BANKS' HOLDINGS

As a result of the expansion of the market in Federal Funds and the Commercial Paper market and of the development of the market in Certificates of Deposits, banks now depend to a smaller degree on their holdings of Treasury bills than they did in the 'fifties. Their holdings have their ups and downs in accordance with changes in business trends and with changes in relative interest rates. A decline in demand for credits by their clients leads to an increase in the banks' holdings of Treasury bills and/or of other market paper, while a business revival produces the opposite effect. They seek to time the maturities of their bill holdings in accordance with their foreseeable seasonal or other cash requirements. Of course from time to time other holdings are more lucrative, but Treasury bills are particularly useful for banks and other holders for the purpose of meeting unforseen cash requirements. Owing to the large size of the market they are in a position to sell substantial amounts without moving the rates against themselves, or at any rate not to the same extent as they would if they had to sell other short-term securities which have a narrower market.

Treasurers of corporations too have got into the habit of holding Treasury bills as secondary cash reserves. Likewise, State Government, Municipalities and various official agencies are among the regular holders. Foreign Central banks hold their dollar reserves, in so far as they are not expected to be required in the immediate future, largely in the form of Treasury bills, bought and held on their account by the Federal Reserve Bank of New York, even though Euro-dollar deposits are a tempting alternative, and for various reasons many Central Banks yielded to the temptation in recent years. Various Trust funds of the United States Government itself are also large holders, and so are Federal Reserve Banks on their own account as well as on account of their clients.

The proportion of marketable public debt in the form of Treasury bills increased, interruptions apart, during the 'sixties from less than 1 per cent at the beginning of the 'sixties to over one-third of the total by the end of the decade. One of the reasons for this was the extent to which the Federal Reserve Authorities used the secondary market in Treasury bills for the execution of their monetary policies in accordance with details elaborated by the Open Market Committee of the Federal Reserve Board.

Although the Bank of England, too, is in the habit of operating in Treasury bills for a similar purpose, the relative extent to which it uses the secondary market in Treasury bills for the purpose of making money easier or tighter is smaller. There are many days when the Bank of England does not intervene at all in the market, and often its intervention does not assume the form of operations in Treasury bills. In New York, on the other hand, the Federal Reserve Bank's operations constitute part of the market's normal daily routine activities. It is in very frequent contact with dealers and with banks.

(8) OPEN MARKET OPERATIONS

Open market operations in New York are not confined to the Treasury bill market. As we saw in Chapter 5, they are executed to some extent in the market in which they had originated – the acceptance market. The Federal Reserve also operates in the market for long-term Government securities, though not to the same relative extent as the Bank of England and not primarily for bolstering up the prices of Gilt-edged securities. The bulk of its operations in Government securities in pursuit of monetary policy ends is in the Treasury bill market.

Official operations in Treasury bills in the United States have a refinement for which there is no parallel in Britain, even though it is applied in several less advanced countries – the method of transferring the ownership of Treasury bills by means of re-purchase agreements or matched-sale purchase agreements. Under re-purchase agreements the Federal Reserve Bank sells Treasury bills on the understanding that they will re-purchase them from the buyer at a fixed price at a given date. Under matched sale-purchase agreements it buys Treasury bills on the understanding that it will re-sell them to the seller at a fixed price at a given date. These transactinos involve no risk of loss or prospects of profits for either party, with the result that the authorities mop up for a brief period any unwanted temporary surplus funds or cover for a brief period any unwanted temporary deficiencies of funds.

The same system is widely applied also in other markets in which the Federal Reserve intervenes. Its advantage over outright sales or purchases is that it enables the authorities to mitigate the effect of their open market operations on interest rates, in

situations in which their aim is solely to influence the volume of
liquid resources and not to influence interest rates as well.

(9) ADVANTAGES OF INTERVENTION BY RE-PURCHASE

If their sole aim is to influence the amount of liquid resources
of banks in given circumstances it may not suit their purpose to
influence interest rates to a large extent as a result of influencing
the amount of liquid resources. According to an opinion widely
held among American bankers and economists, the purchase or
sale of Treasury bills by means of re-purchase agreements and
matched sale-purchase agreements is liable to affect interest rates
to a smaller degree than the outright purchase or sale of the same
amounts.

In given situations the Federal Reserve Authorities are thus in
a position to influence the trend of the domestic economy by
mopping up or releasing bank reserves with the aid of matched
sale-purchase agreements or re-purchase agreements, without at
the same time extensively influencing interest rates as a result of
the full effect of outright purchase or sale of Treasury bills on
domestic interest rates and on the international movements of
balances. The difference is of course merely one of degree, for
interest rates are not immune from the effect of matched sale-
purchase agreements or re-purchase agreements by the authorities
on the volume of liquid funds, even though the effect is largely
indirect. But in given circumstances it is deemed worthwhile to
employ that device in preference to outright purchases and sales
of Treasury bills even for the sake of the relatively limited difference in the extent of an unwanted effect of the intervention.

(10) PARTICIPATION BY ALL DEALERS

The employment of matched sale-purchase agreements or re-
purchase agreements by the Federal Reserve Bank for the purpose
of intervention is not the only difference between British and
American methods of intervention in the Treasury bill market.
Towards the middle 'fifties the Federal Reserve developed a
method of intervention that came to be known as a 'go-around',
meaning that the authorities now give all dealers an equal opportunity to compete for the Treasury bill business of the Federal
Reserve in the same way as they do at the weekly or monthly

tenders. This is considered fair to dealers because all of them are informed about the direction in which the Federal Reserve is operating, and it is advantageous to the authorities because it means keener competition for business in Treasury bills with the Federal Reserve.

This system operates very efficiently. Each trader at the Treasury bill desk of the Federal Reserve Bank contacts almost simultaneously two to four dealers, so that in a matter of minutes the entire market is in possession of the information regarding official operations. Dealers are expected to make their offers or bids in a matter of minutes, so that the whole exercise need not ever take more than three-quarters of an hour. Very often it takes less than half that time. The length of time depends on whether the authorities are interested in a small number of maturities or in a large number of maturities. The amount and maturities required or offered by the Federal Reserve is communicated to all principal dealers who are therefore all in a position to form an idea not only about the direction of the official intervention but also about its extent. This privilege is only shared by active dealers. If the Federal Reserve find any dealer unwilling to operate on a large scale the name is removed from its list.

In London the Bank of England does not pursue this system. The discount house operating on its behalf is at liberty to approach a single bank or discount house, or a small number of them, and the total extent of the operations is only known to the firm in charge until its publication in the next issue of the *Bank of England Quarterly Review*. Meanwhile the market has to depend on second-hand information, guessing or rumours. In given circumstances this secrecy has its advantages, in that unwanted psychological effects of intervention on a large scale can be reduced. But there are valid arguments in favour and against both methods. From the point of view of dealers it is certainly an advantage to be brought into the picture simultaneously with other dealers; they have an equal opportunity to share in the official operations, and also to adapt their own operations to the anticipated effort of the official intervention.

(11) 'BILLS ONLY' POLICY ABANDONED

The methods and techniques of open market operations have been subject to much controversy and the official policy was repeatedly changed.

Over a long period during the 'fifties and up to 1961 intervention was entirely, or almost entirely, in the bill market, and the
Federal Reserve concentrated its purchases and sales mainly to
three-month bills, leaving it to interest arbitrage to adjust longer
and shorter maturities to the three-month rate. The reason why
the authorities decided early in the 'sixties to spread their operations over a wider range of securities was that an increase in the
volume of Treasury bills held by the banks provided the basis of a
degree of credit expansion which often did not suit the official
monetary policy. It could be prevented more effectively by the
sale of securities with longer maturities. The abandonment of the
'bills only' tactics was largely responsible for the marked decline
in the proportion of Treasury bills held by bankers.

A high proportion of business in the secondary market, both
between the authorities and dealers and among private interests,
assume the form of re-purchase agreements or matched sales-
purchase agreements. We saw above that official circles considered
it an advantage to resort to this method in order to keep down the
effect of the operations on interest rates, But private buyers and
sellers too often prefer it to outright purchases and sales. The
advantage from the point of view of both buyers and sellers is that
any risk arising from changes in discount rates is eliminated, so
that both parties know precisely the exact yield they earn on the
transactions.

(12) OFFSETTING EFFECTS OF TAX PAYMENTS

From the point of view of the authorities and of the market it is
an advantage to spread the withdrawal of funds for tax payments
over a longer period instead of causing heavy withdrawals on the
eve of the payments due at the middle of March, June, September
and December. The system of Tax Anticipation bills goes some
way towards ironing out the effect of the ups and downs of tax
receipts on the monetary situation. There is always a heavy influx
of tax receipts during the first half of the fiscal year – that is,
during the second half of the calendar year – while there is a
seasonal deficit during the first half of the calendar year. The
extensive use of Tax Anticipation bills reduces the resulting
seasonal surplus liquidity and seasonal tightness to some extent.
Dealers and banks often acquire such bills for their own portfolios
in the expectation of being able to sell them at a profit.

Although the amount of Tax Anticipation bills is much smaller than that of Treasury bills, they have a good market because many holders in need of immediate cash realise their holdings before the tax payments fall due. The possibility of realising then is the main attraction of these bills. Their British equivalent, the Tax Certificates, are non-transferable and whoever acquires them renounces the use of the amount involved until he uses them for tax payment. They can have no market, and in any case they are available from the Treasury in unlimited amounts. Tax Anticipation bills, on the other hand, are only issued in limited amounts by means of competitive tenders. Their amounts are determined partly as a device of monetary policy, to influence money market trends, while British Tax Certificates are primarily a debt management device.

The Treasury also issues Certificates of Indebtedness with a fixed rate of interest at a fixed price, at a premium or at a discount. They are usually for twelve months, but also for longer periods. Their terms of issue are usually favourable by comparison with market rates for Government securities of corresponding maturities, in order to ensure the oversubscription of the amount offered, for the sake of the psychological effect of the success of the issue. They are alternatives to Tax Anticipation bills.

CHAPTER NINE

Federal Agency Notes

(1) A WIDE VARIETY OF SECURITIES

WHILE most money markets are basically homogenous – if not in the sense of the identity or standing of borrowers at any rate in respect of the basic character of the loans – the newly developed market in Federal Agency securities deals in a multitude of different types of loans. They differ from each other in respect of the institutions that issue them, in the extent to which the Federal authorities guarantee them legally or at least morally, in the extent of tax exemption provisions and in several other respects. In themselves most markets for the issues of particular agencies are relatively small, but the sum total of the outstanding issues of all of them) and their total turnover, is a by no means negligible factor in the American money market.

Owing to the high degree to which such securities are considered to be morally Government-guaranteed, even in the absence of any legally binding formal undertaking to that effect, they are considered a popular form of short-term investment in the United States, even though they are relatively little known abroad. The differentials between their yields and those of Treasury papers with corresponding maturities attract the more sophisticated types of large investors. At the other extreme the small minimum amounts of the units attract small investors who cannot afford to buy most other types of market paper, the minimum units of which are beyond their means.

Originally commercial banks were the principal holders of Federal Agency Securities, but in more recent years various trust funds and individual investors came to hold a high proportion of these issues. Holdings of commercial banks, like their holdings of other short-term securities, tend to fluctuate widely, according to the changes in the amounts of liquid funds at their disposal and according to rate differentials between the alternative forms in which their funds can be invested.

(2) FEDERAL BUDGET RELIEF

Federal agencies that issue notes have been established for some specific purpose of financing some definite programme of the Federal Government, mainly but not exclusively in the sphere of agriculture or housing. Some of these programmes were originally financed out of the Federal Budget, while others were from the very outset autonomous or semi-autonomous institutions. The main issuing agencies are Federal Land Banks, Federal Intermediate Credit Banks, Banks for Co-operatives, Federal Home Loan Banks and the Federal National Mortgage Association. At the end of the 'sixties these institutions were responsible for about nine-tenths of the total outstanding Federal Agency securities, not counting Participation Certificates which were the Federal Government's direct liabilities.

Federal Agencies which also issue short-term securities in addition to those listed above include the Export-Import Bank, the Commodity Credit Corporation, the Tennessee Valley Authority, the Housing Assistance Administration, the Small Business Administration, etc. Eximbank discount notes are issued in denominations from $5,000 to $100,000 and for maturities between thirty and 360 days. Tennessee Valley Authority short-term notes are auctioned at regular intervals.

(3) SPECTACULAR EXPANSION

The expansion of the market – or, to be correct, markets (in plural) since each Agency paper has a separate market, and most of them have both primary and secondary markets – was indeed remarkable. According to official figures published by the Federal Reserve Bank of Richmond in its brochure *Instruments of Money Markets*, the outstanding total volume of these securities rose from $1·5 billion in 1950 to $16·3 billion in 1965 and to over $34 billion in 1969. The main cause of this rapid growth, in addition to the general expansionary trend, was the basic change in Budgetary policy aimed at relieving the Treasury of the financial burden resulting from the financing of various autonomous or semi-autonomous operations. They are now financed by the Federal Agencies concerned, with the aid of securities issued by them. A high proportion of these securities matures within one year, representing an appreciable addition to the volume of market paper.

Most of these securities are not guaranteed legally by the Federal Government, any more than the liabilities of Local Authorities in the U.K. are guaranteed legally by the British Government. There are some exceptions, such as the issues of the Farmers Home Administration and the Federal and Participation Certificates which are the Government's direct liabilities. Apart from these the Federal Agency issues are usually described as 'non-guaranteed' securities, to lay stress on the absence of a legal guarantee.

(4) ORAL GUARANTEE

Yet since the Agencies that issue them and are responsible for them are officially-owned and controlled, their securities are considered to be quite safe – just as those of British Local Authorities are assumed to be – and in the absence of a formal guarantee there are merely relatively modest differentials in the rates at which they are issued or in the yields at the prices at which they change hands in the secondary markets. Even such differentials are largely due to the narrowness of the markets in such securities compared with the much larger market in Treasury paper.

But there are also differentials between rates quoted for the various Agency issues for identical maturities, not only according to whether they are formally guaranteed or not, but also because not all of them are eligible to serve as collaterals for loans by Federal Reserve Banks, as legal reserves for savings and loan associations and as collaterals for loans of various kinds which have to be secured by Government loans. The Federal Reserve Authorities can only use some of them in their open market operations.

This is unquestionably a most untidy situation which prevents the development of a large homogenous market similar to the British market in Local Authorities deposits. Nevertheless, broadly speaking, most types of notes are quite popular among investors looking for higher yields on safe short-term investments.

(5) FISCAL CONCESSION

Most Federal Agency issues are exempt from State and Municipal taxation – issues of the Federal National Mortgage Association are amongst the exceptions – but are subject to Federal taxation. There are, however, some notes which are altogether tax-free. They include the temporary notes of the Housing Assistance Administration and the preliminary loan notes of the Renewal Assistance Administration. These Agencies are under the Department of Housing and Urban Development, and their issues are besides being free of tax, fully Government-guaranteed.

Practically all short-term notes issued by Federal Agencies bear fixed interest payable on maturity. But the notes of the Commodity Credit Corporation and some of the National Mortgage Association are issued at a discount. In respect of some notes the Agencies reserve the right to call the issues as from a certain date. The Export-Import Bank grants holders of its notes an option enabling them to recover their money on certain terms. On the other hand, in the case of some notes such as those of the Farmers Home Administration, it is the borrowing agency that has the option to renew the notes when they mature.

The market for these issues is in New York and the issuing Agencies have fiscal agents there. The terms of the issues of some Federal Agencies are fixed by the fiscal agents in consultation with the Federal Reserve Bank of New York and with the Treasury. These terms are usually fixed in such a way as to ensure that the issues are over-subscribed. Other Agencies employ different methods. For instance the Tennessee Valley Authority invites tenders for its issues of notes. Owing to these and other complications, it took a long time before investors other than commercial banks and other big institutions came to take an active interest in this market, in spite of the higher yield on such notes compared with Treasury issues. But dealers and banks are gradually educating their clients to acquire and keep Federal Agency securities.

(6) SECONDARY MARKETS

The extent to which issues of Federal Agencies have secondary markets varies widely. Dealers are mostly the same firms which are active in the market for Government issues. Since they are thoroughly familiar with Federal Agency issues they do not hesitate to acquire and hold large amounts of them in their own portfolios.

The turnover in many of them is good, with narrow spreads

between bid and offered rates, and the market is capable of absorbing fairly substantial amounts.

The Federal Reserve System plays an important part in the secondary market, for Federal Agency notes, partly by accepting them as collaterals and partly by engaging in open market operations in some of these in the same way as in Government securities. Federal Reserve Banks are also entitled to conclude re-purchase agreements involving some Federal Agency securities.

According to the publication of the Federal Reserve Bank of Richmond quoted above, during 1969 dealers' daily positions in Federal Agency securities averaged $583 million, of which 57 per cent represented notes maturing within one year. Their daily turnover averaged $61 million, of which over 60 per cent was in short-term securities. These figures give an idea of the size of the secondary market, even though it must be borne in mind that 1969 was a particularly active year. The primary market, too, has been increasing during the late 'sixties almost without interruption, from $2·9 billion in 1965 to $7 billion in 1969. In that year Federal Agencies between them provided many more funds for financing mortgages than the private sector.

(7) WIDENING OF INTEREST DIFFERENTIALS

In spite of the expansion of Federal Agency issues during the late 'sixties there was a distinct widening of the differentials between the yield on their securities and those of Treasury issues for the corresponding maturities. While in 1963 the differentials for various maturities up to one year ranged between twenty and thirty basis points compared with Treasury bills of identical maturities, at the close of the 'sixties the range was between thirty and sixty basis points. This was in spite of the increasing realisation in a number of quarters that Federal Agency issues are virtually Government securities. But largely because of the extremely heterogeneous character of the market its securities are of course not nearly as easily marketable in large amounts as Treasury bills. As far as long-term Federal Agency securities are concerned, the differentials are sometimes as wide as 100 basis points compared with Government securities of corresponding maturities.

One of the reasons why differentials between the yields on Federal Agency issues and those on Treasury issues persist lies in the possibility of changes in the status of the various agencies.

For instance, even though the capital of the twelve Federal Intermediate Credit Banks established under the Federal Farm Loan Act was originally held largely by the Treasury, the Government aims at transferring them into the ownership of the Production Credit Associations. In 1967 some two-thirds of their capital stock was still owned by the Government. But even if they should become privately-controlled, indeed even if their entire capital stock were to become privately-owned, the Government could not divest itself of its moral responsibility for their issues.

Most Federal Agencies issue short-term notes solely for the purpose of being able to select the right moment for the issue of long-term loans on favourable terms. Since, however, their capital requirements are continuous, they have short-term notes outstanding almost all the time.

CHAPTER TEN

Interplay Between the American
Money Markets

(1) IMPROVEMENT SINCE THE WAR

THE facilities of the New York traditional money markets have greatly improved since the war. As we saw in earlier chapters, there is now a good acceptance market, an important market in Treasury bills and a big market in commercial paper. The market in call money no longer caters mainly for the ups and downs of Wall Street requirements but for the much steadier market in Government loans and short-term paper. What is perhaps even more important, some parallel money markets that have developed or expanded in New York have surpassed the corresponding markets in London. For instance the market in Federal Funds, which existed before the war, has become a most important market, even more important than the London inter-bank deposit market. In 1961 New York led the way in the adoption of a market in CDs, and it took some years for London to follow the American example.

On the other hand, the emergence and spectacular expansion of the London Euro-dollar market has more or less restored the balance in favour of London as the leading money market, even if New York assumed from time to time virtual control of the London Euro-dollar market.

Progress was both in the London market for fine trade bills and in the American market for commercial paper. London is well ahead of New York in respect of the primary market in Local Authority deposits. On the other hand, dealing in CDs has developed much more in New York, even though the London market is not exposed to anything like the same extent to the effects of unpredictable changes in official regulations.

(2) CHOICE BETWEEN ALTERNATIVE FACILITIES

Between them the parallel money markets in the various financial centres in the United States – unlike Britain, where London is still the sole money centre, whereas there are several big money centres in America, even if New York still predominates — now form a highly developed and sophisticated system which offers as wide a range of facilities for both lender and borrower as London. From the point of view of its role as a centre for international arbitrage, too, New York almost rivals London now. Its importance is kept down by its geographical position, but its technical position will improve when the proposed reform under which all payments connected with foreign exchange and Euro-dollar transactions would be made in Federal Funds instead of clearing house funds comes to be finalised. Possibly by the time this book appears it will be an accomplished fact.

There is keen competition between the alternative facilities offered by the American parallel markets, and because of this their rates tend to move in sympathy with each other – just as the rates of the London parallel markets do – even though differentials between the respective rate structures are apt to fluctuate and are also subject to institutional changes. Arbitrage between the American parallel markets is very active and tends to prevent abnormal discrepancies between rates for corresponding maturities. But as in London, in the United States the various parallel markets, and also the traditional markets, take turns in being the favourite markets that virtually monopolise the attention of dealers.

(3 A NATION-WIDE MONEY MARKET

An important change that has developed gradually has been the creation of a nation-wide money market, as a result of the institutional and technical changes that have occurred since the war. The creation of a multiplicity of financial channels through which funds can now flow between New York and every part of the United States, and of a network of telephone and teleprinter connections, has made it practically as easy to transact business in short-term funds between two different states of the Federation as between two offices in Wall Street – allowing of course for the difference in business hours in the three time zones.

This development has been contrary to the spirit of the American federal system which, in the financial sphere, aims at safeguarding the less advanced districts from being 'exploited' and dominated by the superior financial power of New York and other leading financial centres. The creation of the Federal Reserve System had pursued that objective, as had the restrictive legislation preventing American commercial banks from opening branches outside their own states. Having taken all this trouble to financially isolate the individual states, the United States Government, Congress and the Federal Reserve Board have in recent times tolerated, and even encouraged, the development of financial channels which have gone a long way towards removing the previously erected banking and monetary barriers between the states of the Federation. As a result of the present system of operation of the various parallel money markets, it is now almost as easy for New York to siphon out the financial resources of some less advanced state of the Mid West as it would be if New York banks were entitled to operate branches there and if the United States had one single Central Bank instead of twelve Federal Reserve Banks. It is almost as easy for the banks of the big cities to compete with local banks both as holders of deposits and as lenders as if they were represented on the spot by branches. It is true, that the Federal Reserve Banks have retained the initiative for changing their re-discount rates, but thanks to the multiple financial channels across the borders of states, the effects of changes in any district become dispersed in a matter of hours, if not minutes.

This is not the place to try to answer the highly controversial and involved question whether this frustration of the efforts to insulate various areas of the United States financially is on balance a good thing or a bad thing. I merely aim at describing the situation created, for better or for worse, by the development of a nation-wide money market.

(4) A *DE FACTO* CONSTITUTIONAL CHANGE?

Because of this basic consideration the change brought about by the development of parallel money markets has been much more far-reaching in the United States than in Britain. It has brought about a *de facto* change in the American constitution, at any rate in the sphere of banking and, as a result, in the broader economic sphere, even though the legal *status quo* remains unchanged. In practice the United States is no longer divided into fifty financial areas, or even into twelve financial districts corresponding to the Federal Reserve Districts. The extent to which the local Federal Reserve Banks are in a position to insulate their respective districts from the rest of the United States has become reduced to a considerable degree.

At the same time, the development of local markets with a network of connections between them, together with other developments since the war, has changed the financial balance of power as between New York and the rest of the country.

(5) NEW YORK'S REDUCED MONOPOLY

New York's monopolistic position as the financial centre of the United States has become reduced to an appreciable extent. Even though the creation of the market in CDs has gone some way towards restoring the *status quo*, the emergence and expansion of other leading financial centres in the Mid West and the West and the increased sophistication of out-of-town banks has made the situation less one-sided.

Admittedly some individual markets still tend to operate in a unilateral sense. In the CD market, for instance, big New York banks are primarily sellers and smaller out-of-town banks are buyers. But the money attracted to New York by such means is apt to find its way back to the places of its origin through the operation of the market in commercial paper in the reverse sense.

The development of a number of money markets has attracted additional funds into short-term investments and has broadened the basis of the market for such investments. Until the slump of 1929 short-term funds seeking temporary employment were attracted mostly into the Wall Street market for brokers' loans, which was a major factor making for instability both on the Stock Exchange and in the monetary and economic system. The widening of the choice between various forms of employment of call moneys has made, therefore for a higher degree of stability.

(6) RE-ALLOCATION OF FUNDS

The evolution of parallel money markets in the United States has greatly facilitated the re-allocation of funds between advanced and less advanced areas of the Federation. It should go a long way towards allaying the reasonable fears of less advanced states that, unless they are financially insulated from the more advanced states, their financial resources would tend to become attracted by the latter, and that, as a result, the difference between their relative pace of progress would widen further, in accordance with the pessimistic prediction of the New Testament: 'Whosoever hath, to him shall be given, but whosoever hath not, from him shall be taken away even that that he hath'. Thanks to the plurality of money markets, funds are now liable to move in both directions simultaneously – from the relatively poor states to the rich states through one market, and at the same time in the opposite direction through another market.

Admittedly there are periods when all markets but one tend to be neglected, and funds then can only flow in one direction through that channel. But normally funds tend to flow in all directions through the various channels. As a result the less advanced regions receive, by and large, their fair share of the financial resources of the country through the intricate network of the parallel money markets. At any rate, they now stand a better chance to obtain satisfaction of their financial requirements than they did prior to the development of the parallel markets.

As several markets are of recent origin they are still liable to undergo institutional and technical changes until their mechanisms settle down in their permanent form. In any case the systems and activities of American parallel money markets are more liable to become subject to changes as a result of new official regulations than the London parallel money markets which are allowed a much higher degree of freedom to develop their own rules and practices.

One of the economic effects of the emergence of multiple money markets is a tendency towards an increase in the velocity of circulation of money in the United States. Their operation creates a tendency for funds to flow into hands which make more active use of them. Quite apart from the increase in money market turnover, which need not in itself produce any profound economic effects, the new monetary channels provide opportunities for additional borrowing, not only for productive purposes but also for speculative purposes. Given a 'neutral attitude' on the part of the authorities, the super-imposition of the new markets to the conventional markets tends to produce an expansionary effect. This view is, however, open to argument.

Reference was made in various chapters to the re-allocation of banking resources as a result of the operation of various parallel markets. The question whether such re-allocation tends to produce on balance an effect on the total volume of banking resources, and whether its influence on the velocity of circulation of the balances is liable to produce an inflationary or deflationary effect, is highly controversial and is likely to be subject to lively debate by generations of economists and practical experts. What we must always bear in mind is that the Federal Reserve is always in a position to offset any unwanted effect.

(7) THE COMPLICATION OF BANKING

One of the results of the development of parallel money markets in the United States, as in London, is that banking has become much more complicated. The Bank treasurers' task has become even more difficult, not only because their tight-rope walking between having unwanted excess reserves and being short of liquid resources has become even more precarious, but also because they have to choose between a larger number of alternative investment facilities and borrowing facilities. Their banks' reserves are now exposed to unexpected reductions or increases from more directions. Also it is now their job to follow closely a larger number of differentials if they want to avoid missing profitable short-term investment opportunities.

The change has affected big non-banking institutions in the same sense. Being often in possession of substantial liquid resources, they can now ill afford to ignore the differentials between yields obtainable to their various alternative forms of investment. Their treasurers have to keep an eye on the interplay between the parallel markets and endeavour to switch their funds from one market to another at the right moment. It is no longer sufficient to have sound judgement – and lucky hunches – about the general prospects of interest rates. Treasurers have to also take a view about the prospects of changes in differentials between the rates in the various parallel markets.

(8) INTERNATIONALISATION OF THE NEW YORK MARKET

Another effect of the development of parallel money markets is further progress towards the internationalisation of the New York market. Until comparatively recently domestic business kept American banks well occupied, so that even in New York international business was for most banks of relatively small importance compared with the volume of their domestic business. Today New York is the leading international banking centre and the international operations of its banks have assumed considerable importance both in an absolute and in a relative sense. A number of foreign branches and affiliates have been established there. The number of American branches and affiliates established outside the United States is many times larger than it was before the war, their main object being to gain direct access to foreign money markets.

Even the differences between business hours in New York and other financial centres is no longer the same handicap to the maintenance of closer relations between money markets. As stated in Volume 1, a number of American branches in London and other London banks maintain some degree of contact with the New York money market during the hours when the latter is open and the London market closed. There is, moreover, active business in Euro-dollars and other money market transactions between the Nassau branches or affiliates of American banks or other Nassau banks and New York banks while London is closed. These operations are not confined to arbitrage, unless we use the term in its broad sense which includes 'borrower-arbitrage' and 'lender-arbitrage' – that is, operations to take advatnage of discrepancies between rates prevailing in various parallel markets in the other centre.

PART II

MONEY MARKETS OF CANADA

CHAPTER ELEVEN

Creation of an Advanced Mechanism

(2) THIRD ADVANCED MONEY MARKET

NEXT to the British and American money markets, the Canadian money market is easily the most highly developed and possesses the most highly sophisticated mechanism. This in spite of the small population of the country compared with that of other countries which, in spite of their advanced economic system, have less advanced money markets. The relative economic and financial importance of Canada is in many respects quite out of proportion to the size of its population, but this alone would not account for the high stage reached by her money market. Close financial association with the United States may possibly have a great deal to do with it.

The Canadian money market, unlike that of Britain, the continental countries apart from Switzerland, the United States and Japan, is not concentrated exclusively or overwhelmingly in a single financial centre. It is true that Toronto claims to be the leading Canadian money market, but Montreal contests that claim, and financial opinion outside the two cities is divided as to which claim is justified. Moreover, the head office of the Bank of Canada is in Ottawa, whence the monetary policy of the country is guided. During the hours when Toronto and Montreal are closed there is a small market in Vancouver, but most transactions are deferred to the following morning when they can be executed in Toronto or in Montreal. Business hours are from 9 a.m. to 5 p.m., but there is a difference of two hours between the time zone of Toronto and Montreal and that of Vancouver. But in these times of telecommunication the dipsersion of monetary activities between several cities does not prevent the existence of a unified money market in Canada, any more than it does in Switzerland.

(2) LARGE TURNOVER

The turnover in the Canadian money market, in spite of the small size of Canada's population, bears comparison from time to time with that of the money markets of Germany or France. And it surpasses all but New York and London in respect of the variety of her money market instruments and the number of her markets. Indeed in some respects Canada surpasses even New York and London from the point of view of the refinements of her monetary practices and techniques. One or two of her money market's methods of dealing and of its types of operations, described in later chapters, are even more advanced than anything practised in the two leading money markets.

The Canadian money market follows the world trend in extending its activities to the 'no man's land' between money market and capital market – medium-term credit instruments. The maximum maturities of money market paper vary from country to country and within countries from market to market. They are apt to lengthen during prolonged periods free of trouble. In Canada there is, however, a definite time limit for medium-term paper – three years, because that is the Bank of Canada's time limit for securities eligible for collateral for dealers or banks borrowing from it. However, in Canada as in other countries the overwhelming majority of money market transactions is for periods not exceeding one year.

(3) AN ARTIFICIAL CREATION

One of the peculiarities of the Canadian money market is the extent to which it is the artificial creation of the monetary authorities – the Finance Ministry and the Bank of Canada. The London money market is almost entirely a natural growth, its institutions have developed spontaneously through private initiative, though not without official guidance of a varying degree. The same is largely true of the New York money market, with the difference that official influence played in its development a much more active part than in the London market. Frankfurt, Amsterdam and Brussels developed largely independently of official policies, while the French authorities were unable to achieve the degree of development of the Paris money market which their policy had aimed at. The Swiss money market emerged largely in the face of official disapproval, or at any rate in the complete absence of any official encouragement.

As far as the Canadian money market is concerned, the authorities are entitled to claim credit for its remarkable progress achieved within a very brief period. Had it not been for the official efforts in the 'fifties to create a market in Treasury bills and in call money, there would be a very limited money market in Canada today. Although official efforts were, and still are, focused on those two markets, several others have emerged on private initiative once the foundations for them have been laid by the existence of a call money market. Thus the market in commercial paper, in finance paper, in Certificates of Deposits and in bank acceptances might not have come into existence – at any rate not for a long time – if the authorities had not encouraged the emergence of an active market in day-to-day money that has enabled banks, other financial institutions, commercial corporations and other investors to acquire and hold Treasury bills, short-term bonds and other kinds of money market paper without having to jeopardise their liquidity.

(4) THE CALL MONEY MARKET

The only Canadian money market which has come into being independent of the officially encouraged creation of the call money market, is the market in U.S. dollar deposits – the Canadian equivalent of the Euro-dollar market. But for the emergence of a market in day-to-day money in terms of Canadian dollars the turnover in the Canadian money market might have developed almost entirely in terms of U.S. dollars. A much more active market in U.S. dollar call money would have developed than the one that exists today. Swapped U.S. dollar deposits would have been used on a much larger scale than they are actually used, in the absence of similar facilities in terms of Canadian dollars.

The evolution of an advanced money market in Canada has been influenced to a large degree by her close financial links with the United States and, to a smaller degree, with Britain. Various institutions and methods of the Canadian money market are in fact a compromise between the American and British systems, though they are nearer to the former than to the latter. The spectacular commercial and industrial development of the country, especially since the war, also had its share in generating influences making for the emergence of a highly developed monetary mechanism.

Last but by no means least, Canadians are highly gifted in the sphere of finance and are able not only to copy successfully institutions and methods of other countries but to invent innovations of their own. They are essentially international-minded in the commercial and financial sphere and possess a great many financial links with other countries. The relatively high percentage represented by their foreign trade in their economies is not the only reason for the creation and maintenance of bank branches and affiliates in a number of foreign countries and in the participation of Canadian banks in a number of international financial transactions in which Canada is not directly concerned.

For all these reasons the description of the Canadian money market deserves more space than would appear to be justified solely on the basis of its actual size. In any case, the market, like the country itself, has immense potentialities for expansion.

(5) AUTHORISED DEALERS

The most important element in the Canadian money market mechanism is the dealer – the Canadian equivalent to the London discount house – who has the privilege to use the Bank of Canada as lender of last resort. Originally twelve in number, there are at the time of writing fifteen of them. But in addition, many smaller dealers who are less active in the money market are not on the Central Bank's select list of houses with re-discount facilities. The qualification that enables dealers to get on the list is large turnover and willingness to hold bills and short bonds in their portfolios – in other words, willingness to assist in the creation and maintenance of a good market.

Dealers are allowed a limit up to which they may rely on the facilities of the Central Bank and these limits are reconsidered in frequent intervals. They have to submit weekly returns to the Bank of Canada. These limits are relatively low, because it is against the official policy to encourage dealers to resort to the facilities frequently, on a large scale or for prolonged periods instead of trying to meet their requirements and those of their clients in the market or through borrowing from banks. On the other hand, as we shall see in the next chapter, dealers have other privileges which place them in an advantageous position compared with banks and other operators, borrowers or investors in money market paper.

In his evidence before the Royal Commission on Banking and Finance in 1963, Mr Louis Rasminsky, Governor of the Bank of Canada, stated that there was no rigid ceiling fixed for the grand total of limits for all dealers, and that if additional dealers are admitted to the market that grand total may be increased. Nevertheless, he added, it would be against the Bank's policy to increase the grand total considerably, because such an increase would have an expansionary effect and might result in inflation.

(6) ROLE OF CHARTERED BANKS

Chartered banks constitute another important element in the Canadian money market. They were originally almost the only large-scale buyers of Treasury bills but gradually their relative share declined and that of 'near-banks' – financial institutions of various classes other than chartered banks – and of non-banking investors increased. A most important role of chartered banks in the money market is that they lend dealers day-to-day money and grant other forms of short-term credits to dealers, thereby enabling the latter to buy and hold Treasury bills and other kinds of market paper without having to fall back upon the Bank of Canada for financing their holdings. This role will be discussed in greater detail in Chapter 12.

While in London the Bank of England insists that the functions of dealers and those of brokers must be kept apart, at any rate technically – affiliates of dealers may act as brokers – no such rule exists in Canada. There is a firm of dealers which combines its functions with those of a broker. Its sphere of activities is confined largely to commercial paper, finance paper, acceptances and CDs.

(7) OPEN MARKET OPERATIONS

The Bank of Canada is of course the focal point of the money market. Although its head office is in Ottawa it has dealing agents in Toronto and in Montreal. They are in constant touch with their head office and with each other and are largely independent of the managements of the Toronto and Montreal branches. It is the Central Bank's task to execute the Finance Ministry's monetary policy decisions largely under the influence of the Central Bank's

E

advice, especially in trying to determine the volume of money and the level of interest rates. This task is performed largely by buying and selling Government securities. But while in New York and London intervention largely assumes the form of open market operations, the Bank of Canada prefers on the whole to play a more passive role. Instead of taking the initiative for changing supply-demand relationship in the Treasury bill market or on the market of day-to-day loans, it merely provides the counterpart to transactions which are initiated by market operators and which, unless met by official buying or selling, would tend to influence the trend in a sense unwanted by the Bank. The difference between the two policies is largely one of method and the result is the same. But it is an important difference nevertheless.

The Bank of Canada is the executive hand of the Finance Ministry, not only in respect of monetarypolicy but also in respect of debt management. In that sphere its duty is to maintain the stability of Treasury bill rates and of prices of Government securities in general. This task is apt to come into conflict with its task as the guardian of the stability of the Canadian dollar and of the Canadian economy. According to Mr Rasminsky's evidence quoted above, the Central Bank deems its foremost duty to give priority to the latter task. Thus it broadens the spread between its buying and selling price of Treasury bills when it does not wish to buy too large amounts in face of a selling pressure in the market, even though in doing so it abstains from preventing a fall in the price of bills, which is contrary to the Finance Ministry's policy.

The relative extent of official operations in the Treasury bill market is comparable with that of the Federal Reserve in the U.S. bill market. It is considerably higher than that of the Bank of England in the London market.

In respect of the degree of discipline in the Canadian money market, the system bears much more similarity to the informal British system than to the formal American system. Although minimum reserve requirements are statutory, as in the United States, the activities of banks and dealers are influenced by informal hints from the Bank of Canada rather than by rigid rules laid down by the Government or the Central Bank. If the Bank of Canada informs a dealer that certain types of transactions, though legally permissible, are not welcome in official quarters, the dealer will abstain from engaging in such transactions.

CHAPTER TWELVE

Day-to-Day Money

(1) THE CENTRE OF THE MONEY MECHANISM

In Canada, as in most other countries, the call money market or day-to-day money market constitutes the centre of the money market mechanism. Like the Canadian market for Treasury bills, it is an artificial creation and not a natural growth, but it is none the worse for that. It is a highly efficient market which satisfactorily fulfils the purpose of providing convenient facilities for banks to adjust their cash positions. At the same time it greatly facilitates the task of the monetary authorities to apply their monetary and economic policies by means of regulating the volume of credit through their open market operations.

As in Britain, in Lombard Street, call money in Canada has to be fully secured with a small margin which is not so wide as in London. Collaterals that borrowers have to provide to lenders include all securities issued or guaranteed by the Government of Canada and maturing within three years. This includes Treasury bills and short Government bonds or near-maturing loans. Provincial and Municipal issues and eligible bankers' acceptances also qualify for serving as securities.

Next to cash and to deposits with the Bank of Canada, day-to-day money and call money are looked upon as the most liquid assets banks and other lenders can hold. Provided that lenders call their loans by noon, they are repayable on the same day, not later than 3.30 p.m. Calling of day-to-day loans is, therefore, a more effective and simple way of raising cash for immediate requirements than selling bills or borrowing, because under either of the two alternative devices, money is received in the form of cheques which have to be passed through the clearing house. This entails two days delay, while call money has to be repaid in certified cheques which count for cash. Of course it is possible to stipulate payment by certified cheques also in connection with other deals, but it is a departure from routine not resorted to regularly.

(2) AN ALTERNATIVE TO BORROWING
FROM THE BANK OF CANADA

Calling of day-to-day money obviates the necessity for banks to sell bills or to borrow from the Bank of Canada on occasions when it is not in the interests of the bank concerned to resort to either device. Canadian banks are reluctant to borrow from the Bank of Canada and seldom do so if they can conveniently avoid it, partly because they prefer to reserve the use of their facilities with the Central Bank for unforeseen contingencies, or for situations in which other methods of raising cash are either inconvenient, or too expensive, or difficult. In any case, for banks to borrow from the Central Bank is usually an expensive method of raising funds. The Bank of Canada lends to banks for a minimum period of seven days, so that if the money is only required for a day or two it is costly to have to pay interest at Bank rate for seven days. For this reason alone it is in the interest of banks to hold enough day-to-day money to meet their probable requirements, even if it means some loss of interest compared with the yield obtainable on bills or other forms of liquid investment.

There is no inter-bank dealing in Canadian day-to-day money or in any form of deposit or loan in terms of Canadian dollars. Banks transact day-to-day loans with dealers or with non-banking customers, but not with each other. There is keen competition between dealers for day-to-day loans from Chartered banks or other lenders so that rates on day-to-day money, as on time loans, truly reflect supply-demand relationships.

(3) TIME LOANS

Time loans are usually for standard maturities – seven, thirty sixty, ninety, 180 days and twelve months – but it is possible to deal for odd dates. The market in call money is much more active then the market in time loans.

Apart altogether from the banks' cash requirements to meet probable withdrawals, day-to-day money serves the important purpose of enabling banks to bring their cash reserve ratio to the legal minimum. This means that, since any withdrawal of deposits reduces the bank's cash reserve in so far as this brings the cash ratio below the limit, the difference has to be replaced to make good the reduction of the reserve below minimum requirements brought about by the reduction of the deposits.

The market for day-to-day loans was initiated in 1954, as part of the general scheme of the monetary authorities to create a money market. It is linked closely with the market in Treasury bills. The rates are almost always slightly lower than the yield on Treasury bills, so that it is worthwhile for dealers to acquire and hold Treasury bills and finance them with the aid of call money. This is usually done on an extensive scale. The chartered banks are the principal lenders, but near-banks and other financial institutions, too, often employ in that form purely temporary surplus funds, or even some permanent near cash reserves.

(4) NO SECONDARY MARKET

The call money market is an active market, but there is no secondary market, for dealers do not re-lend their call money to other dealers or to anyone else. Nor do lenders of call money lend to each other. They either use their surplus holdings of day-to-day loans for reducing their liabilities to the Bank of Canada or to other banks, or for investing in Treasury bills or other market paper, or for keeping in readiness a sufficient amount of meet cash requirements without having to resort to their facilities with the Bank of Canada for assistance, and without having to sell bills or other assets at a moment when this would entail actual loss or at any rate loss of probable profit.

The minimum amount transacted in the market is $100,000, but usually much larger single amounts change hands, anything up to between $10 million to $25 million. The turnover fluctuates widely, but it is fairly high on the average, because every day some banks have surpluses to lend while others have to call the amounts they had lent to meet deficiencies. On busy days banks may lend right up to 3.30 p.m., which is often necessary in Toronto or Monteral.

(5) DIFFERENCE IN TIME ZONES

Owing to the different time zones, the requirements of Vancouver or Halifax bank branches or customers might not reach Toronto or Montreal banks till late.

Although, as already observed, day-to-day money rates are normally slightly lower than Treasury bill rates, this need not necessarily be so. During spells of tight money sudden calls might induce dealers to pay higher rates, so that call money rates might reach and even exceed Treasury bill rates for brief periods. Needless to say, if dealers take the view that this state of affairs is likely to continue for more than a few days they realise some of their Treasury bill holdings rather than carry them at a loss. But it may not be worth their while to incur the cost and inconvenience to interfere with their portfolios for the sake of avoiding a minor loss for a day or two.

CHAPTER THIRTEEN

Bankers' Acceptances

(1) MARKET CREATED IN 1962

THE market in bankers' acceptances made its appearance in Canada in 1962 by a decision of the Canadian Bankers' Association under which banks were authorised to accept, buy or sell bills of corporations other than finance companies, with maturities from thirty to ninety days. Such bills are treated as bankers' acceptances if they are accepted by a chartered bank. Under the Bank of Canada Act the bills have to serve the purpose of financing transactions in 'goods, wares and merchandise' which definition includes, in addition to manufactures, products of mines, quarries, agricultural products, products of the sea, lakes and rivers.

Marketable acceptances must mature within ninety days from the date on which they are acquired by the buying bank. The minimum amount of inter-bank transaction in acceptances is $100,000. Bankers' acceptances are eligible for re-discount by the Bank of Canada and for serving as collaterals for loans by chartered banks and by the Bank of Canada.

(2) PROGRESS A SLOW PROCESS

The development of the Canadian market in acceptances was a slow process. The amount of outstanding acceptances only reached $10 m. after the first two years of its existence. Most business corporations considered the commission of $1\frac{1}{2}$ per cent charged by the accepting banks – the same as in London after the war – too high, as it raised the cost of this form of financing above the cost of financing by means of issuing commercial paper. Firms whose bills are accepted by banks must have a high credit rating, and are therefore in a position to borrow also in the commercial paper market, usually at a lower cost. Firms of less high standing have no access either to the commercial paper market or to the acceptance market and cover their short-term requirements by bank advances.

In 1965 one of the chartered banks reduced its acceptance commission to ½ per cent per annum for first-class borrowers and some other banks followed its example. As a result the expansion of the market became accelerated and by the end of 1970 the outstanding total was around $250 million. Most of this amount is believed to be held by dealers who earn a profit margin by financing their holdings with the aid of day-to-day loans.

(3) INVESTORS PREFER COMMERCIAL PAPER

In the course of its open market operations, the Bank of Canada buys bankers' acceptances, though on a much smaller scale than its operations in Treasury bills. In spite of their liquidity and security, bankers' acceptances have not succeeded in achieving popularity among investors, most of whom prefer to hold commercial paper. Even though the acceptance or endorsement of a bill by a bank makes it a safer short-term investment than commercial paper, most investors prefer to benefit by the higher yield of the latter, provided that the issuing firm is of high standing. Unless this attitude changes the acceptance market is bound to remain a relatively unimportant section of the Canadian money market.

The amounts of acceptances in market operation must be in multiples of $5,000 for the sake of expeditious transaction of business. This does not mean that business firms have to adjust the amounts of their bills to the nearest round figure, as in relationship between banks and their customers broken amounts can be dealt with. It is only when the banks, having concluded a transaction, or several transactions, with customers, want to cover their commitments in the market that they have to deal in the nearest figure divisible by $5,000.

CHAPTER FOURTEEN

Treasury Bills

(1) EXPANSION DUE TO DAY-TO-DAY MARKET

THE Canadian market in Treasury bills is of even more recent origin than the American market. The issue of Treasury bills by tenders was initiated in 1934 and from 1937 the system of fortnightly tenders came into existence. In the mid-'fifties, the Canadian authorities stepped up their efforts to create a money market and weekly tenders were introduced in 1953. A kind of one-sided primary market came into existence. The bills offered were taken up mainly by chartered banks and dealers. The initial volume was very modest and its expansion was slow. The secondary market consisted at first very largely of purchases and sales by the Bank of Canada itself on the basis of its two-way quotations of prices. There was, and still is, no direct dealing between chartered banks. Dealers were originally reluctant to carry portfolios of bills, owing to the high cost of the financing of their holdings by means of bank loans. This difficulty was overcome through the creation of an active market in day-to-day money, discussed in the last chapter. As a result of the accessibility of financing facilities – in addition to those provided to dealers and bankers by the Bank of Canada itself – the volume and turnover of Treasury bills increased considerably during the late 'fifties and in the 'sixties.

(2) RULES OF THE MARKET

Treasury bills are for ninety-one days and 182 days – about four-fifths of the amount offered is for the shorter maturity – though occasionally bills for longer maturities are issued. They are of $25,000, $50,000, $100,000 and $1,000,000 denominations. Amounts applied for must be $25,000 or multiples thereof. Only banks and dealers can apply, others have to apply through banks or dealers or have to acquire bills in the secondary market. Tenders have to be submitted by 12 noon every Thursday. The same applicant may submit several tenders offering different prices. The Bank of Canada itself usually submits two tenders, one for its own account and on behalf of its clients, and another to cover the entire amount offered by the Finance Ministry. This practice is a precaution against the possibility of cartels by banks and dealers aiming at uniform bids at low prices, and also against the risk that total private tenders might not cover the entire amount offered.

Applicants are informed at 2 p.m. on the same day about the amount allotted to them and the price at which they are allotted. This system is identical with the British system. Unlike the American system it does not distinguish between two categories of applicants, and the allocation is strictly according to the prices offered. The Bank of Canada informs applicants about the highest, lowest and average prices offered by applicants for each maturity. At the same time the amount of next week's offer is announced. Applicants inform the Bank of Canada by 4 p.m. of the denominations in which they want the bills allotted to them. Delivery and payment take place by 3 p.m. on the following day.

(3) CENTRAL BANK'S TECHNICAL ASSISTANCE

Applicants are able to prescribe the branch of the Bank of Canada at which the bills are to be delivered. The Bank of Canada has a system of wire network between its branches through which it can arrange to deliver bills, or accept delivery of bills, at whichever branch it is convenient to the party concerned, without any extra charge. Payments must be made in bankers' drafts, certified cheques or clearing house settlement on the day following the transaction, but settlement on the same day can also be arranged.

Treasury bills are similar to those in Britain and in the United States. They bear no interest and their yield is represented by the discount at which they are allotted. In the secondary market the bills are discounted on a 365-day year basis. Treasury bills play an important part in debt management and in the execution of monetary policy, and they provide investors of every kind with a convenient short-term investment. Owing to the well-developed secondary market and the willingness of the Bank of Canada and the chartered banks to accept them as collaterals, they are a highly liquid form of investment with a relatively high yield.

(4) NON-BANK HOLDERS PREDOMINATE

Originally investors acquired and held the bulk of Treasury bills, but gradually the proportion of non-banking holders declined, because other market instruments offered a higher yield on short-term investment than Treasury bills. The latter, together with other market instruments, tended to compete with time deposits, offering higher yields and facilities for realising them before maturity without undue loss. As Professor J. S. G. Wilson pointed out, until 1955 the banks made premature withdrawals of time deposits rather difficult for time deposit holders who had to forfeit their interest for the entire period of the deposit if they reclaimed it even a few days before maturity. This practice produced an effect similar to the rigidity imposed on American bank deposits by Regulation Q – it diverted deposits from banks.

In 1955 banks relaxed their rule as far as deposits over $100,000 for periods of at least ninety days were concerned, in order to check the drain on their time deposits held by large depositors. Many of them became by then sufficiently sophisticated to switch their money into Treasury bills or other market paper which they were in a position to realise without having to submit to the degree of penalty inflicted on them by banks under the old practice. But by that time many customers had come to acquire the habit of investing their liquid funds in Treasury bills or in other market paper, so that the change of the rule had only a partial effect. To recover lost deposits, banks resorted to the issue of marketable Certificates of Deposit in the 'sixties.

(5) FISCAL ADVANTAGE

Investors found that from a fiscal point of view the holding of Treasury bills had an advantage compared with the holding of bonds. Although technically the difference between the purchase price and redemption price or sale price of Treasury bills constituted a capital gain it was not subject to capital gains tax.

If buyers of Treasury bills are non-residents they are subject to a witholding tax of 15 per cent on the yield, to be deducted when they acquire the bills, for the unexpired period. Until recently, if they sold their bills before maturity, they could reclaim the over-payment from the Canadian revenue authorities. This was a clumsy and cumbersome procedure which did discourage to some extent foreign demand for Canadian Treasury bills, especially as there were considerable delays in the repayment. But it was better than the situation created in 1971 when the concession was withdrawn.

A high proportion of transactions in Treasury bills in the secondary market, or with the Bank of Canada, is on a buy-back basis. The official policy is to aim at ironing out fluctuations of Treasury bill rates without diverting too much business from the market. To that end, the Bank of Canada, having originally fixed too narrow a spread between its buying and selling prices, broadened the spread, for otherwise it might be more profitable for many people to deal with the Central Bank rather than with dealers or bankers in the market. The same tactics are applied also when the Bank of Canada is not keen on buying or on selling. It does not actually refuse to buy or sell but tries to make it more profitable to deal in the market where the spread is narrower. Another way in which the Bank of Canada tries to encourage dealing in the market is to grant purchase and resale facilities on more favourable terms to dealers than to banks.

(6) PRE-TENDER CONTRACTS

One of the sophisticated devices alluded to in the last chapter, which is not familiar in other money markets, is the pre-tender contract. Under it a dealer sells Treasury bills to banks or others prior to the announcement of the result of the tenders, at an agreed price. The price is usually based on the average tender yield to be announced, less two basis points, provided that this price does not exceed the highest price paid at the tenders. As Professor Wilson points out, from the bank's point of view such a contract is a hedge when the tender is likely to be too tricky. This device is somewhat less risky than tendering at different prices to avoid being left without new bills.

Yet another privilege of dealers aimed at stimulating the market is their ability to borrow bills and other Government securities from the Bank of Canada. The transaction must be reversed within thirty days, but in given circumstances this period can be extended to ninety days. This device enables dealers to sell to their customers maturities required by the latter, even if they themselves do not hold such maturities in their portfolio and if they are not easily obtainable at short notice. It gives them a chance to look round for the required maturities, and should they be unable to buy them on acceptable prices they can bide their time.

(7) DAYLIGHT OVERDRAFTS

Another facility, one provided by chartered banks to dealers, is 'daylight overdrafts' to bridge over the time lag between the purchase of the maturities required by their customers and the receipt of payment from the customers later on the same day.

As in London and in New York, the Canadian equivalent of our discount market extended its activities to short bonds – in the case of Canada bonds up to three years and near-maturing long-term loans and referred to in the market as 'short Canadas'. Capital gains by buyers on such transactions are subject, however, to capital gains tax. Nevertheless very short bonds compete with long bills, so that the authorities decided to discontinue offering 273-day bills which were offered experimentally in 1953.

As already stated above, bonds transacted in the money market are up to a maturity of three years, because bonds of longer maturities are not eligible to serve as collaterals for day-to-day loans from the Bank of Canada or from chartered banks. The bonds are of C\$1,000, C\$5,000, C\$25,000, C\$100,000 and C\$1 million denominations. The short bond market deals also in short-term Canadian National Railway issues, and in provincial and Municipal securities. Provincial bonds are issued either by the Provincial Governments or under their guarantee by electric power authorities and similar agencies. Some of the issues assume the form of Treasury bills.

Some issuing authorities, such as Quebec Hydro and Ontario Hydro, issue bonds for any short- or medium-term maturities to suit the investors' requirements. The spread between the yields of Provincial and Dominion Government issues fluctuates widely, owing to the absence of a regular secondary market for most Provincial bonds. This means that only investors or dealers who are prepared to hold the bonds to maturity bid for them. There are also differences between the relative credit rating of the various Provincial issues.

Unlike British Municipalities, Canadian Municipalities do not bid for deposits. But the respective Provincial Governments authorise them to issue short-term bills, with maturities ranging from fourteen to 270 days. Their minimum denomination is C$100,000. Their yields fluctuate in sympathy with those of Provincial issues and are slightly higher than the latter. Most of them have no regular secondary market.

CHAPTER FIFTEEN

Commercial Paper

(1) CREDIT RESTRAINT STIMULATED ISSUES

CANADIAN commercial paper, like American commercial paper, is a one-name paper. It is referred to sometimes as corporation paper or industrial paper, to distinguish it from promissory notes of a similar kind issued by finance houses. While in the United States business firms preceded finance houses in initiating the development of a market in their promissory notes, in Canada promissory notes issued by finance houses, to be dealt with in the next chapter, were first in the field. It was under the influence of credit squeezes in the 'fifties that leading corporations decided to supplement their short-term credits raised by means of bank advances by issuing commercial paper.

Apart from the need for additional borrowing facilities, considerations of interest charges also played a part in inducing business firms to resort to this form of borrowing. Commercial paper issued by Canadian industrial and commercial firms – some of which are subsidiaries of leading American firms – is substantially similar to American commercial paper.

(2) 'SECURED' BY OPEN OVERDRAFTS

The notes are legally unsecured and are one-name paper and, for this reason, only firms of high credit rating are in a position to issue them. The American practice of nominally 'securing' them by arranging an open unused credit line during the duration of the notes has also been adopted. Only the smaller firms have to cover the whole amount; in the case of larger firms a bank credit up to 50 per cent, or even less, is sufficient. Firms of absolutely first-class standing are able to issue notes without having to arrange such credit lines.

Commercial paper can be either fixed interest-bearing or it can be issued at a discount. All dealing in the secondary market is on a discount basis. The minimum amount of individual rates is $100,000. Higher amounts are usually multiples of $50,000.

Maturities vary from one day's notice to fixed maturities of twelve months. In theory either party can call the notes subject to notice, but in practice the issuing firms seldom, if ever, exercise their rights, for in doing so they would discourage investors from acquiring their paper in future. Because of their borrowers' willingness to repay the notes if the investor needs the money, no secondary market has developed in notes subject to notice, but there is a secondary market in notes with fixed maturities. Dealers may act as intermediaries not only in the original placing of the notes, but also in their subsequent re-sale. Some borrowers deal directly with banks or with large investors, but most of them issue the notes through dealers, especially if large amounts are involved.

(3) EITHER FIXED INTEREST OR DISCOUNT

In many instances a maximum amount of issue is fixed and investors are given the choice between buying fixed interest-bearing notes and notes sold at a discount. In other instances, notes of one type or the other, or both, are on tap. Notes with fixed maturities are usually a matter for negotiation and issuing firms endeavour to meet the investors' requirements. Some firms are permanently in the market on a large scale.

The total of commercial paper issues made by one single leading firm was just under $2 billion by the beginning of 1971 and the average amount outstanding during the concluding years of the 'sixties was somewhat under $300 million. These figures give an idea of the scale of operations in the market.

Apart from questions of availability of additional credit and of the cost of borrowing, notes are often issued in anticipation of issues of long-term or medium-term bonds. This is done if the borrowers expect interest rates to decline and prefer not to commit themselves for a long period on the basis of the prevailing rates, or if the amounts required in the near future are not sufficiently large to justify long-term or medium-term bond issues. When the total of commercial paper that has been placed gradually reaches a high figure, the borrowing firm might deem it expedient to consolidate its floating debt by arranging medium- or long-term issues, thereby clearing the ground for issuing further notes without having too large amounts of floating debt outstanding.

(4) ARBITRAGE WITH THE U.S.

Commercial paper subject to a day's notice is taken up by banks or near-banks, also by treasurers of corporations wanting to obtain a yield on their liquid reserves. Notes with definite maturity are placed with institutional investors of every kind, both in Canada and in New York and London. The notes are issued by some borrowers either in Canadian dollars or in U.S. dollars, according to whether the prevailing swap rates make it attractive for U.S. investors to acquire notes in Canadian dollar denomination, or for Canadian residents to acquire notes in U.S. dollar denomination, with the exchange risk covered. When the Canadian dollar is expected to appreciate – as it was after the return to the floating system in 1969 – many non-resident investors acquire the notes issued in Canadian dollars without covering the forward exchange even if the forward Canadian dollar is at a premium.

Owing to the important part played by the swap rates of the U.S. dollar and, to a less extent, of sterling, the Bank of Canada intervened from time to time in 1970–1971 to keep down the premium on forward dollars. The object of such intervention was to make the acquisition of promissory notes in Canadian dollars, and other Canadian short-term investments by non-residents, less profitable and to discourage thereby the unwanted influx of hot money.

(5) NOTES ISSUED BY U.S. AFFILIATES

There is a fairly active arbitrage with New York in some Canadian commercial paper, especially with those issued by affiliates of big American corporations which issue commercial paper also in the United States. The issues of their Canadian affiliates usually secure a somewhat higher yield, especially if the premium of forward Canadian dollars becomes overvalued compared with its interest parity with the U.S. dollar. Holders are then able to sell forward their notes at an advantageous price.

There is a fair demand for Canadian commercial paper also in London, whether they are issued in Canadian dollars or in U.S. dollars. There is, however, no secondary market in them either in London or even in New York.

(6) EFFECT OF U.S. BUYING ON THE EXCHANGE

American buying of Canadian commercial paper is an important factor affecting the Canadian dollar. When the Canadian Budget of 1971 stopped a loophole through which the deduction of the 15 per cent withholding tax on commercial paper sold abroad could be evaded, the Canadian dollar, which was very firm until then, became distinctly weak. Until then it was possible to evade the withholding tax if the U.S. buyer of the commercial paper re-sold it to a Canadian resident before maturity. But now that the Canadian resident is responsible for the tax if he acquires the notes before maturity, there is no advantage in such a transaction.

As a general rule the rates on commercial paper are slightly higher than the rates on finance paper issued by firms of com-parable standing. This is because the latter are secured by the hire-purchase contracts they finance, while commercial paper is unsecured even if a credit line is kept open, unless it is guaranteed by the bank which has opened the credit line. Otherwise there is nothing to prevent the bank concerned from cutting the credit just when difficulties of the firm issuing commercial paper would make its use necessary.

In addition to lending money at call or at short notice to in-vestment dealers, chartered banks and others lend also to stock-brokers. The amounts of such loans are much smaller than those of loans to dealers.

CHAPTER SIXTEEN

Notes of Finance Companies

(1) FINANCE PAPER PRECEDED COMMERCIAL PAPER

THE issue of short-term notes by finance companies began in Canada much later than either in Britain or in the United States – to be exact, in 1951. Even then it did not assume noteworthy dimensions until official action resulted in the emergence of a market in short-term Treasury bills in 1954, which paved the way for other market instruments. Although the official policy was directed primarily towards the creation of a market for Treasury bills, its incidental effect was that it also created facilities for the issue and secondary sale of other kinds of market paper.

As already mentioned in the last chapter, while in the United States the appearance of commercial paper preceded that of finance paper, in Canada finance paper was first to come into existence. Amongst them promissory notes issued by wholly-owned Canadian subsidiaries of American finance companies figured prominently. Demand by American investors for Canadian finance paper issued by subsidiaries of American firms whose names were houshold words played an important part in encouraging the new departure made by these subsidiaries, and in paving the way also for the development of a market for Canadian issues proper.

Finance companies issue certificates secured by parcels of hire purchase contracts with similar maturities. Originally most of these certificates were brought by banks. Even though the certificates were transferable, it took some time before a secondary market developed in them.

(2) SETBACK THROUGH A FAILURE

The progress of both primary and secondary markets suffered a reverse, however, in 1965, as a result of the failure of a leading Canadian finance company. It took some time for finance paper to live down this setback, and even up to the time of writing it has

failed to recover fully the popularity it enjoyed among investors
before the failure. It is now bought mainly by dealers who keep it
in their portfolio or sell it to banks.

The notes of wholly-owned subsidiaries of American finance
companies are guaranteed by the parent companies. In spite of
this, as in the case of commercial paper issued by wholly-owned
subsidiaries of American business firms, their yield is higher than
the paper issued by their parent companies.

(3) U.S. AFFILIATES' PAPER FAVOURED

After the failure of 1965 notes of American subsidiaries came to
command higher prices than those issued by local finance companies. Prior to the incident of 1965 American investors were also
actively interested in finance paper issued by local Canadian
finance companies. After a few years they came to be interested
once more in first-rate issues. Nevertheless the fact that brokerage
on finance paper is twice as high as commercial paper shows that
even after a number of years it is more difficult to place the
former than the latter, unless they are issued by firms of very high
standing, such as, for instance, the Canadian subsidiary of General
Motors.

Finance paper of a totally different type, promissory notes
issued by Canadian bank affiliates, also made its appearance
during the 'sixties. On the other hand, finance paper issued in the
United States by holding companies of American banks has no
equivalent in Canada.

CHAPTER SEVENTEEN

Bank Deposit Instruments

(1) THE CANADIAN EQUIVALENT OF CDS

THERE is a well-developed market in the Canadian equivalent of American and British Certificates of Deposits. Those issued by chartered banks are called Bank Deposit Instruments; those issued by trust companies are called Guaranteed Investment Certificates. Apart from this terminological difference they are substantially identical with the CDs. The main difference is that in the primary market investors are not in a position to obtain the maturities they require and their choice is usually limited between thirty-day, sixty-day and ninety-day deposits. But this fact does not prevent investors from obtaining deposits for the required maturity, for in the secondary market dealers are usually able to accommodate them either from their own portfolios or through acquiring deposits for the required maturity from some other dealer or holder.

As the market has been in existence for some time there is in existence a certain amount of certificates maturing on any day. The secondary market is fairly active, so that it is possible to acquire certificates maturing on odd dates, All chartered banks issue certificates on their own behalf and not through their affiliates. The certificates are in Canadian dollars.

U.S. dollar and sterling CDs of firms with Canadian affiliates are sold in Canada and there is arbitrage between certificates issued by the American parent company and those issued by their Canadian affiliates.

The minimum amount of Deposit Instruments is $10,000, but for such a small amount the interest rate is well under market rates. In market transactions the minimum is usually $250,000, but amounts may be as high as $20 m. or $25 m. for a single transaction. Maturities are usually for standard dates, but some issuing banks or area banks are prepared to meet the depositor's requirements. In this respect the practice varies between various banks. Most of them are prepared to issue either registered receipts or bearer receipts, according to the depositor's choice.

Dealers usually hold portfolios in Certificates in order to ensure a good market by meeting demand without having to negotiate with a bank. All Certificates are in terms of Canadian dollars. No Certificates are issued in swapped U.S. dollars.

CHAPTER EIGHTEEN

U.S. Dollar Deposits

(1) THE CANADIAN EQUIVALENT OF EURO-DOLLARS

THERE is a very active market in Toronto and in Montreal in the Canadian equivalent of Euro-dollars and, to a very much less extent, in the equivalents of other Euro-currencies – that is, in deposits in terms of currencies other than Canadian dollars. The fact that total foreign currency assets and total liabilities of the chartered banks exceeded the equivalent of 12 billion Canadian dollars throughout 1970 indicates the magnitude of the market. U.S. dollars are virtually a second currency besides Canadian dollars in the Canadian money market.

Business in U.S. dollar deposits was brisk long before the emergence of the Euro-dollar market in London and other European financial centres in the late 'fifties, during the floating period of the Canadian dollar up to 1962. It is regarded as part of the activities of foreign exchange departments. There are no restrictions to inter-bank dealing in deposits in terms of U.S. dollars or other non-Canadian currencies. Re-stabilisation of the Canadian dollar in 1962 did not mean a decline in the activity in U.S. dollar deposits. For one thing, the volume of U.S. dollars in Canada increased materially in the 'sixties, partly because of fiscal considerations which made it advantageous for U.S. residents to transfer their capital or the proceeds of their capital to Canada, partly because of the expansion of American business interests and investments in Canada, and partly owing to the development and expansion of the Euro-dollar market in London and other centres across the Atlantic, which provided a permanent alternative outlet for Canadian holdings of U.S. dollars besides their investment in the New York market.

(2) FLOW OF FUNDS FROM THE U.S.

The rising trend of interest rates during the late 'sixties encouraged the flow of funds across the border, because Canadian banks, being unhampered by interest rate ceiling on time deposits, were able to pay higher interest rates on U.S. dollar deposits than banks in the United States which remained hampered by Regulation Q until 1970. The flow of American deposits depends from time to time to a very large degree on the swap rates compared with interest parities and on the view taken of the necessity to cover the exchange.

(3) CAUSES OF EXPANSION OF U.S. DEPOSITS

Another reason why deposits in terms of U.S. dollars held by Canadian banks tended to increase faster than their deposits in terms of Canadian dollars was the increase in the number of Canadian bank branches and agencies abroad and the expansion in the volume of Canadian commercial and financial transactions abroad. Canadian banks became more active in the Euro-dollar market.

Finally, the U.S. dollar deposits of Canadian banks increased in the late 'sixties as a result of the outflow of American capital owing to the anticipation of a reinforcement of the informal exchange control adopted by President Johnson's 'guidelines' in order to defend the dollar. Large amounts of dollar notes were constantly smuggled across the border. Since under the anti-hoarding legislation adopted in the 'thirties and never repealed, the banks were under obligation to report to the Revenue authorities any unusually large withdrawals of deposits in cash, a 'black market' in large amounts of notes exists in New York where such large amounts command a premium of anything up to $1\frac{1}{2}$ per cent over their nominal value. Once smuggled across the border, they are paid into Canadian banks and become U.S. dollar deposits held in Canada by non-residents. But New York agencies of Canadian banks, and Canadian banks in general, also obtain large U.S. dollar deposits transferred from the United States in a legitimate way. Owing to the closeness of U.S.-Canadian business and financial reasons there is ample justification for U.S. residents to hold dollars with Canadian banks.

Canadian banks employ their U.S. dollar deposits to a large extent in their original denomination by lending them to their New York agencies which place them in various forms in the New York money market. Such transactions are usually profitable, because even though deposit rates paid on such deposits are higher than those paid by American banks, they are lower than the yields obtainable on various American money market instruments. The dollar deposits can also be re-lent in their original denomination in the Euro-dollar market in London, Paris or other centres. In fact for a long time during the late 'fifties and the early 'sixties, that market was supplied mainly from Canadian deposits. During the late 'sixties American bank branches in Canada borrowed U.S. dollar deposits in the same way as American branches did in London, and lent them to their head offices.

(4) IMPORTANCE OF SWAP RATE

But Canadian banks also employ a large part of their U.S. dollars in the Canadian money market or in advances to their customers. To that end they swap them into Canadian dollars. The fact that the assets and liabilities of chartered banks in terms of foreign currencies are almost equal indicates that Canadian banks avoid taking exchange risk by being long or short in dollars. The market is to a very large extent in 'swapped dollar deposits' which is similar to the 'swap and deposit' business transacted in European markets on a large scale during the inter-war period. Most Canadian banks take great care that their assets and liabilities in U.S. dollars are always balanced.

One of the advantages of the accumulation of large U.S. dollar deposits from the point of view of Canadian banks is that, unlike their deposits in Canadian dollars, they are not subject to rules regarding cash ratio or liquidity ratio. Nevertheless owing to the fluidity of a large proportion of these deposits, the banks practice self-imposed restraint and employ a high proportion of them in an essentially liquid form, to be able to meet unexpected withdrawals.

(5) WINDOW-DRESSING ADVANTAGE

Another advantage of the influx of U.S. dollars is that it enables Canadian banks to show impressive increases of their deposits in their balance sheets. There is therefore keen competition between the Canadian banks for U.S. dollar deposits, and this contributes towards the increase of the turnover in the U.S. dollar deposit market, at the same time as keeping interest rates at a relatively high level. Owing to the existence of active arbitrage with the Euro-dollar market there should be no major discrepancies between rates for the same maturities for any length of time, allowing for the swap rates. But, as mentioned above, the Bank of Canada intervenes in given circumstances to maintain forward rates at an artificial level, in order to influence the influx or efflux of funds through covered arbitrage.

CHAPTER NINETEEN

Economics of Canada's Money Market

(1) CANADA'S EXAMPLE IN CREATING A MONEY MARKET

THE brief experience of the Canadian money market has conclusively proved that an economically advanced country need not remain handicapped by inadequacy of choice between alternative devices for short-term financing. The remedy lies in its own hands. The Canadian authorities have proved the possibility of developing within a brief space of time a money market which offers borrowers and lenders a variety of facilities and which achieves the creation of a highly advanced monetary mechanism.

A number of developed countries, such as some countries of Western Europe or Japan, which are at least as highly developed industrially and commercially as Canada and which possess equally developed banking systems and ample financial resources, are at the time of writing still not only very far behind Britain and the United States but also distinctly behind Canada in respect of the devices of their money markets. This has the disadvantage of depending for short-term credit and investment facilities largely on foreign money markets, and in many instances on local money markets for loans in terms of foreign currencies. The experience of Canada has proved that such countries would be in a position to make good their deficiencies. The Government, the Central Bank and the banking system of any advanced country is in a position to follow the Canadian example by bringing into existence a money market which is capable of offering a variety of useful facilities and has potentialities for further development.

(2) MONETARY AUTHORITIES HAVE THE LAST WORD

Admittedly the mere existence of a money market need not in itself create additional financial facilities to meet growing credit requirements, unless this is in accordance with the policy of the monetary authorities. They are in a position to keep down or mop up the money supply if it increases above a limit that is considered to be in accordance with the official policy. But in the absence of official resistance to expansion of credit an advanced local money market can and does provide additional facilities which could only be obtained from abroad in the absence of a a local money market. The basic condition is an efficient banking system which commands confidence.

(3) IS CANADA LESS DEPENDENT ON THE U.S.?

This argument appears to point to the conclusion that, thanks to the development of her money market, Canada is now less dependent financially on the United States than she was before she had a money market of her own. This is true in a sense, but we must bear in mind the extent to which American financial interests dominate the Canadian money market, both as investors and, since more recently, as borrowers. Although Canadian firms are now in a more favourable position to meet their short-term credit requirements in Toronto or Montreal instead of depending on New York, the trend in Toronto and Montreal is influenced to a very high degree by movements of American short-term funds in and out of the Canadian money market. On the other hand, Canadian firms – and Canadian subsidiaries of American firms – are now in a position to employ their liquid funds at home instead of having to employ them in New York or London for lack of short-term investment facilities in Canada. They do so to a substantial if varying degree. In that sense at any rate the Canadian economy does not depend on the United States to the same extent as before the emergence of the Canadian money market.

(4) WHY A FIXED EXCHANGE RATE WAS ABANDONED

Nevertheless the trend in the New York money market and in the economy of the United States does influence the trend in the Canadian money markets and in Canada's economy, and the creation of additional financial links between the two countries tends to increase the extent to which the Canadian money market and the Canadian economy react to changes in the trend across the border. This may have been one of the reasons why the Canadian Government decided in 1969 to abandon once more the system of fixed parities and to allow the Canadian dollar to fluctuate in terms of U.S. dollars and of other currencies.

No doubt the Canadian monetary authorities based their decision on the assumption that with the aid of the system of floating exchanges they would be in a better position to regulate the flow of funds between the money markets of the two countries. It would be premature at the time of writing to pronounce a definite judgement on that decision. But since owing to a number of circumstances the range of fluctuations between the spot rates of the two dollars tends to be very narrow it is doubtful whether they provide a shock-absorber to a sufficient extent to ensure the desired degree of independence of the monetary trend in Canada from the monetary trend in the United States. On the other hand, intervention by the Bank of Canada in the forward market does moderate to some extent the unwanted influx of short-term funds.

During the greater part of the previous period of floating exchanges in Canada, the money markets in Toronto and Montreal were still in their infancy, so that the experience gained during that period does not in itself help us very much to form a definite opinion about the chances of the new experiment in floating exchanges amidst changed circumstances. Moreover in the interval the relative strength of the two dollars has changed to the detriment of the U.S. dollar. Even though the Canadian dollar is still largely its satellite currency in the international field, the U.S. dollar is now largely on the defensive and there is a somewhat higher degree of reciprocity in its relationship with the Canadian dollar. Time alone will show how this change, together with the development of a more advanced Canadian money market, will affect the relationship between the American and Canadian money markets.

PART III

MONEY MARKETS OF EUROPE

CHAPTER TWENTY

The Paris Money Market

(1) FACILITIES IMPROVED BUT INADEQUATE

'STRICTLY speaking there is no true money market in France, as there is . . . in other countries, in which supply and demand for short-term capital can be matched through the free play of interest rates'. This observation made in 1962 in an official Common Market publication *The Instruments of Monetary Policy in Countries of the EEC*, is no longer valid to the same extent as it was in the early 'sixties. For in the meantime the French money market has made noteworthy progress. Even so, Paris is still without a good secondary market in bills in which fluctuating prices would adjust supply and demand to equilibrium. But it has developed an active market in overnight loans and in call money, and a reasonably good market exists now in time deposits of a wide range of maturities. Paris has also good Euro-currency markets.

It is true that progress towards a market with elastic supply and demand on an adequate scale, and towards the creation of a true system of parallel money markets offering lenders and borrowers a choice between a variety of lending and borrowing facilities has not kept pace with the increase in the importance of the French franc among the leading currencies. But it can no longer be contended that there is no true money market in France.

Nevertheless it remains correct to say that the facilities provided by the Paris money market bear no comparison with those of other first-class financial centres. In their report to the French Government prepared in 1968 by Robert Marjolin, Jean Sadrin and Oliver Wormser, *Rapport sur le marché monétaire et les conditions de crédit*, they emphatically state that, amidst the prevailing conditions of international competition, the absence of a satisfactory money market was still a handicap for the French economy. In spite of their widely-approved recommendations of improvements, there is even now much left to be desired, largely because the

F

disadvantages of a lack of certain facilities are greatly aggravated by the existence of various official restrictions.

(2) REGIONAL MARKETS ARE UNIMPORTANT

The popular saying *Paris c'est la France* applies to a very high degree to the French money market. It is true that there are several French provincial centres with important regional banks which act as intermediaries between their respective regions and Paris. But their relative importance compared with Paris is limited. Such inter-bank money market as exists in France operates almost exclusively in Paris. The relative importance of French secondary markets of Lille, Marseilles, Lyons, Bordeaux, etc., bears no comparison with that of Düsseldorf, Hamburg and Munich in Germany, or that of Boston, Philadelphia, Chicago, San Francisco and Los Angeles in the United States, not to speak of the relative importance of Basle and Geneva in Switzerland.

Before embarking on the description of the Paris money market it is necessary to cast a glance at the background against which it operates. There is a fundamental difference between the basic principle of banking relationship between the Central Bank and the banks of the private sector in France and the corresponding relationship in Britain, in the United States, in Germany and other countries where the Central Bank plays the part of lender of last resort.

(3) BANK OF FRANCE AS 'LENDER OF FIRST RESORT'

So far from playing that part, the Bank of France plays the part of 'lender of first resort'. Instead of lending only when banks are unable to meet their requirements from other sources, French banks usually avail themselves of the Bank of France's facilities whenever they can, in preference to borrowing elsewhere. It is only if they are unable to cover their requirements by borrowing from the Bank of France, or if the Central Bank's facilities are too costly, that they resort to other sources.

Consequently the Bank of France is a permanent creditor of French banks, though the extent of their indebtedness to the Central Bank is subject to wide fluctuations. The explanation of this state of affairs lies to a large extent in the deeply engrained hoarding habit of French people. Instead of depositing their money with banks, as their opposite numbers in other advanced countries do, they hoard it. As a result the total bank deposits in France fall short of the credit requirements of her advanced economy. In France credits need not necessarily create deposits, and they do not create deposits to anything like the extent they do in Britain, because a very high proportion of French people hoards the proceeds of the credits as soon as the money reaches them through the intermediary of the borrower. The banks are therefore unable to meet the credit requirements of their customers without drawing permanently on the Central Bank's facilities.

It is normally easier and cheaper for banks to borrow from the Bank of France through re-discounting or giving in pension eligible securities, up to the ceiling fixed for each bank. It is to their advantage to make systematic use of their facilities so long as they are able to do so without being charged penalising rates. It is only if their credit requirements exceed their *plafond* – the limits to which the Bank of France is prepared to lend them at Bank rate – or if they are relucatnt to exhaust their limits, wanting to keep in reserve some unused facilities, that they borrow outside the Bank of France.

(4) PENALISING RATES

The Bank of France has a very effective way to divert demand for credit to the market, by charging penalising rates on loans in excess of the *plafond*. Although this system of penalties on excessive borrowing exists also in other countries, in no other leading country is it so elaborate and so extensively institutionalised as in France. In other countries there are usually no hard and fast rules about the application of the penalties which depends largely on the view taken by the Central Bank about the situation. In France a higher rate, popularly known as the *taux d'enfer* is charged on any borrowing in excess of the ceiling, up to 10 per cent of the ceiling, For any borrowing more than 10 per cent in excess of the ceiling a much higher rate called *taux de super-enfer* is charged. To give an idea of the extent of the penalties, let it be sufficient to recall that during the squeeze of 1957 when the Bank rate was 5 per cent the *taux d'enfer* was raised to 8 per cent and the *taux de super-enfer* to 12 per cent. The Bank of France is at liberty to change these penalising rates independently of any changes in the Bank rate.

Plurality of official rates exists not only above the Bank rate but also under it. Various special categories of bills benefit by lower rates, especially export bills, equipment bills, agricultural bills, etc. There are something like ten different rates at any given moment at which the Bank of France may lend. But some of these special rates have a very limited application.

(5) CREDIT CONTROL IS SELECTIVE

The overall effect is that, unlike the Anglo-American system of controlling the total volume of credit, the French system is one of largely selective credit control. The reason why quantitative credit control would not be satisfactory in France is, according to Engberg, that French banks allow their cash ratios and liquidity ratios to fluctuate within very wide limits. Monetary policy devices affecting the total of liquid resources have to be supplemented, therefore, by selective credit control devices. In any case, the French discount market is too narrow for large-scale open market operations. The Bank of France is not permitted to operate in long-term securities which have an adequate market. But other official or semi-official financial institutions are not inhibited from engaging in such operations, even though their sales of Government securities are more likely to be connected with debt management than with monetary policy. Selectivity is enforced not only by applying different ceilings for various credits but also by means of applying different lending rates for various purposes. Although certain special rates are applied also in Britain and in the United States they are applied much less systematically than in France.

Apart from the plurality of official rates, the French system differs from the British system also in respect of the active interest taken by the Bank of France and other official or semi-official institutions in financing medium-term credits for exports, capital equipment and construction. Rates charged on bills rediscounted for those purposes are of course higher than rediscount rates but they are usually lower than the *taux d'enfer*. Indeed, if medium-term credits are for the purposes of financing exports the rates are below the Bank rate.

The Bank of France automatically re-discounts short- and medium-term bills for a number of special institutions such as the *Crédit National*, the *Caisse de Dépôts et des Consignations*, the *Crédit*

Foncier, the *Caisses de Crédit Mutuel,* the *Caisses de Crédit Co-opèratif,* the *Caisses de Crédit Agricole,* the *Caisse National des Marchés de l'Etat,* etc. Subject to the consent of the Bank of France, banks may re-discount special bills with the above institutions, in addition to their direct re-discount facilities with the Bank of France.

(6) MUCH SPECIAL CREDIT GRANTED

The grand total of all general re-discount ceilings with the Bank of France is relatively small but various types of bills can be re-discounted in addition to the credit limits (*hors plafond*). The total amount of such borrowings is usually higher – often several times higher – than the aggregate of credit ceilings, i.e., the amount that can be re-discounted up to the *plafond.* Bills qualified for re-discounting outside the ceiling include cereal bills, export bills, medium-term bills financing equipment and construction, etc.

French banks are under obligation to keep a reserve with the Bank of France, representing a small percentage of their liabilities and varying according to the length of maturity of the liabilities and according to other circumstances. But this reserve ratio does not play such an important part as in other countries because, apart from other reasons, the amounts of the banks' debts to the Bank of France are usually well in excess of the amounts of their balances with it.

(7) NO MARKET IN COMMERCIAL BILLS

The weakest spot of the Paris money market is the complete absence of any inter-bank market in commercial bills of any kind. Banks usually keep in their own portfolios the bills drawn on them by their customers. But they are in a position to realise their claims before maturity not only through re-discounting them with the Bank of France but also through re-discounting them with one of the specialised institutions referred to above, which, in turn, are in a position to re-discount them with the Bank of France.

Banks are also able to borrow on the security of the bills. The form of such borrowing is to give the bills *en pension* – that is, to pawn them. But if the bills are given *en pension* to the Bank of France the amounts involved come under the re-discount ceilings of the banks concerned. One of the reasons why re-purchase arrangements are more popular in France than straight lending is that from a fiscal point of view the difference between the buying and selling price of the bills does not count as income.

(8) OPEN MARKET OPERATIONS

The Bank of France often takes the initiative for such operations if it wants to expand credit. Such transactions are referred to as *'open market operations'* or just *'open market'* (in English) in French financial literature and in official reports. This in spite of the absence of an open market in bills in the real sense of the term. These transactions usually assume the form of lending to the banking community on a day-to-day basis. The Bank of France does not buy bills outright, nor does it take them in pension for long maturities. It influences the volume of liquidity by increasing or reducing the outstanding amount of bills taken in pension for short maturities. The sum total involved is relatively small and the extent of the influence of open market operations on the volume of liquid resources and on interest rates is usually moderate.

It is not the aim of the French authorities to influence the basic credit situation and the business trend with the aid of open market operations, but merely to mitigate or exaggerate a trend according to whether it suits the official policy. While in other countries – notably in the United States and in Britain – open market operations are often the principal device determining the volume of credit available to trade, or at any rate the amount of liquid money market resources, and of course the level of interest rates, in France they seldom pursue such ambitious ends. They are not an instrument of monetary strategy but merely a tactical device.

(9) ALTERNATIVE MEANS FOR INFLUENCING LIQUIDITY

The Bank of France has the choice between the following means for influencing the basic credit situation:

(1) It may change the aggregate re-discount ceilings and other credit ceilings, or the ceilings of individual banks.

(2) It may change the re-discount rate, the *taux d'enfer* and the

taux de super-enfer, as well as the special favourable re-discount rates.

(3) It may change the minimum balances to be kept with it by banks against their liabilities. According to the Marjolin Report, in 1968 an increase of the minimum balances by each per cent would have reduced liquid resources by Frs. 1,200 m.

(4) It may change the rates for loans against securities *en pension*.

(5) It may change the grand total of credits banks are authorised to grant to their customers.

(6) It may change the minimum percentage of Treasury bills banks have to hold.

(7) It may mitigate or reinforce its rules relating to the eligibility of various types of bills for re-discount or for security for loans against bills taken *en pension*.

(8) It may change the *coefficient de liquidité* – the ratio of cash, Treasury bills in excess of legal minimum holdings and eligible commercial bills in excess of the *plafond* – to sight liabilities.

(9) It may change the *coefficient de trésorerie* – the ratio of the total of the above items, plus all other eligible or marketable securities, to total liabilities.

(10) It may increase or reduce the selective character of its credit policy by changing the differentials charged for various types of facilities.

(11) Finally, it may influence the basic credit situation as distinct from ironing out fluctuations, by making more extensive or less extensive use of open market policy.

(10) CREDIT CEILINGS OFTEN ADJUSTED

Credit ceilings are subject to frequent changes. The Bank of France' revises them monthly and changes them not only in accordance with the requirements of monetary policy but even to allow for seasonal fluctuations of credit requirements. It may also reduce the ceilings of individual banks as a penalty for offending against its rules.

With the aid of these various means the Bank of France is in a position to induce banks to change the rates they charge to their customers, or to change the volume of credit facilities they grant, or to change the purposes for which they grant credit, or to change the length of maturities of their credits. Above all, it is in a position to influence money market rates in inter-bank trans-actions.

One of the bank of France's most important functions is the management of the public debt, a function which is apt to produce important incidental effects on monetary trends. During the early post-war years French banks drastically reduced their holdings of Treasury bills in order to employ their resources more profitably in the private sector. This trend was embarrassing to the Treasury, and in order to moderate it the authorities fixed a minimum percentage for bank assets (*planchers*) to be held in the form of Treasury bills. Originally very high, this percentage came to be reduced gradually. The device of adjusting changes in the *planchers* now serves the purposes of monetary policy rather than those of debt management.

(11) LIQUIDITY RATIO IS FLEXIBLE

In most countries the liquidity ratio of banks is uniform for all sight liabilities and is fixed, if not permanently, at any rate for very long periods. In France it varies according to the types of liabilities and the types of banks and is subject to many more frequent changes than in most other countries. It is thus used very actively as a device of monetary policy to influence the liquidity of the monetary system.

The banks have to submit monthly returns to the Bank of France on the twenty-first day of each month, showing their average liquidity ratios for the entire month. If the ratio is not high enough when the return date approaches the banks en-deavour to raise additional liquid resources, largely through obtaining from their clients additional commercial bills which are eligible for re-discount or for being given *en pension*.

While there is no secondary bill market in Paris or an inter-bank franc deposit market, there are very active Euro-currency markets, to be dealt with later. Although there is a foreign exchange market at the *Bourse*, all transactions in money or bills take place by telephone, either direct or through the inter-mediary of money brokers who are in some instances identical with foreign exchange brokers. The size of the market is com-parable with that of Frankfurt but is of course much smaller than that of London or of New York.

There are seven re-discount houses which act as intermediaries between banks and the Bank of France, operating on their own accounts, and a score of brokers. *The Compagnie Parisienne de Réescompte* is by far the most important amongst them, because of its close association with the Bank of France.

(a) THE OFFICIAL MARKET

(1) DISCOUNT HOUSES

We saw in the last chapter that French banks have re-discount facilities with the Bank of France up to a certain ceiling that is subject to changes. They may avail themselves of these facilities either for the purpose of re-discounting their bill holdings or for the purpose of giving bills 'in pension', by borrowing on the security of Treasury bills or commercial bills through the intermediary of one of the seven discount houses, the largest of them being the semi-official institution, the *Compagnie Parisienne de Réescompte*. Commercial bills, in order to be eligible, must bear at least three signatures.

The other six discount houses, established by commercial banks or by *banques d'affaires*, engage in operations similar to those of the *Compagnie de Réescompte*, but the total of their operations falls short of those of the latter. It acts as the agent of the Bank of France in executing most of the open market operations, although from time to time the Bank of France also deals through the discount houses or direct with banks.

(2) RATES FIXED BY BANK OF FRANCE

The rates for loans do not necessarily fluctuate according to changes in supply-demand relationship – except indirectly – but are fixed by the Bank of France which controls the *Compagnie de Réescompte* very closely. They are announced at 10.30 a.m. every morning. They are arrived at on the basis of the requirements or surpluses of the banks which the banks communicate first thing every morning to the *Compagnie de Réescompte*. Of course the Bank of France also takes other factors into consideration. Euro-dollar rates in particular play an important part, especially when the situation is such as to prevent franc-dollar swap rates from adapting themselves to changes of interest parities between Paris and

New York in general and between Euro-dollar rates and the Bank of France's 'pension' lending rates in particular. In more recent times Euro-Deutschemark rates played from time to time a similar part. French banks often borrow through discount houses even before the daily lending rate is announced, accepting in advance the rate to be announced at 10.30 a.m. The same rate remains in force for such loans during the rest of the day.

(3) THE USUAL DEFICIENCIES OF BANKS

If banks have surpluses the discount houses borrow these funds. Their borrowing rate is the same as the lending rate. They borrow from the Bank of France only the net requirements of all banks. On occasions when the surpluses of banks lent to them exceed the deficiencies covered by borrowing them, they lend the net surplus to the Bank of France. But most of the time there is always a deficiency which the Bank of France meets in full at the rate fixed by it that morning. The reason for this is in part the perennial expanding trend of credit requirements and in part the fact that, while it is usually more advantageous for banks to borrow from the Bank of France it is usually more advantageous for them to lend in the market or to customers.

In order to be able to borrow through discount houses, the banks must possess bills which are eligible for that purpose. If they have no such bills available, or if they do not wish to reduce their portfolios, or if they do not want to increase the amounts they have borrowed from the Bank of France, they have the alternative of borrowing in the unofficial market which will be discussed in the next chapter.

(4) NO SECONDARY MARKET

As mentioned in the last chapter, as an alternative to borrowing through discount house, the banks may make direct use of their re-discount facilities with the Bank of France within the ceiling fixed for them. They can also re-discount various kinds of special bills with special financial institutions. But unlike banks in London, New York or Canada, they do not have the alternative of recovering before maturity the possession of their money lent to customers against bills by selling the bills in a market, for in France there is no secondary inter-bank market in bills.

Rates paid by banks on money brorowed *en pension* through discount houses are higher than the Bank rate charged on bills re-discounted with the Bank of France, and a great deal higher than the rates at which certain of the special bills referred to in the last chapter – such as export paper, cereal paper, etc. – can be re-discounted with special institutions. But they are not so high as the *taux d'enfer*. It is to the interests of banks to induce their customers to draw bills on them instead of borrowing in the form of loans, because amounts lent against bills may be mobilised through the intermediary of discount houses at a relatively low cost. In so far as the banks have not exhausted their re-discount *plafonds* those facilities are also at their disposal. But often they prefer to keep some unused re-discounting facilities in reserve, so that when they are approaching their ceiling they prefer to fall back upon other facilities rather than exhaust their ceilings altogether and expose themselves to the necessity of borrowing at *taux d'enfer*.

In outward form the official market of Paris bears some similarity with Lombard Street. The *Compagnie de Réescouple* plays the part of the London discount houses, with the difference that it is controlled much more closely by the Bank of France than the discount houses are by the Bank of England. It obtains loans from the Central Bank against eligible securities, with a margin providing for the possibility of a depreciation of the securities. In Paris the margin is much wider than in London. Any depreciation of the securities has to be made good by providing additional securities. Any borrowing which the Central bank considers excessive is penalised by charging higher interest rates. But while in London the differentials are fractional in Paris the difference between the normal discount rate and the *taux d'enfer*, let alone *taux de super-enfer*, is very substantial.

(5) NOT AN AUTOMATIC MECHANISM

A more important difference is that the Paris official market is not an automatic mechanism. The rates in Paris are much more rigid than in London, fixed by the Bank of France arbitrarily above the Bank rate, even though it has to allow for supply-demand relationship and for other influences. In London the rates in Lombard Street fluctuate freely under the official rate, in accordance with the ever-changing supply-demand relationship.

Because in Paris the rates in the free market are practically always higher than the rates in the official market, borrowers who are able and willing to provide the necessary security and have not reached their ceiling naturally prefer to borrow in the official market. It is mainly for this reason that, while the Bank of England is considered to be the lender of last resort, the Bank of France is considered to be the lender of first resort. Another difference is that while the Bank of England intervenes in the free market the Bank of France intervenes in the official market, thereby increasing or reducing the amount of funds available in the free markets.

(b) THE PRIVATE MARKET

(1) SIMILARITY WITH INTER-BANK DEPOSIT MARKET

The only unofficial money market in Paris, in the sense of inter-bank dealings in short-term credits at rates fluctuating in accordance with changes in supply-demand relationship, is the private money market which corresponds roughly to the inter-bank deposit market in London. No securities are required by lenders of short-term money, and for this reason the turnover is not handicapped by the volume of eligible securities available to would-be borrowers. Since borrowers do not have to deposit securities with lenders and do not therefore retrieve them on repayment of their credits, the method of transacting business is naturally much more informal and expeditious than in the official market.

But because the loans in this market are unsecured the rates are normally $\frac{1}{4}$ to $\frac{1}{2}$ per cent higher than those paid in the official market. Differentials between official and unofficial rates are apt to fluctuate more widely for overnight loans and for day-to-day loans than for time deposits. The differentials between rates quoted for short and long loans depend on the views the market takes of interest rate trend prospects.

As seen in the last chapter banks are willing to pay higher rates in the unofficial market if they have exhausted or even approached their re-discount ceilings. They have to pay higher market rates willy-nilly if they have no eligible securities which they could give *en pension* for loans from official quarters.

(2) HOW THE PRIVATE MARKET OPERATES

A high proportion of the business in the unofficial market is transacted through the intermediary of brokers or of dealers operating on their own account, but there is also much direct inter-bank dealing as in the London inter-bank deposit market. Non-banking financial institutions, too, participate in the private market indirectly through the intermediary of bankers, dealers or brokers. French discount houses do not accept deposits from non-banks or from banks abroad, because they are not supposed to compete with banks.

Brokers are not permitted to transact business on their own account, a rule which was established under Louis XIV. But this rule can be circumvented, not by brokers acting as dealers but by dealers acting as intermediaries between two parties as well as dealing on their own account. As in London, some deposit brokers function also as foreign exchange brokers.

(3) EXPANDING TIME DEPOSITS

Amounts of individual transactions are multiples of Frs. 1 m. Some individual transactions nowadays are as high as Frs. 1,000 m. or even higher. The private market is usually very active. Although the market in overnight loans and loans at call is still much larger than the market in time deposits, relative size of the latter has expanded considerably in recent years. This is partly because non-banking institutions have gained access to the market, for which reason banks have now to compete with market rates to obtain and retain large deposits which their customers would lend otherwise in the market. They may want to replace deposits withdrawn by their customers. There is much more freedom of competition for customers' deposits in France than in the United States or in Britain. The long period of rising trend in interest rates in the late 'sixties tended to encourage dealing in time deposits.

Time deposits are usually for two and seven days, one, two, three, six and twelve months, but it is possible to deal in other maturities in terms of weeks or months, and for broken dates. There is much dealing for the end of the current month or for the end of any month up to the twelfth month.

The spread between borrowing and lending quotations by

dealers for deposits to first-class banks is normally between $\frac{1}{4}$ and $\frac{3}{8}$ per cent. Different rates are quoted according to the borrower's standing. There are no marketable CDs. Although banks may issue *bons de caisse* to depositors, they are not marketable, even though they may be accepted as collateral. If lending banks need the money before the deposits mature they can always re-borrow it at current rates for the remaining duration of their time deposits.

(1) THE POPULAR OVERNIGHT MARKET

French provincial banks transact their money market business mostly with the regional banks of their districts, and the latter cover the resulting net deficiency, or unload the resulting net surplus, in the Paris money market. Most of the big regional banks have Paris branches which play an active part in the private market.

Specialised financial institutions which raise medium- or long-term loans lend their temporary surpluses in the private money market pending the employment of the funds for the purposes for which they had been raised. The overnight market is a particularly popular medium for the employment of such temporary funds. It is usually larger than the call money market.

The turnover in the private money market is subject to seasonal fluctuations. Taxation dates and Government disbursements are among the main causes of these fluctuations. Disbursements of dividends and holiday seasons are also liable to influence the turnover. The basic economic trend also affects the trend in the private market.

The market provides facilities for lenders of long-term deposits to undo their commitments by borrowing in the short-term deposit market and rolling forward their short deposits. Money lent for months and even years is often financed by this method. There is much active time arbitrage of lending short against long deposits or *vice-versa*. Foreign banks may participate in the market as lenders but not as borrowers.

(5) LIMITS FOR NAMES CHANGE FREQUENTLY

Because the loans are unsecured lenders have necessarily limits for names. These limits are liable to be changed more frequently than in London where limits are apt to be maintained at times long after the change in the situation of the banks concerned would necessitate a reduction or would justify an increase of their amounts.

Interest rates in the private money market are apt to lose touch with those of the official market when money conditions are very plentiful. Amidst such conditions it is easy to borrow without security and the official rate has to be lowered considerably in order to restore contact with the private rate. But amidst tight money conditions, when most banks have exhausted their re-discount ceilings, the demand for loans in the private market tends to push the private rates well above the official rates. The cost of borrowing in the private market is increased by the commission payable to brokers or discount houses.

When deciding whether to borrow in the private market or from the Bank of France, banks have to take into consideration the fact that the Bank of France only lend for minimum periods which may exceed the period for which the money is needed. If borrowing assumes the form of re-discounting bills the transaction is irreversible, so that if a borrower expects a decline in interest rates before the bills mature he might prefer to borrow in the private market in the form of day-to-day loans even if the rate is higher.

(6) FULL USE OF CENTRAL BANK FACILITIES BY BANKS

But in the majority of instances the choice between the two methods of borrowing does not arise, because banks are inclined to make full or nearly full use of their re-discount limits with the Bank of France most of the time. Very often amidst conditions of tight money the choice is not between borrowing in the private money market or re-discounting bills on the basis of the Bank rate but between borrowing in the private market and re-discounting bills on the basis of the *taux d'enfer* or even the *taux de super-enfer*.

In theory the rates in the private market cannot decline below the Bank rate or the rate at which the banks with surplus funds have borrowed from the Bank of France. For since all banks are in debt to the latter they usually prefer to reduce their debt rather than level in the market at a lower rate. In given situations it is conceivable, however, that a bank with a purely temporary surplus employs its funds in the market rather than disturb its debt to the Bank of France.

(c) EURO-CURRENCY MARKETS

(1) THE LEADING MARKET IN EURO-STERLING

Although the initiative for the development of the Euro-dollar market had come from London, it did not take very long before Paris followed the example, albeit on a more limited scale. By the end of the 'fifties Paris had a distinct market in Euro-dollars which was second in size to that of London. Even though the Frankfurt market in Euro-dollars made considerable progress in the late 'sixties and early 'seventies, Paris has probably retained its position as the second largest market in Euro-D. marks and Euro-Swiss francs, and as the leading market in Euro-sterling. From the outset Italian banks transacted a high proportion of their Euro-currency business through Paris.

The volume of turnover in Euro-dollars in Paris is of course usually distinctly smaller than the volume of turnover in London. While the London market can usually easily absorb individual transactions amounting to $100 m. or more, in Paris such transactions are usually divided into several tranches, or a counterpart is sought for them in London. Nevertheless precisely because the turnover is smaller and the rates are therefore more sensitive than in London, the resulting discrepancies often provide opportunities for space arbitrage between London and Paris.

This arbitrage is not necessarily always in one direction. On occasions one-sided local pressure in London causes London rates to deviate from Paris rates and London dealers may then find it profitable to undo their commitments in Paris.

(2) DIFFICULTY IN DEALING IN LONG MATURITIES

Although dealers in Paris are usually somewhat earlier at their dealing desks than their opposite numbers in London, active dealing in Paris does not begin as a rule until there is some indication about the trend in London, unless some developments overnight induce French dealers to take a distinct view about the prospective trend in London.

Standard maturities in Paris for Euro-dollar transactions are identical with those of the London market. There is a great deal of time arbitrage. It is more difficult in Paris than in London to deal in maturities exceeding one year, unless the transaction is undone immediately in London.

In Paris the markets in Euro-D. marks, Euro-Swiss francs and Euro-guilders are, if anything, more active than in London, and there is a fair amount of dealing in Euro-sterling, though the bulk of borrowing or selling of sterling is transacted by means of swap transactions combined with borrowing or lending sterling in London. Whenever there was a speculative attack on sterling during the 'sixties, to a large degree it assumed the form of buying Euro-sterling deposits in Paris and selling the sterling.

During the Euro-dollar boom of 1968–1969 American bank branches in Paris were borrowers on a very large scale. There is often much borrowing of Euro-dollars for selling the proceeds against D. marks whenever a revaluation of the D. mark is anticipated by speculators, or whenever an appreciation of the floating D. mark is anticipated.

CHAPTER TWENTY-ONE

The Frankfurt Money Market

(1) BERLIN v. FRANKFURT

GERMANY possessed money markets during the *Renaissance* thanks to the Fuggers and other leading merchant bankers. There was an all-round relapse in the 17th century, but in the 18th century Frankfurt emerged as one of the leading money markets of Europe. After the unification of Germany in 1871 it ceded the lead to the capital of the Reich. The Berlin money market played an increasingly important part between 1871 and 1914. It resumed its activities after the stabilisation of the German currency in 1924 until the financial crisis of 1931.

The second re-stabilisation of the currency in 1948 and the remarkable increase in the importance of the Deutschemark during the 'fifties and 'sixties was not followed, however, for a long time by a comparable increase in the importance of the German money market. This in spite of the fact that by the late 'sixties Western Germany came to surpass considerably the economic achievements of the Reich before the Second World War.

In itself the detachment of Eastern Germany and the isolation of West Berlin from the Federal Republic would not have prevented the re-emergence of a leading money market in Western Germany, the importance of which would be in keeping with the strength of the Deutschemark. Of course, owing to the political status of West Berlin and its precarious position due to being surrounded by Communist territory, it could not have functioned efficiently as the financial centre of Western Germany or as an international financial centre. It was therefore natural that Frankfurt should resume its former role of the financial capital of Germany as soon as she succeeded in emerging from the chaotic monetary conditions inherited from the Second World War.

(2) GOOD INTERNATIONAL CONNECTIONS

Even during the period when Berlin acted as Germany's monetary centre Frankfurt retained much of its previous financial activities.

A number of well-established private banks remained there and the leading commercial banks with head offices in Berlin had important branches in Frankfurt. Although Frankfurt was a secondary banking centre of Germany between the wars, it continued to have direct relations with foreign banking centres. When owing to the political circumstances referred to above Berlin was prevented from resuming its pre-war role as Germany's main money market, its place was taken by Frankfurt as a matter of course, even though Düsseldorf was Western Germany's principal industrial centre, Hamburg her principal commercial centre and Bonn her political and administrative centre. There are secondary money markets in Düsseldorf and Hamburg and also in Munich and Cologne, but Frankfurt's supremacy has become incontestable.

(3) IMPLEMENTING MONETARY POLICY

The head office of the *Deutsche Bundesbank* is situated in Frankfurt where all important German banks have their head offices, or at least important branch offices. Central offices of co-operative banks, agricultural banks and mortgage banks add to the importance of the Frankfurt money market, and so do the head offices of leading industrial and commercial corporations and the growing number of foreign bank branches or affiliates.

One of the main reasons why Frankfurt has become the incontestable monetary centre of Western Germany is the fact that the German monetary authorities conduct the operations implementing their monetary policy in the Frankfurt market. We shall see in the next chapter the active part played by the Bundesbank in the daily fixing of a quasi-official call-money rate. Its open market operations greatly increase the importance of Frankfurt. Also in the next chapter the part played in Frankfurt by the *Privatdiskont A.G.*, which is the nearest German equivalent of the London discount houses, will be outlined.

Although some banks authorise their branches situated in other German monetary centres to transact inter-bank business in the respective local money markets, most of the money and foreign exchange transactions of branches are transacted through their Frankfurt offices. The existence of secondary money markets in Germany does not in itself prevent Frankfurt from becoming a rival to London and New York as a leading money market, any

more than the existence of similar secondary markets in the
United States has prevented New York from achieving and maintaining supremacy.

(4). EFFECT OF THE 'GERMAN MIRACLE'

There is no lack of liquid funds, German or foreign, in the Frankfurt market. The 'German miracle' heralded in two decades of
almost uninterrupted prosperity and business expansion and frequent and prolonged periods of influx of foreign balances in addition to an almost chronic import surplus. For a long time it was
contrary to the official monetary policy to try to set up Frankfurt
as a rival to London and New York as an international monetary
centre. From the beginning of the 'sixties until 1970, the influx of
foreign balances was in fact actively discouraged. The Germans,
although rightly proud of the strength of the D. mark, are far
from keen on taking advantage of its strength for attracting 'hot
money'.

The call money market and the market in time deposits are
practically the only really important money markets in Frankfurt.
While its market in foreign currency deposits is at least equal in
importance to Paris, Zürich and Amsterdam and is inferior only
to that of London in Europe, its local money market was until
recently not so important as that of Paris, though it was more
important than those of other continental centres.

Owing to the spectacular expansion of liquid financial resources and of the West German banking system, the creation of
an active money market in which German banks dispose of their
cash surpluses and cover their cash deficiencies was of course
inevitable. The German authorities came to encourage the emergence and evolution of such a market.

(5) ACCEPTANCE MARKET NOT ENCOURAGED

But there has been no effort to encourage the creation of a really
active market in bank acceptances or trade bills or Treasury bills.
While the Canadian money market – which from time to time
bears comparison in size with the German money market, in spite
of the striking difference between the size of the population and
wealth of Canada and of Western Germany – sought to emulate
the United States and Britain in respect of the creation of various

parallel money markets in recent years, the German money market seems to have entertained so far no such ambitions.

However, within its self-imposed limits, the Frankfurt money market has achieved an active turnover and a high degree of efficiency by the early 'seventies. It is probably a mere question of time before the German authorities and banks decide to make a deliberate bid in the international financial sphere for leadership for the Frankfurt market. They have already succeeded in creating a market in long-term and medium-term capital issues which exceeds considerably in importance the German capital market between the wars and the pre-1914 capital market of Imperial Germany. There is no reason why they should not be able to create an equally efficient and active market in a variety of forms of short-term credits.

The daily meetings of money market dealers at the *Börse* are no longer important, as most business is transacted on the telephone. Nevertheless the practice is maintained if only for the sake of keeping a tradition alive and maintaining personal contact.

(a) CALL MONEY AND DAY-TO-DAY LOANS

(1) MARKET IN CENTRAL BANK BALANCES

As already pointed out in the last chapter, the Frankfurt call money market is a very important money market. It is an inter-bank market in which sight deposits of banks with the *Landes-Zentral-Banken* (Central Banks of the member states of the Federation, which are virtually branches of the *Bundesbank*), are lent and borrowed without any security. In this respect the German call money market bears much more similarity with the London inter-bank deposit market than with the traditional market of Lombard Street where all loans have to be secured.

Participants in transactions in call money are the German banks, the *Bundesbank* and the *Privatdiskont A.G.* about which more will be said in the next chapter. Transactions with foreign banks are not in funds with *Landes-Zentral-Banken* but in sight deposits with German banks.

The German banks have to keep with the Central Bank a certain proportion of their liabilities in the form of sight deposits.

The reserve ratio depends on the type of liabilities. It is usually much higher on non-resident deposits than on resident deposits and is subject to adjustments according to *Bundesbank* policy. Banks have to submit four returns each month, and on the return days their ratio – which does not include cash holdings – must not be under the official limit. The demand for call money largely arises from the banks' efforts to comply with their statutory reserve requirements.

Lenders in this market instruct their Central Banks to transfer from their accounts the amounts lent to the accounts of the borrowing banks. When the loans are repaid the transactions are reversed. The borrowers then instruct their Central Bank to transfer to the lenders' account the amounts borrowed plus interest.

(2) TWO TYPES OF LOANS

Loans may be definitely for one day only, repayable on the following business day in the absence of specific agreement to renew them. They may assume the form of exchanging cheques, in which case the lender's cheque is dated for the day of the transaction and the borrower's cheque is dated for the following day. But in that form the loan and its repayment are deferred until the cheques are cleared. Transfers from one Central Bank account to another is more expeditious. When the two parties agree to renew a loan it is renewed on the basis of the interest rate prevailing on the day on which repayment is due.

The bulk of the transactions does not assume this form but of money at call. Such loans are repayable at one day's notice. Although either party is entitled to exercise its right at any time, they often informally indicate their intention to the other party – for instance the lender may inform the borrower that he would call the loan at the end of the month, or the borrower may inform the lender that he intended to repay the loan after the turn of the month – which statement of intent does not legally prevent them from calling or repaying the loan at some earlier date should unexpected need for it arise. In many instances the right is not exercised by either party for weeks or even for months. Interest rates on loans at call which are not called are adjusted to changes in call money rates. Notice for repayment on the following business day may be given at any time during business hours.

(3) *BUNDESBANK* FIXES RATE WITH 'BIG THREE' BANKS

The *Bundesbank* announces the call money rate whenever it changes from the rate announced previously. The rate is fixed on the basis of the *Bundesbank*'s close contact with the three leading commercial banks and with other financial quarters. These rates are not binding for operators in the market where rates are determined by an ever-changing supply-demand relationship. They merely indicate the official view of the trend of the market.

While before the war a high proportion of call money operations was transacted at the *Börse*, today most business is transacted by telephone or, between various centres, by teleprinter. But there is still much personal contact between the principal participants in the market, especially between the leading commercial banks. Their object is that the prevailing rates at which their respective surpluses and deficiencies offset each other should represent truly the prevailing supply-demand relationship and should not be distorted by speculative operations. This high degree of co-operation is at the cost of making the market less competitive for the sake of avoiding unwarranted fluctuations of interest rates. In any case call money rates and day-to-day money rates are subject to much wider fluctuations than rates for time deposits, to be dealt with in the next chapter.

(4) HOW THE MARKET OPERATES

When the market opens the initial rates quoted are mostly not dealing rates but are quoted for information only. Later when the dealers are able to form a better idea of the market trend as well as of their requirements they make firm quotations. Some banks make two-way quotations, but the leading banks are usually either borrowers or lenders, even though they are liable to change the trend of their operations several times in the course of a day.

All transactions in the market are in round figures. The smallest transaction may be as low as DM.100,000, the largest may be as high as DM.100 million or over. As the loans are unsecured there are limits for the amount lent to any one borrower, and rates at which small banks are able to borrow may be $\frac{1}{8}$ to $\frac{1}{4}$ per cent above current market rates.

The main object of the market, from the point of view of banks which are subject to reserve requirements is to keep any surpluses above the statutory minimum in a highly liquid form and to enable banks to avoid a decline of their reserve ratios below the statutory minimum. The existence of an efficient call money market obviates the necessity for keeping too much cash or Central Bank balances for fear of a sudden tightening of conditions.

Although direct participation in the market is confined to banks, other financial institutions too borrow and lend through the intermediary of banks. Thus mortgage banks and other long-term borrowers on a large scale re-lend part of the proceeds of their issues on the call money market, pending their use for the purpose for which the capital has been raised.

(5) END-OF-MONTH INFLUENCES

Before the crises of the 'thirties a high proportion of the call money was borrowed for financing Stock Exchange transactions, and for this reason money rates tended to rise on the eve of the *medio* and *ultimo* Stock Exchange settlements. Now the financing of such transactions usually represents a small proportion of the demand for call money. Nevertheless call money rates tend to rise at the end of the month.

Cash requirements for tax payments also constitute a regularly recurrent influence affecting interest rates. The banks are affected by their depositors' tax payments about a fortnight in advance of the dates of 10 March, 10 June, 10 September and 10 December. During these periods the amounts involved in tax requirements run into many billions of D. marks. The authorities, in order to mitigate the effect of this demand on interest rates, are inclined to relax their rules concerning payment dates.

There is a very large turnover immediately before and after the dates for which banks have to declare their liquidity position – on the seventh, thirteenth, twenty-third and last business day of each month. End-of-year window-dressing also affects the turnover in the usual way.

(6) INFLUENCE OF OFFICIAL POLICY

The call money rate is affected by official policy in several ways – through changes in the Bank rate or the Lombard rate (the rate charged by the Central Bank on loans against eligible security), and by official intervention in the market. The fixing of the rate by the *Bundesbank* also influences the market trend. Taking everything into consideration it seems that the influence of the *Bundesbank* on the German money market, though not so decisive as the influence of the Bank of France on the Paris money market, is very strong.

In theory the ceiling of the call money rate is the Lombard rate, because banks in possession of eligible securities are unwilling to pay a higher rate in the market. In practice, in given circumstances, the call money rate is apt to rise above the Lombard rate, when demand for liquid resources is particularly strong and a number of banks have exhausted their portfolios of eligible securities, or at any rate they have reduced their holdings to such an extent that they prefer to pay higher rates on unsecured loans rather than pledge more securities against secured loans for the sake of saving the interest differential. In any case the procedure for borrowing in the market is simpler and more expeditious, so that for that reason alone most banks prefer to pay a marginally higher rate to obviate the necessity for raising Lombard credits.

Banks which have no borrowing facilities with the Central Bank often have to pay rates for call money well in excess of the Bank rate and of the Lombard rate. On the eve of window-dressing dates all banks want money and have to attract money to the market by offering sufficiently high rates to induce other financial institutions or corporations to part with some of their liquid resources for the sake of the temporary high yield obtainable. Most banks prefer not to leave their window-dressing arrangements till the last minute. They want to avoid the risk of having to pay abnormally high rates. While it might be worth their while to borrow from the Central Bank for longer periods, the additional cost of higher rates paid on call money which they intend to repay in a few days is too small to make it worth while to have recourse to the lender of last resort.

(b) TIME LOANS

(1) INCREASED TURNOVER

In addition to the market in day-to-day loans and in money at call, Frankfurt has also an increasingly active market in unsecured deposits for various maturities. It is possible to borrow and lend money repayable at longer notice and there is a large and increasing turnover in deposits for fixed dates. Standard maturities for such loans are one month, two months, three months, six months and twelve months, but there is a growing turnover also in longer maturities. The turnover in loans for fixed maturities was until recently incomparably smaller than in call money or day-to-day money, but now there is little to choose between the size of their respective turnovers.

In the market in time loans the largest turnover is in deposits for three months, and transactions for longer maturities are intermittent and usually a matter for negotiation. The spread between bid and offered rates for longer maturities is usually wider.

According to Lipfert, one of the advantages of the existence of a good call money market is that by its existence it encourages banks to assume time money commitments. For it enables them to raise, if necessary, temporary loans at short notice to meet maturing time money commitments if the lenders do not want to renew their loans and if the borrowers have immobilised the proceeds of those loans in investments or in loans to customers. Banks are more reluctant to lend to customers for periods in excess of, say, three months, and even for three months, if there is a possibility that the latter might want their credits to be renewed, were it not for the facilities for covering deposit withdrawals by borrowing on the call money market. In the absence of such facilities they would be dependent on their limited Central Bank facilities whenever the influx of new deposits and the possibility of borrowing time loans at advantageous rates falls short of maturing time loans and of withdrawals of deposits.

(2) RENEWAL A MATTER OF NEGOTIATION

Time inter-bank deposits are not renewed as a matter of course; their renewal can seldom be taken for granted. Thanks to the availability of call money, banks are in a position to await the favourable moment for borrowing time deposits.

One of the objects of time money is to enable banks to cope with end-of-month or end-of-year pressures. There is usually much borrowing of time money for the purpose of window-dressing arrangements, or for the purpose of meeting withdrawals made for window-dressing.

The Frankfurt market in time loans, like the London market in long inter-bank deposits, assists banks in offsetting loans to customers of identical maturities.

(c) THE DISCOUNT MARKET

(1) HISTORY OF GERMAN BILLS

In Germany the modern market in bills came into being in 1876 as a result of the establishment of the *Reichsbank*. Under its statutes German banks were allotted quotas of re-discount facilities enabling them to raise funds by re-discounting bills they discounted for their clients and held in their portfolios. Eligible commercial bills were re-discounted with the Reichsbank at Bank rate. As the re-discount quotas were relatively small and credit requirements tended to increase with the expansion of the economy of the Reich, the market rate of discount was usually higher than the Bank rate throughout the period when in London it was always lower than the British Bank rate.

The *Reichsbank* willingly acquired commercial bills not only in order to facilitate the financing of trade but also to acquire and hold in bills the proportion of its assets prescribed by its statutory rules concerning note cover. For some time the *Reichsbank* engaged also in open market operations to that end, but from 1896 till 1914 the discount market was left to its own devices. German and foreign banks were the principal buyers of commercial bills.

Advanced inflation during the early years after the First World War made the operation of the Berlin bill market impossible. But it resumed its activity in 1925 after the return of normal conditions. Under the Reichsbank Act of 1924 a bill issued by a business firm, in order to become eligible for re-discount by the *Reichsbank*, had to be accepted by a bank of good standing and endorsed by another bank of good standing or by a bill broker. To comply with this rule, leading German banks adopted the practice of swapping their holdings of bills, so as to ensure that, if and when they should wish to have them re-discounted, the bills should bear the required three signatures.

(2) UNSOUND PRACTICES

In spite of these strict rules, the discount market assumed an unsound character in the late 'twenties. While before 1914 dealings were mostly in genuine self-liquidating commercial bills, in the middle and late 'twenties the bills became to an increasing degree finance bills. They served the purpose of financing long term loans through the repeated renewal of short-term bills which were not self-liquidating. Owing to the high standing of the German banks, through whose intermediary these bills came into circulation, they were readily discounted in Germany and if issued in terms of foreign currencies, they were willingly accepted abroad. As already noted in Chapter 4, Volume 1 and Chapter 4, Volume 2, dealing with the inter-war acceptance markets of London and of New York, British, and American banks eagerly accepted bills drawn upon them by German firms under acceptance credits arranged for them by German banks, even though these bills quite obviously did not serve the purpose of financing current self-liquidating short-term trade transactions. Likewise, in the Berin bill market it was easy to place finance bills of a similar character provided that they were endorsed by a leading German bank.

Under the strain of the succession of crises triggered off by the Wall Street slump of 1929, culminating in the failure of several German banks, all German bills which had been accepted and placed abroad became frozen in 1931. But within Germany a kind of officially-controlled domestic bill market was maintained, with the aid of two newly created institutions, the *Akzeptbank A.G.* and the *Diskont-Kompanie A.G.* The market thus created dealt mainly in 'employment-creating bills' which were eligible for re-discount by the *Reichsbank*. Public works and rearmament were financed largely through the issue of such bills. The *Deutsche Golddiskontbank*, too, issued bills. These, together with Treasury bills to be dealt with in the next chapter, played an important part in the financing of rearmament and of the war itself.

(3) STRICT PRECAUTIONS AGAINST RECURRENCE OF EXPERIENCE

When the German financial system emerged from the chaotic conditions resulting from the Second World War, as a reaction to the pre-1931 misuse of the bill market steps were taken to prevent a repetition of that experience. The rule was laid down in 1948 that bank acceptances were only eligible for re-discount by the Central Bank if the bank concerned vouched for its genuine commercial and self-liquidating character and provided detailed information about the transaction which the bill financed. This cumbersome regulation was revoked some years later, to facilitate the creation of an active bill market. In 1959 the *Privatdiskont A.G.* was established in Frankfurt, with the participation of all banks in its share capital. This institution, referred to in Chapter 22, plays the role of intermediary between the bill market and the *Bundesbank*. It is prepared to re-discount bills of German banks offered by the *Privatdiskont A.G.* up to a limit fixed for each bank. It is the only bill broker and discount house in the Frankfurt market. Its representatives, in consultation with those of the *Bundesbank*, fix every day at 1 p.m. the daily market rate of discount.

(4) A NEW BILL MARKET

The rule adopted in 1948 under which eligible bills must bear three names has been upheld, and in order to comply with it bills have to pass through the market – that is, they have to be endorsed by the *Privatdiskont A.G.* – before they become eligible for re-discount. Banks accepting bills from their customers may keep them in their portfolios, or may place them in the market through the intermediary of the *Privatsdikont A.G.* It is only if the latter is unable to find a counterpart that the bills are offered to the *Bundesbank* for re-discount. The maximum rate at which this is done is $\frac{1}{4}$ per cent above the Bank rate, but normally the *Bundesbank* is prepared to re-discount them at Bank rate. The spread around the middle rate fixed by the *Bundesbank* is usually $\frac{1}{16}$ per cent on each side, but it might widen to $\frac{1}{8}$ per cent. Once a bill is endorsed by the *Privatdiskont A.G.*, however, it may be sold at a mere $\frac{1}{32}$ per cent above the official middle rate. It is not obligatory for banks to deal with *Privatdiskont A.G.* They are entitled to deal with each other and in such dealings the rate may diverge appreciably from the official middle rate. Outside the market and the *Girozentrale*, the big banks which have quotas with the *Bundesbank* buy commercial bills from smaller banks which have no such quotas and from specialised banks whose bills are not eligible for re-discount.

The practice of swapping bills between big banks has been discontinued, among other reasons because banks are reluctant to disclose to their rivals the business of their non-banking clients. German banks sell bills to foreign banks on occasions when the interplay of discount rate and forward premium on the Deutschmark makes the operation profitable.

(5) BILLS GIVEN IN PENSION

Already before the First World War, and again between the wars, it was a widespread practice among German and other continental banks to borrow in London or elsewhere on the security of trade bills which were given in pension to the lender. That practice was revived during the period of the restriction on paying interest on foreign bank deposits. A foreign bank's deposit assumed the form of a loan against bills in pension.

It is now mostly bonds and not commercial bills that are given in 'pension'. The transactions are in substance similar to the 'buy-back transactions in the U.S. and Canada. They provide an alternative to outright purchases and sales, and in given circumstances they have distinct advantages compared with outright purchases or sales.

The rates fixed at 1 p.m. are for 'long' bills (sixty to ninety days) and 'short' bills (thirty to fifty-nine days). In addition to fixing the middle rate the buying and selling rates are also fixed. It is only if the *Privatdiskont A.G.* is unable to find buyers at the officially fixed rate that it offers the bills for re-discount, provided that its maturity does not exceed twenty-nine days. Eligible bills of longer maturity are bills arising from imports, exports, re-exports and from loan transactions with non-German banks, or from commercial or financial transactions between non-German firms or banks. To be marketable, their maturity must not exceed ninety days.

The minimum amount of individual bills admissible to the bill market is DM.100,000 and their maximum amount DM.1,000,000. Their amounts must be multiples of DM.5,000.

Although the *Privatdiskont A.G.* plays a part similar to that of the discount house in London, there is a basic difference between the British and German systems. Under the latter, commercial banks have direct access to the discount window of the *Bundesbank* provided that the bills they present for re-discount are eligible and that their re-discount limit is not exhausted.

(d) TREASURY BILLS

(1) TWO TYPES OF PAPER

The virtual disappearance of bank acceptances from the Berlin market after the crisis of 1931 provided an opportunity for the development of a market in Treasury bills and other official market paper. After the revival of the German money market after the Second World War and following on the success of the currency reform, the German authorities sought to encourage the expansion of the demand for Treasury bills and Treasury notes by banks. This end was pursued by accepting such paper as collateral for Lombard loans, without deducting the amounts thus lent from the banks' unused re-discount quotas.

There are two types of Treasury bills, fixed interest-bearing notes sold at par and what are called 'non-interest-bearing' bills sold at a discount. The former type includes Federal Railway notes, Federal Post Office notes. They are for longer maturities for six months, twelve months, eighteen months and two years. The *Bundesbank* issued under the provisions of the currency reform of 1948 '*Mobilisierungspapiere*', notes payable by the Treasury, for the purpose of assisting in the revival of the economy affected by the fate of the Reichsmark at the end of the war, to compensate certain classes of claimants for losses arising from the post-war depreciation of their holdings of currency.

(2) A LIMITED MARKET

Treasury bills and other paper of the public sector can be dealt in between banks, but that market is limited, so much so that open market operations of the *Bundesbank* mostly assume the form of direct buying from the banks or selling to the banks. Non-banking institutions have to deal in Treasury bills through banks. The Bundesbank sells Treasury bills either in its capacity of agent of the Finance Ministry for debt management purposes or in its capacity of Central Bank for purposes of monetary policy. Thus in 1959 the Bundesbank sold Treasury notes to the amount of

DM.1,000 million to the commercial banks – the transaction came to be known as the 'Blessing billion' after the name of the President of the *Bundesbank* in order to mop up excessive liquidity. The inter-bank market in Treasury paper is not sufficiently wide to allow for operations on such a scale.

The *Bundesbank* also sells Treasury bills outside the market to certain public and semi-public institutions. There are also bills issued by the various States of the Federation. Whether papers issued by the public sector are sold to banks or to other buyers, their sale tends to reduce the volume of bank deposits. But of course the extent of Treasury bill dealings in Germany bears no comparison with its extent in Britain, in the United States or even in France.

(3) AN INTEGRATED MARKET

The various German money markets present in normal circumstances the picture of a well-integrated system. German operators are thoroughly sophisticated and are prompt in seizing the opportunity for engaging in arbitrage transactions whenever discrepancies occur between rates, whether within the same market or between different markets – allowing, of course, for normal differentials.

Even the Euro-Deutschemark market outside Germany is well integrated with the German money market. While discrepancies are liable to occur for longer maturities, the fluctuations of day-to-day money rates – which are of considerable importance – follow very closely the movements of rates in the Frankfurt market.

CHAPTER TWENTY-TWO

The Zürich Money Market

(1) MARKET IN CALL MONEY ONLY

ALTHOUGH Switzerland has three important financial centres, Zürich, Basle and Geneva, which share between them her capital market and her foreign exchange market, the relatively limited money market she possesses is concentrated almost entirely in Zürich, at any rate as far as transactions in short-term credits in Swiss francs are concerned. Basle and Geneva share with Zürich the turnover in Euro-dollars and other Euro-currency deposits. But the market in call money in terms of Swiss francs operates in Zürich only. And there are virtually no other money markets in Zürich or in any other financial centre in Switzerland.

There is no Swiss market in commercial bills. To the extent to which trade is financed by means of bills drawn by firms on their bankers they are discounted by their bankers who keep the bills in their own portfolios. If necessary they may re-discount them with the Swiss National Bank, but the proportion of their resources borrowed from the Central Bank – whether through re-discounting or through Lombard credits – which was fairly high before the war is now quite negligible. This is largely due to the almost uninterrupted inflow of foreign moneys which has resulted in a high degree of liquidity.

(2) MOVEMENTS OF HOT MONEY

It is true that the tide of foreign moneys turns sometimes, for whenever confidence returns in the French franc, the lira etc., 'hot money' is repatriated in large amounts. But since Swiss banks maintain the proceeds of the influx of foreign funds in a liquid form – whether in terms of Swiss francs or of other currencies – the repayment of the deposits causes no problem. There always seem to be sufficient refugee funds of one kind or another in addition to domestic deposits to enable Swiss commercial banks to finance their domestic customers without depending on the

G

Central Bank. Should they feel the need for realising their bills they re-discount them with the Swiss National Bank rather than sell them to other banks.

An exception from this rule is provided by the relationship between the leading commercial banks on the one hand and the smaller banks all over the country on the other. The Zürich 'big three' often re-discounts bills for these local banks. Also the *Kantonalbank* of Zürich re-discounts bills for the other *Kantonalbanks*. This is about the sum total of the commercial bill market in Switzerland. It is hardly an open market, as the transactions are based on special relationship between the parties.

(3) LIMITED MARKET IN TREASURY BILLS

Nor is there an active secondary market in Treasury bills. The short-term liabilities of the Federal Government are very small. Treasury bills with maturities up to two years are issued fourteen days after the end of each quarter – presumably mainly in order to mop up the funds released after the reversal of window-dressing operations before the end of quarters – but banks retain these bills usually in their portfolios, and if necessary they discount them with the Central Bank which is under obligation to re-discount any amount offered. Recently the Swiss National Bank obtained authority for issuing notes maturing within two years. These notes are issued from time to time for mopping up surplus liquid funds. This device obviates the necessity for the Swiss National Bank to persuade the Federal Treasury to issue such notes when it is not convenient to do so from the point of view of the management of the public debt.

The Kantons are also authorised to issue such notes, but the sum total of their issues is not sufficiently large to affect the money market.

All these bills change hands between banks and their customers or banks and the National Bank. In Switzerland there are no financial institutions corresponding to discount houses or bill brokers in London and in other financial centres.

There are also special bills that originated during the war for the purpose of financing food and other commodity reserves. These bills continue to be renewed and are eligible for re-discount with the Swiss National Bank to an unlimited extent.

(4) INFLUENCES ON CALL MONEY RATES

The sum total of inter-bank transactions in all bills issued by the public sector does not amount to very much. On the other hand the call money market has a fair turnover and becomes rather active from time to time. Commercial banks lend call money to local banks regularly. Call money rates usually fluctuate largely independently of the Bank rate, rising at times well above it and declining on other occasions well below it over prolonged periods. The rates are influenced largely by changes in the trend of the flow of foreign funds, which is the reason why the Swiss National Bank discourages the influx of foreign funds. Rates are also subject to seasonal influences such as window-dressing demand towards the end of the year and, to a less extent, towards the end of each quarter. The summer and winter holiday seasons are also important factors in influencing call money rates. To a very large degree the Swiss money market in call money, and even more in time deposits, is either in terms of Euro-currencies or in terms of Euro-Swiss francs deposited with banks outside Switzerland. There is a fairly important market in Euro-dollar deposits in the three Swiss financial centres. In fact, the practice of lending dollar deposits to Italian banks originated in Switzerland before the development of the London Euro-dollar market. Even today Italian banks transact a large part of their Euro-dollar business in the Swiss market.

The Swiss banks themselves make extensive use of the Euro-currency markets, both in Switzerland and in London and other centres abroad, for employing their own liquid resources in addition to investing their customers' money, owing to the lack of domestic short-term facilities for investment in a liquid form.

(5) RE-CYCLING OF HOT MONEY

In any case, owing to the perennial state of liquidity in Switzerland, short-term interest rates are relatively low and it is often profitable for Swiss banks and for foreign banks established in Switzerland to invest in Euro-currency deposits in spite of the cost of covering the exchange risk. The Swiss National Bank encourages this practice in order to mitigate the inflationary effect of large-scale influx or foreign funds through their employment in Switzerland. 'Hot money' is thus re-directed from Switzerland to other countries, instead of being invested in the Swiss money market.

Foreign holders of deposits in terms of Swiss francs – on which no interest is allowed and a commission of $\frac{1}{2}$ per cent is charged – re-lend these deposits outside Switzerland where they can earn reasonably high interest on them, even though borrowers have to allow for the cost of covering the exchange risk if they swap their francs into some other currency.

Owing to low interest rates in Switzerland and to world-wide confidence in the Swiss currency – confidence which gave rise to the anticipation of revaluation from time to time – forward francs were usually at a premium, so that the covering of the exchange risk by non-resident borrowers of Euro-francs was usually costly. Only if they deemed it safe to leave the transaction uncovered, or if the premium on forward francs declared for some reason below its interest parities, was it worth-while for borrowers to borrow in the Euro-Swiss franc market mainly in Frankfurt and in Paris. But owing to the persistent world-wide shortage of money many firms deemed it necessary to borrow Euro-Swiss francs regardless of the cost of covering. The resulting relatively high interest rates made it worth-while for foreign holders of Swiss francs to lend Euro-Swiss francs deposits abroad.

(6) MOPPING UP EXCESSIVE LIQUIDITY

The Swiss National Bank resorts to a variety of mopping up measures whenever there is an excessive degree of liquidity. The commercial banks usually comply with the Central Bank's requests to buy from it or sell to it bills or securities, in spite of the fact that, owing to their perennial liquidity and to the Swiss National Bank's statutory obligation to re-discount certain types of paper without limit, they do not depend on the Central Bank's goodwill to the same extent as commercial banks do in other countries.

The Swiss National Bank aims at mitigating tight money conditions on the eve of window-dressing dates. To that end it buys Euro-dollars from Swiss banks outright, or concludes swap arrangements with them, under which the Euro-dollars acquired from them on the eve of window-dressing dates are resold to them for delivery after such dates. Similar transactions for the same purpose are also made in eligible long-term securities. Likewise, short-term re-discount arrangements are made for the purpose of tiding over window-dressing dates. But the Swiss banks are usually in a position to increase their liquidity during tight periods independently of the Central Bank, by realising some of their Euro-currency holdings, even though in the absence of official intervention the operations would be distinctly costlier for them.

(7) ROLE OF EURO-MONEY MARKET

It is largely because of the facilities provided by the Euro-money markets that there is no imperative necessity for Swiss banks to develop an active domestic money market. Even so, having regard to the exchange risk and the cost of its covering if they convert the proceeds of Euro-currencies into Swiss francs, and to the commercial risk involved, it seems strange that one of the most advanced banking systems in the world should be without a mechanism comparable with those operating in other advanced countries. The Swiss authorities do not go out of their way to encourage the emergence of some such system, even though the issue of Treasury notes and the Swiss National Bank's interest-bearing notes has been a step in that direction. The existence of an active Euro-Swiss franc market in foreign countries offers the possibility of the development of a large Swiss money market which is abroad in a geographical sense but which is Swiss nonetheless. The absence of exchange control in Switzerland makes contact between the Euro-Swiss franc market and the Swiss money market much easier. The excessive revaluation of the Swiss franc in May 1971 might lead to the development of a more active domestic money market.

CHAPTER TWENTY-THREE

The Amsterdam Money Market

(1) IMPORTANT HISTORICAL ROLE

FOLLOWING the decline of the Antwerp and Lyons money markets in the late 17th century, Amsterdam became the principal money market in Europe. It reigned supreme during the 18th century, even though it had to face the growing competition of the London market. It had a good market for short loans, also for acceptances. But the conquest of the Netherlands by the French revolutionary army and her prolonged domination by Napoleon greatly reduced the importance of Amsterdam as a financial centre. During the 19th century it was unable to recover its previous position, because by that time London achieved an incontestable lead and Paris was a good second.

It was not until after the First World War that the Amsterdam money market succeeded in coming once more into its own. From 1922, as a result of the simplification of the procedure of rediscounting bank acceptances and trade bills by the Netherlands Bank, there was a revival of the bill market. Indeed during the 'twenties Amsterdam came to be considered third in order of importance as an acceptance market, after London and New York.

The crises of the 'thirties caused an eclipse of the Amsterdam bill market, as of all other acceptance markets, and to this day it has failed to recover its previous prominence. Although Amsterdam now ranks high among the Euro-bond markets, its functions as a money market are largely confined to dealings in call money, inter-bank deposits and Treasury paper. Even the turnover in Treasury bills declined in the late 'sixties and early 'seventies, owing to low rates compared with those quoted abroad, and to the consolidation of much of the Government's floating debts.

(2) THE CALL MONEY MARKET

In the Amsterdam call money market all business is transacted by telephone. While there is very active foreign exchange dealing at the *Bourse* during a brief mid-day session every day, hardly any business is transacted in bills or in call money through personal contact. There is mostly direct dealing between banks, but brokers are employed in transactions between banks and non-banking borrowers or lenders. The inter-bank market in deposits is entirely without the intermediary of brokers.

Dealing by telephone begins at 10 a.m. and ends about noon. By about 12.30 the discount houses – who combine that function with the function of brokers – are able to square their positions, if necessary by having recourse to the Netherlands Bank. Collaterals are transferred through the intermediary of a special clearing institution set up for that purpose. Transactions concluded by telephone are confirmed by the exchange of standard contracts.

The turnover varies widely from day to day, especially in bills. On some days there is very little business even in short Treasury bills. On the other hand, transactions in call money are apt to be very high both between banks and with non-banking parties transacting business through the intermediary of brokers.

Inter-bank call money and deposits are unsecured, but loans to brokers or to non-banking borrowers are against collateral of an equivalent amount of Treasury paper.

(3) FINANCING TREASURY BILLS

Brokers borrow mainly for the purpose of buying and holding Treasury bills. Like banks they have re-discounting facilities with the Netherlands Bank. But in recent years their main activity consists of acting as intermediaries in the call money market, and in the deposit market. Such deposits are known under the name of 'call-fixe'; they are lent for a definite period, usually for a number of days or weeks, but at times for periods of up to one year, after which the arrangement come automatically to an end. Individual amounts transacted in the market vary from Fl. 1 m. to items of between Fl. 20 m. and Fl. 30 m.

The Treasury paper is sold either by the Agent of the Ministry of Finance or by the Netherlands Bank out of its own holdings. For the purpose of dealing in banks Treasury bills are issued in denominations of Fl.100,000 or multiples of that amount. Treasury bills mature within one year, Treasury bonds are for two, three or five years. The latter carry half-yearly coupons and are issued at par, while Treasury bills are issued at a discount.

They are issued either on tap over the counter, at rates announced by the Finance Ministry's agent, or through offers at a definite discount rate announced in advance, or by tenders. Bills issued by tenders are allotted at a uniform discount rate, which is the highest rate that the issuing authority has to pay in order to place the amount of paper to be determined after receiving the tenders. The amount to be allotted is not announced in advance but depends on the amount of the applications and the rates offered.

Local authorities, too, issue short-term paper, but there is no secondary market in their loans.

(4) THE 'CALL-FIXE' MARKET

The market in commercial bills is very narrow, because banks prefer to discount their own acceptances rather than sell them on behalf of their clients or leave it to their clients to sell them. This is because the banks do not like their acceptances to find their way into the portfolios of other banks. If they need cash they prefer to borrow call money or deposits, or to sell Treasury bills, or to re-discount Treasury bills or commercial bills with the Netherlands Bank.

There is an increase in the turnover in 'call-fixe'. It often assumes the form of re-purchase agreements – the sale of Treasury paper with simultaneous re-purchase for a fixed date instead of using the Treasury paper as collateral to the deposits. Banks place deposits with each other without collateral. There is an inter-bank deposit market similar to that of London but its extent is relatively smaller. Altogether the money market is, relatively speaking, less important in Amsterdam than in London or New York.

(4) OFFICIAL FIXING OF CALL MONEY RATES

There is an 'official' quotation of call money rates, fixed daily by a committee representing the leading banks. It is possible, however, to deal at different rates and this is done to some extent between non-banks or with non-banks. Either party to a call money trans-action may give notice up to 12 noon and the loan is repayable on the same day.

Occasionally the Government borrows call money, as do Local Authorities and the Netherlands Bank. But the main borrowers are usually commercial banks, the central institutions of agricultural banks and bill brokers. They are also usually large lenders, offsetting each others' surpluses with each others' deficiences. In addition, the Netherlands Bank, the Postal Cheque and Giro Transfer Service, institutional investors of all descriptions, savings banks, large business firms and Local Authorities are also in the habit of lending their temporary surpluses.

Interest rates are influenced considerably by the extent of borrowing by the Government and Local Authorities and by the policy pursued by the Netherlands Bank. Bank acceptances are re-discounted at $\frac{1}{2}$ per cent above the Bank rate. The rates for Treasury bills sold across the counter vary according to market conditions. Seasonal agricultural industrial and, commercial requirements and seasonal Government receipts and disbursements play an important part in determining the trend of interest rates.

Brokers enjoy a unique privilege in the Netherlands. When the Bank rate is raised they are entitled to re-discount with the Central Bank a certain percentage of their portfolios at the old Bank rate during the day of the change. This concession is in recognition of the useful function they perform by keeping a range of maturities in their portfolios. There is a good forward market in bills, especially in Treasury bills of long maturities. Both brokers and banks are active in time arbitrage in Treasury bills and commercial bills. Brokers usually combine their function, with those of foreign exchange brokers.

(6) OPEN MARKET OPERATIONS

Open market operations play an important part among the Netherlands Bank's devices of monetary policy. When the Central Bank does not wish to influence the trend its open market operations are confined to offsetting temporary surpluses and shortages usually through the sale or purchase of Treasury paper at current market rates. In given situations the Netherlands Bank pursues its policy – in a passive sense – by abstaining from intervening to counteract the effect of any excess supply or excess of demand. In other situations it engages in active intervention, buying or selling to counteract or reinforce the prevailing trend. When the pressure on the market appears to be only temporary the open market operations assume the form of re-purchase agreements for brief periods, such as ten to fourteen days.

Open market operations hardly ever assume the form of purchases or sales of long-term Government securities, for the
Netherlands Bank has a large portfolio of Treasury paper out of
which it is able to operate when its aim is to mop up unwanted
liquidity. If additional paper is needed the Finance Ministry
converts part of its book debt to the Central Bank into Treasury
paper.

The Central Bank may influence the trend of the market also
by altering the minimum reserve ratios of the banks or by pursuing a discount rate policy by changing the Bank rate. The
money market can discount eligible paper with the Netherlands
Bank provided that its maturity does not exceed 105 days. Banks
and brokers can also obtain current account advances at a rate
$\frac{1}{2}$ per cent above the Bank rate. Banks usually prefer the second
alternative. Advances are against collateral of Treasury bills or
eligible commercial bills. There is no limit to the eligibility of
Treasury paper. Bank acceptances and trade bills are eligible on
the basis of general arrangements with a number of banks and
brokers fixing the limits. Additional special arrangements may be
made on application by the banks.

(7) RELUCTANCE TO RESORT TO CENTRAL BANK

Dutch banks aim at avoiding having recourse to the Netherlands
Bank and the latter too prefers to confine its assistance to covering
purely temporary requirements. It takes the view that the use of
Central Bank credit should not lead to a lasting increase in the
liquidity of the market. Banks usually prefer to borrow in the
market even when they would be in a position to borrow from
the Netherlands Bank at a lower cost.

Only acceptances covering foreign trade transactions are automatically eligible for re-discount, bills originating from other
commercial transactions are subject to previous arrangement or
consultation. Possibly this is one of the reasons why the market in
commercial bills in Amsterdam has remained relatively limited.
Banks prefer to hold Treasury bills as liquid reserves, because
they can be re-discounted unconditionally and because they have
even now a larger market in spite of the decline of their turnover.

Amsterdam has active Euro-currency markets, especially in
Euro-dollars, Euro- Deutschemarks and Euro-sterling. The transactions are concluded mostly with foreign banks, Dutch banks

acting as intermediaries. As their foreign currency assets and liabilities must balance, they employ funds they received from abroad for reinvestment abroad.

Inter-bank deposits maturing in less than one month are counted as liquid assets for the purpose of reckoning the banks' liquidity ratio. Deposits maturing in one month or more can only be included if they are secured by collateral.

One of the unusual features of the Amsterdam financial centre is that the connection between the market for short-term credits and the capital market is not nearly as close as in most other markets. This is partly because the Netherlands Bank hardly ever intervenes in the capital market in order to influence short-term interest rates indirectly, and partly because of the division of labour in the Dutch banking system – issuing houses do not operate in the money market on a large scale while commercial banks hardly operate in the capital market. The link between long-term and short-term interest rates, which exists nevertheless, is therefore more psychological than material.

CHAPTER TWENTY-FOUR

The Brussels Money Market

(1) THE ROLE OF EURO-BOND CLEARING

IT is generally assumed that Brussels will play an important part in an integrated money market of the E.E.C. But monetary integration is a long way away. Nevertheless the Brussels money market has already benefited to some extent from the role of Brussels as the administrative capital of the Common Market. A number of foreign banks and big corporations established branches and affiliates there, in addition to a number of international companies. All this means that additional liquid funds are made available for money market operations.

The operation of a clearing system in Euro-bonds has also helped in the development of the Brussels money market. But in spite of the resulting increase in its turnover, it is still inferior to the Amsterdam market, not to speak of Frankfurt, Zürich and London.

(2) CALL MONEY AND TIME MONEY

There is a call money market and a market in time deposits for maturities of one, two, three and six months in Brussels. Some foreign branches are very active lenders and borrowers, especially when uncovered interest arbitrage appears to be safe. The absence of a really satisfactory market for swap transactions in Belgian francs makes it at times difficult to undertake interest arbitrage operations with the Brussels market, for such transactions are liable to affect swap rates to a sufficient extent to wipe out the narrow profit margin on arbitrage.

The standard amount transacted between banks is Frs. 50 m. The turnover between Belgian banks – only about half a dozen of them take an active part in the market – is relatively moderate. This may be largely due to a restriction adopted in 1969, under which only banks which do not accept deposits exceeding three months are entitled to operate in the market.

Another restriction is that banks participating in the call money market are required to lend during each quarter amounts that are at least equal to the amount they borrow during the same quarter. This rule does not of course apply to the Securities Stabilisation Fund, which is charged with regulating the market, or to the Re-discount and Guarantee Institute specialising in financing foreign trade. One of the main objects why the Securities Stabilisation Fund operates in the market is to obviate the necessity of obtaining advances from the *Banque Nationale de Belgique*.

American banks in the late 'sixties were borrowers in the deposit market through operating in the market for external francs, the exchange rates in which are usually quoted virtually at par with those prevailing in the foreign exchange market.

(3) OFFICIAL INTERVENTION

The task of the Securities Stabilisation Fund is to engage in open market operations which influence the trend of the market considerably. It aims at preventing a decline of rates when this would cause an unwanted pressure on the exchange rate.

The market's trend is also influenced by the National Bank's policy of adjusting re-discount ceilings of banks. These ceilings are subject to frequent adjustments for the sake of regulating cyclical trends and also for the sake of influencing trends in the foreign exchange market. Moreover, banks which disregard the National Bank's wishes about credit restraint are apt to be penalised by a reduction of their ceilings.

(4) LIMITED MARKET IN BILLS

There is a limited market in bank acceptances. Banks may re-discount with the *Institut de Réescompte et de Garantie* their customer's bills bearing three signatures. Eligible paper is submitted by that institution to the National Bank for approval. The *Institut* charges a lower discount rate for bills approved by the National Bank.

Apart from such transactions, most bills discounted by banks are kept in their portfolios. This practice has increased considerably compared with pre-war practice when banks financed their customers mostly by means of advances. Bills financing capital equipment are often re-sold by banks to insurance companies and to other institutional investors, but there is also a small inter-bank market in them.

Nor is the market in Treasury bills very large. On a number of occasions the Treasury borrowed in the Euro-dollar market for lack of adequate facilities in the domestic money market.

CHAPTER TWENTY-FIVE

The Luxembourg Money Market

(1) FINANCING EURO-ISSUES

LUXEMBOURG has become a banking centre of some importance largely as a result of the development of a very active market in Euro-bonds. This market, together with fiscal privileges and other advantages, has attracted a number of foreign bank branches and affiliates and foreign participations in international or local banks. The Euro-bond clearing system established in Luxembourg as a rival to the system operating in Brussels assisted in the development of a banking centre and of a money market. Euro-bond transactions assist in the development of an active market in Euro-currencies.

The main function of the foreign banks established in Luxembourg is to share with the greatly expanded local banks the Euro-issuing activity and the activity in the secondary market in Euro-bonds. That activity is encouraged by fiscal and other privileges given by the Luxembourg Government and by the *Bourse*. Issues and operations in the secondary market are financed to a large degree in the Euro-currency markets.

Large amounts of liquid funds are always held in Luxembourg prior to their investment or re-investment in Euro-bonds. It is often convenient to hold them in Euro-deposits with local banks or with local branches of foreign banks instead of borrowing such deposits in other centres. Even though the proximity of the Brussels, Amsterdam and Frankfurt Euro-currency markets offers ample facilities, in given circumstances it is more convenient to meet the requirements locally. This provides a certain amount of Euro-currency activity in Luxembourg. Luxembourg banks acting as agents for investors in Euro-bonds often borrow Euro-currencies in the local market and re-sell locally the proceeds of Euro-bonds realised on the Luxembourg *Bourse*.

(2) ACTIVITY OF GERMAN AND AMERICAN BANKS

But German and other banks represented in Luxembourg, some of them by large branches, affiliates or correspondents, often operate in the local Euro-currency market independently of Euro-bond transactions. For geographical and other considerations it is a convenient market for them. American banks and firms issuing Euro-bonds found Luxembourg convenient for fiscal reasons until they discovered that they could benefit by the same advantages if they operated nearer home, in the State of Delaware. This discovery has led to a decline in Euro-dollar operations by Americans in Luxembourg in connection with Euro-bond transactions. But since American banks had already opened branches in Luxembourg their presence there ensured a certain amount of activity by them in Euro-dollars and in other money market transactions.

CHAPTER TWENTY-SIX

The Milan Money Market

(1) A LIMITED MARKET

CONSIDERING that the medieval Italian City-States had been the first to develop financial markets, and that the Italian economy has made remarkable progress since the 'Italian miracle' of the 'fifties, the progress of the Italian money market has been far from adequate. Milan is Italy's economic and financial capital, but its money market is lagging behind that of other leading Western European countries. It is only during the second half of the 'sixties that a noteworthy money market developed.

The *Banca d'Italia* aims at encouraging the development of an adequate money market. Largely to that end, the issue of twelve months Treasury bills by monthly tenders was initiated and the amount outstanding considerably increased. A secondary market gradually came into being. Owing to the increase of the outstanding amount of twelve months bills, an active secondary market developed in shorter maturities. It plays an important part as a device to enable banks to adapt their liquidity to requirements.

(2) CALL MONEY AND TIME DEPOSITS

But the main device to that end is provided by the markets in call money and in time deposits. The call money market in particular has assumed sizeable dimensions, and in more recent years time deposits too came to be dealt in actively, for maturities up to twelve months.

On the other hand, there is no market in commercial bills. Banks discount their customers' bills and either keep them in their portfolio till maturity or re-discount them with the *Banca d'Italia*. Bills are not sold between banks. There are no official open market operations. While the *Banca d'Italia* is actively engaged in foreign exchange transactions through Italian National Institute of Exchange – it confines itself to spot transactions – it keeps aloof from intervention in the money market.

Owing to exchange restrictions there is no inter-bank market in foreign currency deposits. Yet Italian banks were the first to borrow Euro-dollars in the early 'fifties. But all early transactions took place in Switzerland, and even though Italian banks are from time to time actively engaged in Euro-currency operations, they are all transacted in foreign financial centres – Switzerland, London or Paris. They transact Euro-dollar business in Italy with their customers or with the *Banca d'Italia*.

In 1970 the *Banca d'Italia* adopted the practice of differentiating between bills financing exports to E.E.C. countries and to other countries. While the former are all eligible, the latter have to be certified as being eligible. This means that while bills financing exports to the Common Market can be re-discounted in excess of the ceiling for facilities with the Central Bank, the export bills financing exports outside the E.E.C. may or may not be eligible once the re-discount ceiling of the holders is reached. This discrimination tends to affect the discount rate of E.E.C. bills favourably.

CHAPTER TWENTY-SEVEN

The Vienna Money Market

(1) THE ROLE OF SPECIAL INSTITUTIONS

VIENNESE banks have a long tradition in sophisticated money market operations. If in spite of this the Vienna money market is of limited importance it is because the crisis of 1931 left Austria with very few big banks. There are only two commercial banks and both are nationalised. In addition there are some merchant banks but the total number of banks operating in the market is so small that Austrian authors describe the prevailing banking system as a duopoly.

Several large mortgage banks have temporary liquid resources from time to time. They and three special central institutions deal with surpluses or deficiencies of the multitude of small institutions for which they act as intermediaries in relation to the money market.

The *Girozentrale* plays the part of a Central Bank for the Austrian savings banks, most of which are too small to have direct access to the money market. It relieves them of their liquid surpluses and meets their requirements for liquid resources. The net surplus or deficiency resulting from these operations is lent or borrowed in the market. The *Genossenschaftliche Zentralbank A.G.* plays a similar part for industrial agricultural co-operatives and the *Zentralbank der Volksbanken Österreichse G.m.b.H.* functions in the same way for small local banks. The Post Office Savings Bank too operates in the money market.

(2) ADJUSTING LIQUIDITY POSITIONS

According to Scheithauer, Vienna has no money market in the real sense of the term. The inter-bank transactions do not aim primarily at securing a higher yield or obtaining a loan at lower rates. Balances with the Austrian National Bank or with the Post Office Savings Bank are lent and borrowed mainly for the purpose of adjusting liquidity positions. Special relationship between the institutions concerned, or personal relationship between their executives, play an important part in arranging the transactions and in fixing the interest rates. The Vienna market is thus not an automatically functioning mechanism which equalises supply and demand through interest rate adjustments.

The market deals in overnight loans, money at call and, to a much less extent, in time deposits, mostly for three and six months. Money at call is often left with the borrower for long periods but the interest rate is changed on the initiative of either party if the general level of interest rates changes. Since the removal of the exchange control, banks and other institutions are permitted to take advantage of the better facilities offered by Euro-currency markets. Although the Austrian National Bank fixes limits for each bank and institution for such transactions, their volume is usually below the limit – owing to the inadequacy of forward exchange facilities – to enable them to cover the exchange risk.

(3) ISSUES OF THE PUBLIC SECTOR

The turnover in market paper is much lower than the turnover in loans. The Federal Treasury issues Treasury notes in units of one million schillings to the National Bank and the National Bank uses them for open market operations. Such operations are carried out partly at the *Börse*. The Central Bank re-discounts Treasury notes and also export bills which are guaranteed by the Government to the extent of 80 per cent and by banks to the extent of 20 per cent. Commercial bills are re-discounted up to the ceiling of the re-discount facilities fixed by the National Bank for each bank. The National Bank lends on the security of eligible market paper, on Government loans and on eligible securities quoted on the *Börse*.

Inter-bank dealing is limited. Banks feel inhibited from disclosing to their rivals that they are in need of liquid resources, and they therefore operate through the intermediary of some 'neutral' institution. Non-banks other than the institutions mentioned above cannot participate in the money market. Banks prefer to re-discount their commercial bills with the National Bank rather than offer them in the market if they are in need of liquid resources.

Conditions are usually tight at the end of each month, the quarter and the year. Owing to close contact with Euro-currency markets interest rates in the local money market are also influenced by Euro-currency rates and by the influx or efflux of foreign funds.

PART IV

OTHER OVERSEAS MONEY MARKETS

CHAPTER TWENTY-EIGHT

The Nassau Money Market

(1) EURO-CURRENCY TRANSACTIONS

THE Bahamas are one of the havens for capital seeking refuge from high taxation or leaving its country of origin for some other reason. Owing to the large amount of British, American and other capital that found its way there, Nassau has become an international financial centre of some importance. It is particularly important as an active market in Euro-dollars and, to a less extent, in other Euro-currencies.

A number of British, American and Canadian banks have important branches or affiliates, or participate in international banks established there. The fact that even two leading Swiss banks have wholly-owned affiliates in Nassau is in itself sufficient to indicate the importance attached to that centre in the world of international banking.

To a very large degree Nassau transacts Euro-currency business with London, New York and other foreign financial centres. In particular during the hours while the London market is closed New York banks transact their Euro-currency business through their Nassau branches, affiliates or correspondents. During the concluding years of the 'sixties a relatively high proportion of American borrowing of Euro-dollars was arranged in Nassau. Other Euro-currencies, especially Euro-Deutschemarks, Euro-Swiss francs, Euro-sterling and Euro-Canadian dollars, have also fairly active markets.

(2) REFUGE FOR FLIGHT MONEY

It is difficult to ascertain the extent to which there are local inter-bank transactions in Nassau either in Euro-currencies or in the local currency. But owing to the presence of a large amount of flight money there is bound to be always a certain amount of local funds which have to be kept in a liquid form, and the banks may find it to their advantage to deal with each other to offset surpluses against deficiencies.

The absence of a Central Bank – at the time of writing the Bahamas Monetary Authority performs some of the functions of a Central Bank – may delay the development of an active local money market in addition to the very active market between Nassau and other financial centres. But reinforced prolonged exchange control in the United States, Britain and other countries is liable to increase the volume of refugee money in Nassau and to increase the local turnover in the local money market.

CHAPTER TWENTY-NINE

The Israeli Money Market

(1) BANK-GUARANTEED PROMISSORY NOTES

As the combined effect of the credit restrictions imposed on banks by the Government to mitigate inflation during the early 'sixties, and of the statutory limitation of interest paid on deposits, an active market developed in Israel in bank-guaranteed promissory notes. In this market investors were able to obtain a higher yield on such short-term investments than through depositing their money in banks, and borrowers were able to obtain loans in excess of the credit ceiling. Originally the market was operated by brokers, but later the banks gradually came to transact most business of this type. They found buyers for their customers' promissory notes when they themselves were unable to meet their credit requirements because of the credit ceiling. In 1965 the outstanding amount of such paper was estimated at about 700 m. Israeli pounds.

In order to prevent a further expansion the Government imposed restrictions on such transactions. Banks were not permitted to guarantee more than three times their capital assets or $1\frac{1}{2}$ times their liquid assets, whichever amount was lower. It remained possible to place promissory notes without a bank guarantee, but the market for such notes was limited.

The demand for bank-guaranteed notes was later reduced by the removal of the limit to deposit rates that banks were permitted to pay to their depositors. As a result most holders of liquid funds came to prefer depositing their money with banks instead of investing them in promissory notes.

(2) POPULARISATION OF TREASURY BILLS

Another reason for the decline of the market in promissory notes was the popularisation of Treasury bills for short-term investment. These bills are on tap at a rate fixed by the Treasury, subject to frequent changes in accordance with the Treasury's requirements for funds, allowing for the trend of the market. These bills are issued through banks, and the banks are prepared to buy back the bills at current interest rates if holders want to recover their money before maturity. There is, therefore, a kind of secondary market in the Treasury bills. In the early 'seventies the demand for them usually exceeded the supply, so that the market rates seldom declined below the official rates.

Finally, the application of reserve requirements on guaranteed notes issued by banks deprived the latter of the means to circumvent the credit restraint by means of guaranteeing notes. Nevertheless the mechanism is there and in a changed situation it might be used again extensively.

There is also a small market in bank balances with the Bank of Israel. Banks with a surplus in excess of the necessary minimum lend their surpluses to banks which have to increase their reserves to the statutory minimum. The rates fluctuate according to supply-demand relationship, but transactions are relatively few, because only the bigger banks participate in this market.

CHAPTER THIRTY

The Beirut Money Market

(1) DEALING IN EURO-CURRENCIES

BEIRUT is by far the most important international banking centre in the Middle East. It has attracted a very large volume of foreign capital, especially from the Arab countries, totalling billions of dollars. A high proportion of this capital is held in a more or less liquid form and changes hands fairly frequently. There are some seventy banks in this country of two million inhabitants. Although the Lebanon has a relatively high volume of foreign trade and serves as an entrepôt for goods to and from other Middle Eastern countries, its trade would not justify the existence of so many banks. In particular it would not have attracted a number of foreign branches, affiliates and participations in local banks – American, British, French, Italian, Dutch, Canadian, Russian, Belgian and various Arab banks have branches or affiliates and German, Japanese, Austrian, Czech and Swiss banks have representatives – were it not for the high level of international financial activity of Beirut.

A large proportion of that activity assumes the form of dealing in Euro-dollars and other Euro-currencies, especially Euro-D. marks, Euro-Swiss francs and Euro-sterling. Even though the counterpart of most of the transactions has to be found in foreign financial centres, there is also much local inter-bank dealing in Euro-currencies between the local banks and foreign branches in Beirut.

(2) MARKET IN LEBANESE POUNDS

Beirut has also a money market in local currency, the Lebanese pound. It assumes the form of call money transactions and also transactions in time deposits. The banks have to keep a deposit with the Bank of Lebanon. Under the Currency and Credit Act, 1964, this liquid reserve could be raised to 25 per cent for deposits at call and to 15 per cent on time deposits, but at the time of writing the percentage is fixed at 5 per cent. Banks which have not sufficient liquid resources to meet this reserve requirement and to cover their own current cash requirements borrow in the market. Alternatively they may borrow from the semi-official *Banque Commerciale, Agricole, Industrielle et Foncière*, which bank is always prepared to relieve them of their unwanted surplus liquid resources.

There are no money brokers in Beirut, all business being transacted direct between the banks. There is an active market in Euro-bonds, transactions in which are financed partly with the aid of Euro-currencies borrowed in the local market. Kuwait and other oil-producing Arab countries transact much of their investment business through the intermediary of Beirut. The presence of large funds awaiting investment or re-investment, and of balances held by banks in connection with their considerable activities in foreign exchanges, keeps the Beirut money markets active.

CHAPTER THIRTY-ONE

India's Money Markets

(1) AN UNINTEGRATED MARKET

ONE of the characteristics of money markets in developing countries is that their primitive indigenous money markets continue to co-exist with more recently developed modern money markets. The difference between this system and what we know as parallel money markets in advanced countries is that there is very little connection between the two sectors. They are not integrated adequately, if indeed they are integrated at all. They exist side by side, serving the requirements of separate sectors of the community.

The money markets of India provide a characteristic instance of this unintegrated system. On the one hand, India possesses a fairly advanced money market for dealings between foreign banks and more or less big Indian banks. On the other hand, the primitive money markets of the bazaars, which must have existed since time immemorial, continue to exist, with barely any connecting link between the two markets.

So long as India was a British Dominion, she relied largely on the London money market's facilities for the requirements of her banks, her industry and her commerce. Soon after having achieved independence, the Indian authorities adopted the policy of developing a modern money market, while the indigenous money market remained in existence for the requirements of small customers for whom big Indian banks or foreign bank branches were unable or unwilling to cater.

(2) DEVELOPMENT OF A MODERN MARKET

In the early 'fifties the Reserve Bank of India took the initiative for creating a bill market by offering to re-discount eligible bills at $\frac{1}{2}$ per cent below the Bank rate. The banks came to realise the advantages of holding bills in their portfolios which they were able to convert into cash up to the limit of their re-discount facilities allowed by the Reserve Bank. Once the practice of buying, holding and re-discounting bills came to be established the concession of lower re-discount rate was discontinued, except for the benefit of special categories of bills such as those financing exports.

Simultaneously with the emergence of the bill market an interbank market developed in call money, with the active participation of foreign banks and large Indian banks. This, together with the secondary market in bills, was an entirely modern market. At the same time, small merchants, artisans, farmers or private individuals continued to borrow from moneylenders or from small local banks, either direct or through the intermediary of brokers, with or without the latters' guarantee of the repayment of their loans.

These brokers, and also the moneylenders and small local banks themselves, are familiar with the credit-worthiness of the borrowers and are, therefore, in a better position to deal with them than big banks. They grant credits against *hundis* (I.O.U.s) at short notice to meet urgent requirements, often on the borrower's personal credit, for various purposes for which neither banks nor even co-operatives would lend. Rates charged in this market are of course very high and bear little or no relationship with the much lower rates quoted in the modern market.

(3) THE INDIGENOUS MARKET

According to authoritative estimates the number of moneylenders in India is between 300,000 and 350,000. There is a market in *hundis* which are apt to change hands between moneylenders, and moneylenders' funds are shifted regularly between urban and rural districts according to seasonal requirement. In spite of the expansion of commercial banks and co-operative banks, this indigenous money market has retained considerable importance. Its funds consist largely of the capital of moneylenders or what they are able to borrow. Their working capital is increased by what is termed in Indian financial literature 'unaccounted money' or 'black money' – money derived from illicit dealings or money kept away from Banks for the purpose of tax evasion. Although much of that kind of money is hoarded, much of it finds its way into the indigenous market.

There is an intermediate money market between the indigenous market and the modern market – the system of co-operative banks which finance the multitude of agricultural and other co-operatives. Most of them are too small to deal in the market with commercial banks and they operate through the intermediary of district co-operative banks which, in turn, deal with the modern sector through State co-operative banks. The latter have facilities with the State Bank (the former Imperial Bank of India) and with the Reserve Bank, and they have access to commercial banks. The structure of interest rates in this market is lower than those in the bazaars, and the expansion of their activities has gone some way towards lowering the level of the latter rates.

(4) INTER-BANK CALL MONEY MARKET

We saw above that, largely independently of both markets, there is an inter-bank call money market. It is situated in Bombay, Calcutta and to a smaller extent in Madras. There are also dealings in inter-bank deposits. Maximum interest rates which are fixed from time to time do not apply to inter-bank transactions, nor are banks handicapped in competition with each other by any minimum rates on advances.

Most transactions in the inter-bank market are unsecured, but the foreign banks and big Indian banks that are able to operate in the market have to be of high standing. Brokers are seldom used in this market, but they are active in acting as intermediaries between banks and non-bank lenders or borrowers. Banks frequently use the call money market for the adjustment of their cash positions. Their liquid reserves are usually high, owing to the practice of keeping their customers' bills in their own portfolios till maturity. It is their cash ratios which are apt to cause them problems through unexpected withdrawals of deposits. They have the choice between re-discounting eligible bills with the Reserve Bank and borrowing in the market in which their cash deficiencies may be offset by surpluses of other banks.

(5) THE MARKET IN TREASURY BILLS

There is also a market in Treasury bills which are issued by weekly tenders or are on tap. The Finance Ministry sells Treasury bills to the Reserve Bank so that they are available for open market operations. It seems that the modern sector of the Indian money market has all the elements of an advanced money market, even

H

though its turnover is at times inadequate, especially in the bill market. This market, and even the call money market, is apt to be handicapped by the one-sided character of the trend of transactions. Some banks are almost always borrowers, for the purpose of financing relatively short-term advances to their customers, while others are almost invariably lenders. During the late autumn, winter and early spring banks want to borrow, while during the other seasons they want to lend. Similar seasonal influences exist more or less in most other countries, but in few countries is their extent comparable with the seasonal influences in India. Indeed the market could not function at all in the absence of official operations aimed at offsetting seasonal discrepancies between supply and demand. It is the Reserve Bank's task to cover seasonal deficiencies and to mop up seasonal surpluses.

Apart from the part played by the Reserve Bank as lender of last resort through re-discounting bills or lending on their security, there is also the State Bank which is often referred to as the 'lender of intermediate resort'. While the Reserve Bank often engages in open market operations the State Bank does not take the initiative but merely responds to the initiative taken by the private sector.

(6) DISCREPANCIES BETWEEN INTEREST RATES

One of the characteristics of the money market in India is the almost complete absence of connection between the structure of interest rates of the modern market and of the primitive market. Although they are both liable to be affected by basic trends, the inter-bank market, with its access to the lender of last resort and owing to its contacts with foreign centres, is liable to be affected to a more moderate extent than the indigenous market.

Another of its characteristics – especially that of the bazaars market – is the existence of discrepancies in interest rates quoted in the same types of loans at the same moment in various districts. The market is inadequately integrated also from this point of view. The discrepancies do not lead to a sufficient volume of arbitrage to bring about a higher degree of uniformity of rates.

(7) OPEN MARKET OPERATIONS

The scope for open market operations in short-term paper is very limited, owing to the limitations of the secondary markets in them. It is the practice of banks, as already mentioned above, to retain in their own portfolios the bills or promissory notes against which they lend to their customers.

The market in Treasury bills is also too narrow to allow for larg-scale open market operations. Nor can open market operations be carried out on a large scale in Government bonds. The Government is usually in need of funds regardless of the trend of the money market, so that considerations of debt management must often be allowed to prevail over considerations of monetary policy. In any case there are very few big dealers who would be able to create a good market by keeping bills and bonds in their portfolios instead of merely acting as intermediaries.

Credit policy does not play the same important part in India as in more advanced countries. This is partly because an important part of the backward sector has barely emerged from the stage of natural economy, and partly because even many sectors which have reached the stage of money economy transact everything in cash. This state of affairs delays the development of a really large money market that would be in accordance with the increasing importance of the sub-continent and with its economic progress.

The money market in Pakistan, with Karachi as the main centre, is similar to that of India. There is a call money market between foreign banks and large local banks. The loans are as a rule unsecured, though on many occasions they are against collateral in the form of bullion or Government securities. As in India, there is hardly any secondary market in commercial bills which banks like to hold to maturity or, if they need cash, they re-discount them with the State Bank. As in India, the monetary authorities in Pakistan sought to encourage the use of bills for some time by re-discounting them $\frac{1}{2}$ per cent below the Bank rate, but later this concession was terminated.

CHAPTER THIRTY-TWO

The Singapore Money Market

(1) ASIAN DOLLAR DEPOSITS

TOWARDS the end of the 'sixties a small but expanding and potentially important market developed in Singapore in U.S. dollar deposits on lines similar to those of the Euro-dollar market. It is referred to as 'Asian dollar market' or as 'market in Asian currency units'. It came into being on the initiative of some American banks with the encouragement of the Singapore Government which made its existence possible by repealing the withholding tax on interest payments on bank deposits held on non-resident accounts. In 1970 the Government went even further in assisting in the development of this market by authorising the adoption of the system of numbered accounts similar to the one that exists in Switzerland, under which the account-holder's identity is kept a closely-guarded secret. This innovation was expected to go a long way towards attracting flight money from Asian countries which are, or are threatened to come, under Left-wing regimes.

Holders of Asian dollar deposits, whether banks or non-banks, are entitled to transfer their deposits to authorised banks or to non-residents. These dollars can therefore be transferred to the relatively small Euro-dollar market that has existed in Singapore for some time, or to any other Euro-dollar market, or to the United States. In 1970 estimates of the volume of outstanding Asian dollar deposits varied between $150 m. and $325 m. No statistics or official estimates are available.

(2) CHINESE EXPATRIATES' FUNDS

Depositors include some Central Banks of South Eastern Asian countries. Chinese expatriate merchants and other Chinese residents outside China, especially in Indonesia, Indo-China and Malaysia, also use the market, albeit to a relatively moderate extent only. Local Chinese banks operate both as lenders and as borrowers. Considering that the resources of the large number of expatriate Chinese people are estimated at several billions of dollars, a popularisation of the use of the Singapore Asian dollar market amongst them could greatly increase its turnover. There are a number of money brokers active in the market, but most of the business is transacted direct between the banks, especially as far as dealings between foreign banks are concerned.

There is in Singapore also an Asian dollar market in Certificates of Deposits, bought and held mostly by Chinese expatriates. It has a small secondary market which is liable to expand simultaneously with the increase in the turnover in Asian dollar deposits.

Even before the development of the Asian dollar market the number of foreign banks or banks with foreign participation was relatively large in Singapore, in addition to the local banking community. Since the emergence and expansion of this new market the importance of the Singapore banking centre has increased considerably. Although it is not so large as the Hong Kong banking community, many depositors prefer to use Singapore, or to spread their risk by keeping there part of their liquid resources, owing to their doubts about Hong Kong's political future.

(3) SINGAPORE DOLLAR DEPOSITS

The volume of deposits in Singapore dollars is of course a great many times larger than that of deposits in Asian dollars. Owing to the size of the gold and foreign exchange reserve, Singapore dollars are widely trusted, and the reason why in spite of this they have not a larger market lies in the inadequacy of forward exchange facilities. Nevertheless there is a money market in Singapore in Singapore dollars, but for non-residents it is more convenient to deal in Asian dollars. While the development of a money market in Singapore dollars is at the time of writing handicapped by the lack of a Central Bank it does not affect the development of the market in Asian dollars which would be in any case outside the control of a Central Bank.

There is an active inter-bank market in local currency also in Kuala Lumpur. It assumes mostly the form of overnight loans, but it is possible to transact inter-bank business for several days.

The existence in Singapore of a very active entrepôt trade in many commodities, and of an active market in gold, provides opportunities for the additional use of Asian dollar facilities. A high proportion of the business in Asian dollars is transacted by foreign banks – American, British, Japanese, French, German, Dutch, Chinese and Indian.

(4) RIVAL MARKETS TO HONG KONG

The development of the Singapore market depends largely on the political outlook of Hong Kong and on the attitude of the Japanese authorities towards the removal of exchange control in Japan. Possibly the friendlier tone adopted by Peking in 1971 will benefit Hong Kong at the expense of Singapore. But there is ample scope for both centres, and neither of them would be a rival to Tokyo as the leading money market in Asia if and when the largely self-imposed limitations of that centre should come to be eliminated.

It is also anybody's guess whether the present supremacy of the Asian dollar market over the Singapore dollar market is necessarily permanent. The spread between borrowing and lending rates is usually wider in the local currency market than in the Asian dollar market, because the latter is more international and there is much arbitrage between it and Euro-dollar markets. Owing to the large amount of refugee funds in Singapore, money rates tend to be low there. An expansion of the forward market in Singapore dollars would go a long way towards reducing the differentials in the money market in local currency.

Singapore has a small market in Treasury bills which are issued by tenders. Banks seldom sell Treasury bills to each other but they sell them to non-bank buyers or buy them from non-bank sellers, usually through the intermediary of brokers. There is also a small market in commercial bills, mostly relating to foreign trade. They are often sold by small banks to bigger banks.

CHAPTER THIRTY-THREE

The Hong Kong Money Market

(1) INTER-BANK DEPOSITS

AN active money market developed in Hong Kong since sterling became convertible in 1958, its development was handicapped to some extent by the absence of a Central Bank. The Commissioner of Banking and, in some sense, the Hong Kong and Shanghai Banking Corporation, play the part of the absent monetary authorities. During a series of crises culminating in the banking crisis of 1965, the Government acted as lender of last resort in the absence of a Central Bank and assisted a number of local Chinese banks in need of support. The extent of the success of their rescue operation is indicated by the fact that the Hong Kong banking community survived without a major crisis the difficulties arising from the riots of 1967 and the resulting political tension with China.

There is an active market in inter-bank deposits in Hong Kong dollars. American and European bank branches usually take deposits from local Chinese banks. The large number of Chinese Communist bank branches – which includes a branch of the Bank of China – keep mostly aloof from that market and confine their activities largely to financing trade between Hong Kong and the mainland and Chinese foreign trade in general.

The inter-bank market in deposits is in Hong Kong dollars, but there is also a market in Euro-dollars. Chinese merchants and investors outside China use both markets for depositing their funds though not nearly to the same extent as during the Sukarno regime in Indonesia and during the acute troubles in Malaysia. Authorised banks may accept deposits from residents in Hong Kong dollars or in sterling only – apart from foreign currencies for currency requirements – but unauthorised banks deal more freely in Euro-dollars.

Large deposits are held with Hong Kong banks also because of their function in the very active foreign exchange market. Oil companies of the Persian Gulf are entitled to sell sterling up to a certain limit in the official market and beyond that limit in the unofficial market at less favourable exchange rates. The flow of these and similar transactions ensures the presence of large amounts of deposits which find their way into the inter-bank deposit market or in the call money market. Up to the time of writing Hong Kong has not developed a market in Asian dollars.

(2) THE CALL MONEY MARKET

There is active dealing in call money and in deposits for seven days, fifteen days and one month. Borrowers provide no collateral. Most transactions are direct between authorised banks, but authorised banks usually deal with unauthorised banks and with some non-banking customers through the intermediary of brokers. Some of the large number of foreign exchange brokers also act as money brokers. There are special brokers acting as intermediaries between unauthorised banks.

Call money rates in Hong Kong are a very sensitive barometer indicating not only business trends but also the degree of confidence in respect of the political outlook. There is a great deal of hoarding of bullion and coins and even notes, and changes in the extent of hoarding constitute one of the important factors affecting the volume of liquid funds in the market and interest rates.

There is no market in Treasury bills or in commercial bills, but there is a very active market in loans to stockbrokers. The Hong Kong Stock Exchange has a very large turnover and the trend of loans financing its transactions is one of the most important factors determining the trend in the money market.

Operations by the Chinese Government – largely through the Hong Kong branch of the Bank of China – are becoming increasingly important. It is widely believed that the increasing importance of the Hong Kong money market, foreign exchange market and gold market, as well as the role of Hong Kong as an intermediary for Chinese imports and exports, is one of the reasons why Peking, in 1971, has relaxed its former pressure on Hong Kong.

In addition to the large number of Chinese Communist banks and local Chinese banks, a number of foreign banks came to be established in Hong Kong. The use made of Hong Kong by certain Sterling Area holders of sterling for transferring their funds into dollars or other currencies is one of the reasons for the activity in the Hong Kong money market.

CHAPTER THIRTY-FOUR

The Manila Money Market

THERE is a fairly advanced money market in the Philippines. The Manila banks took the initiative in 1961 for the creation of a call money market. Its turnover approached $2 billion in 1970. Business firms and other investors with seasonal surplus funds – especially insurance companies, mining finance houses, but also trust funds and wealthy individuals, acquire bills issued by leading finance companies. They are also attracted by the high yield on commercial paper.

The Government was not slow in trying to take advantage of the new facilities. Through the Philippine National Bank it issued Treasury Notes the bulk of which was taken up by banks and official financial institutions.

Dealers formed the Money Market Dealers Association to regularise the activities on the various markets. There are twelve commercial banks and five other financial institutions actively engaged in the market. The turnover is particularly active in interbank call loans and in commercial paper.

CHAPTER THIRTY-FIVE

The Tokyo Money Market

(1) NO BILL MARKET

FOLLOWING on the troubled period in Japan's monetary system during the years that followed the Second World War, conditions underwent a remarkable improvement as a result of the 'economic miracle' similar to the German economic miracle. Japan was able to stabilise the yen – albeit at a fraction of its original value – before the stage of runaway inflation was reached. Japan, like Western Germany, had prolonged periods of almost uninterrupted expansion and her industrialisation during the 'fifties and the 'sixties was truly spectacular. Her banking system too adapted itself to increased industrial and commercial requirements, so that some Japanese banks are now among the world's biggest banks. Above all, the yen has become one of the strongest currencies, thanks to Japan's series of export surpluses and also to borrowing abroad on a large scale.

Notwithstanding this, the evolution of the Japanese money market, even more than the German and French money markets, has failed to keep pace with the progress achieved by the country's economy. It still consists almost entirely of a very active call money market which was reopened in 1950. There is practically no commercial bill market in Tokyo nor a secondary Treasury bill market. Many large business concerns have a very high credit rating and excellent special relationship with leading banks, so that it would be easy to find buyers for their bills in the market, even without the bills being accepted or endorsed by a bank. But it is the practice of banks, if they discount their customers' bills instead of granting them advances, to keep the bills in their own portfolios until maturity, or to re-discount them with the Bank of Japan. Japanese banks never sell bills to other banks and do not grant to their customers acceptance credits to assist the latter in marketing their bills.

(2) NO TREASURY BILL MARKET

Nor is there in Japan a market for Treasury bills. The Finance Ministry does issue sixty-day bills which are on tap. These bills carry a fixed interest which remains unchanged for long periods, irrespective of the ups and downs of market rates of interest. Banks that invest in Treasury bills keep them till maturity, but they can use them as collateral when they borrow from the Bank of Japan. Non-banking holders use them as collateral when borrowing from banks.

Until recently Japanese banks were permitted to borrow Euro-dollars, even though their operations were subject to various rules. For a number of years they were amongst the largest borrowers in London and in other Euro-dollar markets. But there is no Euro-dollar market in Tokyo itself, because Japanese banks are not permitted to re-lend foreign currency deposits to each other or to other Japanese residents. Owing to the embarrassing increase in official holdings of dollars in 1970–1971, the authorities placed a ban on Euro-dollar borrowing by Japanese banks or other Japanese residents. In 1971 this ban was also extended to Euro-bond issues, except under special circumstances.

(3) IMPORTANCE OF A CALL MONEY MARKET

So long as it was possible for Japanese banks to borrow and repay Euro-dollar deposits as a matter of routine, or the granting of licences was purely a matter of form, they were in a position to adjust their liquidity by increasing or reducing their Euro-dollar commitments. But now that this is no longer possible the call money market provides practically the only device for banks and other financial institutions to adjust their liquid reserves. It is a well-developed market with a large turnover.

There are five types of transactions in the Japanese money market:

(1) Half-day loans, which are either morning loans repayable through the daily clearing settlement at 1 p.m. or afternoon loans received after 1 p.m. and are repayable by the close of the same business day.

(2) Overnight loans which are settled on the next day before 1 p.m. unless the transaction is renewed.

(3) 'Unconditional' loans which, in spite of their names, are only unconditional for two days, after which they are subject to one day's notice.

(4) Term loans which are repayable on a definite date.

(5) 'Over the month' loans which become subject to one day's notice as from certain days on the following months, usually from the second day of the following month.

The largest turnover is in 'unconditional' loans and 'over the month' loans. Both are call money loans, the only difference being the date from which they become subject to one day's notice.

(4) 'ONE-WAY' OPERATIONS

Although call money dealers quote and deal in both ways, other operators in the market are either always or practically always borrowers or always or practically always lenders. Most business goes through dealers, but there is much direct dealing between big banks and also between them and smaller banks or other financial institutions. Normally the main lenders are country banks which obtain deposits from their customers but have only limited opportunities for lending to creditworthy borrowers in their own districts. Other lenders include foreign banks, banks specialising in long-term credits, trust banks, the Central Co-operative Bank for Agriculture and Forestry, the Central Bank for Agricultural and Industrial Co-operatives, the National Federation of Credit Associations and insurance companies. All these institutions often have temporary surpluses prior to investing their funds for the purpose for which they want to invest them. But they and other types of investors are also liable to want to employ part of their capital permanently in the call money market, owing to the high yield usually obtained on call loans, the interest rates on which are often higher than the yield on long-term investments.

Most borrowers are 'City banks' – banks of Tokyo, Osaka, Yokohama, Nogoya and Kobe – which lend to industrial and commercial firms on a very large scale and finance these loans largely with the aid of call money. Although Tokyo is by far the largest call money market, the other cities mentioned above have also minor call money markets of their own.

Security finance companies are perennial borrowers from dealers in call money. They finance more than half of their investments with the aid of secured loans. They deposit the collateral with the Stock Exchange against the issue of 'call loan transactions collateral receipts' and obtain loans from dealers against such receipts. The dealers, in turn, borrow from the Bank of Japan against their own promissory notes to which the receipts are attached. The percentage up to which the receipts are accepted as collateral are adjusted by the Bank of Japan according to whether it wants to encourage or discourage this type of borrowing.

In 1970 some fifteen City banks participated in the call money market, as did over sixty local banks, seven trust banks, three banks for long-term credits, a large number of credit associations either direct or through their National Federation, and institutions enumerated earlier in this chapter. Foreign banks were permitted until recently to lend in the market but not to borrow. This permission is now subject to restrictions owing to the official policy aimed at discouraging the influx of foreign money.

(5) HOW THE MARKET OPERATES

Transactions are settled by cheques drawn on the Bank of Japan. If they are between two different centres the funds are transferred through the Bank of Japan's teletype transfer service that operates in cities where the Bank of Japan has branches.

To an increasing degree the loans assume the form of repurchase agreements, both between participants in the market and between them and the Bank of Japan. The latter concludes such agreements up to a maximum period of one month, subject to one day's notice before the date of maturity, in the absence of which the loan may be renewed for another month at the end of which they are not subject to further renewal. The price differentials for such transactions are fixed on the basis of the median between the highest and lowest call money rates of the day of the purchase or of the day of renewal.

All straight borrowing of call money, whether within or outside the market or from the Bank of Japan, is against collateral. Before the war only Government securities were eligible, but now Government-guaranteed bonds, Local Authorities bonds, certain types of bills – usually those eligible for re-discount by the Bank of Japan – and stock deposit certificates are also accepted.

Normal amounts of individual transactions are of the order of between 500 m. and 1,000 m. yen, but transactions with small local savings banks or credit associations may be as small as 10 m. yen. At the other extreme, inter-bank transactions between leading Tokyo banks are sometimes for amounts of 2,000 m. to 3,000 m. yen.

The spread between lending and borrowing rates is in normal conditions around ¼ per cent, but on hectic days, or during periods when interest rates have a strong rising or falling trend, this spread is liable to widen to ½ per cent or more or to narrow to ⅛ per cent.

(6) HOW RATES ARE INFLUENCED

Call money rates are largely influenced by changes in domestic conditions and by official intervention. There are regularly recurrent factors – the balances at the daily clearing settlements, tax payments at the beginning of the month, wage payment dates, various end-of-month settlements, etc. Rates are sensitive to the cash positions of banks, which again are affected by the influx and efflux of deposits, by the net amount of foreign exchange trans-actions of the Bank of Japan's Foreign Exchange Fund – that is, the yen transactions of the Bank of Japan – by the balance of Treasury transactions and, last but by no means least, by the Bank of Japan's policy. The latter often gives dealers and banks guidance without trying to impose an official limit to their lend-ings or borrowings – though there was one in operation in the 'fifties – and it is in a position to influence the volume of call money or the call money rate by various monetary policy devices.

Foremost among those devices is the Bank rate, which is a very flexible instrument in Japan. Call money rates, which are usually above the Bank rate, are affected by the Bank of Japan's attitude towards its perennial debtors. When they have to reduce their debts they have to borrow in the market, which is one of the reasons why call money rates tend to be above the Bank rate. International influences play a part only to the extent to which they influence the Bank of Japan's foreign exchange operations. In spite of the persistent decline of Euro-dollar rates over a long period in 1970–1971 the Tokyo call money remained in the neighbourhood of 8 per cent in February 1971. City banks were not in a position to take advantage of the differential by borrowing

Euro-dollars, because it would have increased the inflow of dollars which was contrary to the official policy.

(7) HEAVY BORROWING BY CITY BANKS

City banks borrow, on the average, about 80 per cent of the total outstanding amount of call money. Owing to business expansion the demand for call money exceeds supply most of the time. The outstanding amount has been increasing almost without interruption ever since the market came to be re-established after the war. Even though the Tokyo call money rate is apt to diverge from rates abroad, its basic trend was affected by the upward trend in the late 'sixties.

There are firms of dealers in call loans who act as intermediaries in the call money market. Before the war their role was largely confined to that of brokers negotiating deals between banks and also with other institutions. In more recent times they also have come to transact in addition business on their own account. They also buy and sell commercial bills and short-term Government securities. Most dealers also operate as foreign exchange brokers.

Dealers have to be licenced by the Finance Ministry which closely supervises their activities. They play a part similar to that of discount houses in London, with the essential difference that they lend to commercial banks instead of borrowing from them, and that the latter, besides borrowing from dealers, have also direct access to the Central Bank both for re-discounting eligible securities and for borrowing against eligible collateral.

The mechanism for the development of parallel money markets exists and Japanese banks together with foreign branches, are sufficiently sophisticated to create such markets. Conceivably we might witness their emergence before very long. As in other spheres, in this sphere too Japan will undoubtedly catch up with progress made by the most advanced Western countries. But the preliminary condition for the development of parallel money markets would be the removal of the exchange restrictions which are still in operation at the time of writing, and which continue to handicap the emergence of Tokyo as one of the leading international money markets.

CHAPTER THIRTY-SIX

The Australian Money Market

(1) INTER-COMPANY DEPOSITS

As in many other countries the money market developed in Australia in the 'fifties and 'sixties largely as a result of prolonged periods of high interest rates. The evolution of the Australian money market differs from that of other money markets in that it began not with the emergence of a call money market or a market in Treasury bills, but with the popularisation of inter-company deposits and finance company deposits. Systematic transactions of these types can be traced back to the early 'fifties, while in much more advanced countries they did not assume noteworthy dimensions until many years later. Apart from inter-company transactions, the money market consisted mainly of loans at call financing Stock Exchange transactions. Sydney and Melbourne were the principal markets.

These markets have remained in existence after the emergence of an official money market in 1959. Indeed the volume of inter-company deposit transactions has increased very considerably as a result of credit restrictions in the 'sixties. When in 1970 the financial combine Finsec suspended payments it had $A80 m. of inter-company deposit liabilities outstanding. Such deposits are negotiated either direct between business firms or through the intermediary of brokers or of banks.

Inter-company deposits are not guaranteed by banks. But if approved by the Reserve Bank the deposit receipts become marketable.

(2) MARKET IN CALL MONEY AND SHORT LOANS

This unofficial market was later supplemented by an official market in call money and short-term loans, by a bill market and by a market in Certificates of Deposits. As from 1959 authorised dealers were given the privilege to obtain 'last resort loans' – that is, loans from the Australian Reserve Bank to finance their holdings of commercial bills and Government paper. These dealers are the principal borrowers in the call money market and in the market in fixed deposits.

Lenders of loans at call and fixed deposits are mainly commercial banks which adjust their liquidity positions through increasing or reducing their loans to authorised dealers, as clearing banks in London increase or reduce their loans to discount houses. Other lenders include various authorities and institutions of the public sector, savings banks, insurance companies, trusts, pension funds, finance houses, agricultural and industrial concerns, etc.

(3) HOW THE MARKET OPERATES

Dealings with banks and also with non-banking customers are done by telephone. Once the transaction is concluded they send a note by messenger confirming its terms, together with the safe custody certificate issued by the Reserve Bank of Australia, with which institution all dealers deposit Commonwealth Government securities that are to serve as collateral for the loan. In return for this certificate the dealer receives a cheque from the lender. The Reserve Bank accepts securities deposited by dealers at any of its branches.

When the lender calls his loan he has to give notice by 11 a.m. and the dealer repays the loan by cheque on the same day. Occasionally this may necessitate the arrangement of a daylight overdraft to meet an unexpected withdrawal. Such overdrafts have to be repaid by the end of the day, and if there is no other way of raising the necessary funds the dealer borrows from the Reserve Bank, in return for the safe custody certificate receipt which he has recovered from the lender against the repayment of the loan.

Borrowers have to deposit securities with the Reserve Bank to serve as margins to cover lenders in the event of a depreciation of their collateral below the amount of the loan.

The money borrowed by dealers is invested in commercial bills, Treasury paper, Hire Purchase paper, Government securities, etc. The rates paid for money at call tend to adapt themselves to rates of these various market instruments – though relationship is reciprocal – leaving a profit margin to dealers. Rates for fixed deposits are usually higher.

(4) THE RESERVE BANK'S ROLE

If money is tight dealers are in a position to borrow from the Reserve Bank, provided they are prepared to pay rates which are above the yield on their investments. Therefore they only fall back on the Reserve Bank in the last resort, if no money is obtainable at lower cost elsewhere. All loans are secured by eligible securities. Alternatively the dealers can re-discount their eligible securities, or can sell them to the Reserve Bank under re-purchase agreements.

Most of the loan transactions in the market assume the form of re-purchase agreements. Transactions in the market, or between dealers, or between banks and the Reserve Bank, are greatly facilitated by the Reserve Bank's security safe-keeping mechanism. Government securities can be transferred from one centre to another through the Reserve Bank's network of branches. As we saw above, dealers, and other depositors of securities, can use the safe custody certificates issued by the Reserve Bank as collateral for loans.

The Reserve Bank has no formal Bank rate. It charges penalising rates on 'last resort loans' so that banks and dealers do not avail themselves of these facilities unless they are unable to meet their requirements at lower cost in the market or through realising assets. But the Reserve Bank itself often takes the initiative for lending to the market in pursuit of its monetary policy through engaging in open market operations, in which case its rates on straight loans or its terms of buy-back arrangements are more favourable to borrowers than they are if it is the latter who take the initiative.

In the late 'sixties there were nine official dealers. In addition to operating in short Government securities and maintaining a portfolio in them, they also operate in commercial bills. The minimum market transaction in Government securities is $A50,000. Commercial banks are not permitted to participate in the capital of security dealers.

The principal lenders on the short-term market are commercial banks, even though the amounts lent in the market cannot be reckoned as part of their liquid reserves. The amount of their loans is liable to fluctuate widely. Other lenders include savings banks, Local Authorities, semi-official institutions and business firms.

(5) MARKET IN TREASURY BILLS
AND COMMERCIAL BILLS

In addition to the development of markets in call money and fixed
deposits, a market in ninety-one-day Treasury Notes was created
in 1963. It is very active, but the market in commercial bills
endorsed by a bank is limited. The bulk of commercial bills is
retained in the portfolios of the banks, though dealers are authorised to hold limited amounts of them.

By 1970 the turnover in the market in commercial bills amoun-
ted to some hundreds of millions of Australian dollars, and several
hundreds of business firms made use of this method of borrowing
In 1965 three acceptance houses were established. In addition to
bank acceptances, trade bills are also issued. They are marketed
by bill brokers. Owing to their high interest rates – which are at
times about twice the prevailing Treasury bill rates – there is a
fair investment demand for them. Such bills are not re-discounted
by the Reserve Bank, but failures have been very few and far
between. Bills accepted by acceptance houses are considered safe,
because these acceptance houses are backed by very strong
financial interests. Some of the houses are willing to undertake to
re-purchase the bills they sell at any time, at current market rates.

There is a market in short-term debentures issued by HP
finance houses. Since 1969 a market in CDs issued by banks has
come into existence. These certificates are in units of $50,000 and
their maturities range between three months and two years. The
Reserve Bank fixed a maximum interest rate limit of $5\frac{1}{2}$ per cent.
Dealers are entitled to hold a certain proportion of their portfolios
in CDs. During the first ten months of their existence the outstanding amount increased to $A246 m. Most of these certificates
are issued to the issuing banks' depositors, but other investors
too are interested in them. This device has gone some way
towards creating a more competitive spirit amongst the banks.

(6) RE-PURCHASE AGREEMENTS

Most transactions in the market assume the form of re-purchase
agreements. The profit on such deals follows closely the interest
rates on loans of corresponding maturities. The Reserve Bank sells
Government paper without charging brokerage.

The dealers' main task is to borrow short and lend long and to benefit by the resulting interest differential. Although they have access to the Reserve Bank, the high cost of re-discounting or buy-back arrangements with the lender of last resort would make it unprofitable for them, as for banks, to finance their portfolios by making prolonged use of official facilities which are only supposed to serve the purpose of helping them out when money is temporarily tight or abnormally costly in the market.

Even though the Australian money market bears no comparison with that of Canada, its progress during two decades foreshadows the possibility of further improvement of its facilities, especially if as a result of Britain's adhesion to the E.E.C. should reduce the extent to which the Australian banking system can depend on London's facilities. If, as is widely expected, the Australian economy should expand considerably, the mechanism of an advanced money market will be available for its increased requirements.

CHAPTER THIRTY-SEVEN

The New Zealand Money Market

(1) ROLE OF DEALERS

A SMALL money market developed in the late 'fifties and received official recognition in 1962 when a limited number of dealers came to be authorised to transact business in short-term securities. These authorised dealers are entitled to sell Government securities to the Reserve Bank of New Zealand if they need cash to repay call money. The price paid by the Reserve Bank on such occasions is not attractive, so that dealers only avail themselves of the facilities in the last resort. That is why the Central Bank is often referred to as 'buyer of last resort' as well as 'lender of last resort'. Dealers have to conform to strict rules laid down by the Reserve Bank. They have to submit returns once a month.

There is a market in Government loans approaching maturity. It is mainly in loans maturing within three years that dealers invest their call money. Deposits are £10,000 or multiples of £10,000. Dealers have to deposit a small percentage of their portfolios with the Reserve Bank.

Trading banks are not permitted to deposit their money with dealers, so that the latter depend on non-banking depositors, mainly business firms. Dealers are authorised to obtain overdrafts from banks up to a fixed limit and for short periods, but rates on such overdrafts are much higher than money market rates, so that dealers only use these facilities, like those offered by the Reserve Bank, when they are in urgent need of cash and are unable to raise it on acceptable terms by other means.

Funds of Local Authorities reach the money market through the intermediary of an official institution, the National Provident Fund.

There are unofficial dealers who are not subject to the strict regulations imposed on authorised dealers. On the other hand, they have no access to the lender of last resort.

(2) RE-PURCHASE AGREEMENTS

The securities sold to the Reserve Bank by dealers are sold on re-purchase terms. Dealers are also in a position to borrow from the Reserve Bank against short-term Government securities. Buy-back arrangements and loans from the Reserve Bank are for a minimum period of three days. The normal maximum period is one month but the Reserve Bank is prepared to consider applications for renewal.

Dealers obtain deposits from non-banking depositors against Government securities, and in such transactions too the buy-back system is applied. They often retain the securities and hold them on behalf the of depositors who receive a safe custody receipt. Trading banks often act as intermediaries between depositors and dealers.

One of the effects of the development of this money market has been an increase of demand for Government securities which could be employed by dealers as collaterals. This made the Government less dependent on the Reserve Bank for its financial requirements. The Reserve Bank does not engage in open market operations for the purpose of regulating the volume of the banks' liquidity, but from time to time it tests the market to ascertain its trend.

There were inter-bank transactions offsetting the reserve deficiency of one bank by the surplus reserve of other banks long before the development of the inter-bank deposit market in London, according to the Memorandum submitted by the Reserve Bank to the Radcliffe Committee in the late 'fifties. The Reserve Bank is authorised to engage in open market operations in commercial bills bearing two good signatures, or Treasury bills. But the market is not developed sufficiently to provide the authorities with adequate scope for open market operations. Lack of Treasury bills and strictness of regulations is mainly responsible for its inadequate development. This means that, even though the small resources of the country limit the potentialities of its money market, they could be expanded to some extent. But the division of the money market's small turnover between Wellington and Auckland is like 'splitting the atom'.

CHAPTER THIRTY-EIGHT

The Johannesburg Money Market

(1) OFFICIAL INITIATIVE

NEXT to the United States and Canada, South Africa has the most highly developed money market outside Europe. The explanation lies largely in the highly developed gold mining industry which attracted to Johannesburg sophisticated financial managements and various financial interests capable of laying the foundations and developing an advance money market mechanism. The mechanism was created on official initiative, through the establishment of the National Finance Corporation in 1949, for the purpose of making better use of liquid financial resources within the Union and at the same time attracting short-term funds from abroad. It concerned itself exclusively with large deposits, amounting to at least 100,000 rands. This institution was established jointly by the Reserve Bank and the private financial sector.

Further development of the market through private initiative too received official encouragement. Financial and industrial interests in the Union established a number of acceptance houses and discount houses. One of the latter bears comparison in size and in turnover with any of the London discount houses. Johannesburg discount houses play a part similar to those of London – they borrow deposits at call or at short notice, or fixed deposits mainly from banks, and invest the money in Treasury bills, acceptances, trade bills, or short-term Government securities. They have re-discounting facilities with the Reserve Bank.

(2) PRIVILEGES OF DISCOUNT HOUSES

One of the ways in which discount houses are encouraged is their exemption from various banking regulations which are applicable even to near-banks to the extent to which they are engaged in banking activities.

The call money market is often very active and the average

turnover is relatively high. Interest rates are very sensitive to seasonal and other influences. To a very large degree commercial banks and other banks subject to rules concerning minimum cash ratio adjust their ratios through lending or borrowing in the call money market. Discount houses, with their access to the lender of last resort, can fulfil a useful function in absorbing surpluses and covering deficiencies. Nevertheless open market operations by the Reserve Bank are essential to maintain balanced supply-demand relationship.

Although a ceiling was imposed from time to time to deposit rates, this ceiling does not apply to inter-bank deposit rates which are allowed to adapt themselves to supply-demand relationship, subject of course to monetary policy measures applied by the Reserve Bank.

(3) MARKET IN COMMERCIAL BILLS

In South Africa acceptance houses must be segregated from discount houses into separate firms. They, together with other banks, were responsible for the creation of a relatively substantial primary market in commercial bills. It would have developed to a much larger degree, as would the much smaller secondary market, largely because Johannesburg has become less dependent on London during the 'fifties and the 'sixties, if it had not been for the credit restrictions the South African authorities had to adopt to resist inflation.

In addition to the expansion of the banking community, various types of near-banks – finance houses, HP finance houses, building societies, etc. – came into being. They as well as the large mining combines, holding companies and trust companies often possess substantial liquid resources awaiting investment, which are available to the call money market or to the deposit market, or can be invested in market paper of various kinds. All near-banks have to comply with reserve requirements and other monetary regulations imposed on banks in so far as they carry out banking activities.

(4) INTER-COMPANY DEPOSITS

Largely as a result of credit squeezes, the inter-company market referred to earlier in this chapter developed very considerably in Johannesburg and to a less extent in other cities, long before such a market made its appearance in London in the late 'sixties. It came to be known as the 'grey market' as distinct from the 'black market' in deposits without securities or guarantees. Its turnover reached a very high figure in the 'sixties, and since it was outside the control of the monetary authorities they took steps to discourage its further expansion. This was done in part through action taken by the Registrar of Banks who informed non-banking corporations that if they should lend beyond a certain limit the rules of the strict banking legislation would become applicable to them. Banks were asked to limit their guarantees.

Another way in which the increase of the turnover in the 'grey market' was sought to be discouraged was by a request addressed by the Reserve Bank to all banks not to lend to business firms if there was reason to suspect that the borrowers intended to re-lend the money to other business firms instead of using it for their own normal requirements. The object of this exercise was to prevent firms which had not reached their credit ceiling with their banks from borrowing more for the purpose of re-lending the money at a profit to other firms which had reached their credit ceiling with their banks. As the banks were anything but pleased by the expansion of the inter-company market that circumvented the banking system, they willingly co-operated with the authorities in complying with their wish.

(5) TREASURY BILL TENDERS

Treasury bills are issued by weekly tenders and they are also on tap. Their use was encouraged at the early stages by discounting them at attractive rates, but in due course banks and other financial institutions and investors grew sufficiently used to them to obviate the necessity for the authorities to go out of their way to attract subscribers.

There is no cartel at Treasury bill tenders among discount houses or banks, apart from other reasons because they have to compete for the allocation of the bills with mining finance houses, which very often have large liquid funds available for temporary investment in Treasury bills, and with near-banks and business firms.

Although acceptance business is expanding, it serves primarily the purpose of financing domestic trade. Its use for special purposes was encouraged during some phases of the credit squeeze when acceptances and other forms of credit for financing 'strategic' supplies of goods as well as lending to public corporations were exempted from credit ceiling provisions.

One of the main reasons why the market for commercial bills has not kept pace with the expansion of the call money market is that, generally speaking, advances and overdrafts are preferred to acceptance credits. Mainly for this reason the secondary market in bills is not sufficiently large to enable the Reserve Bank to operate effectively its open market policy. For lack of commercial bills the investors referred to above absorb the available supply of Treasury bills, so that open market operations have to be executed largely through purchases and sales of Government loans.

(6) OPEN MARKET POLICY

It is not the object of the open market policy to determine the basic trend in the money market. The aim of the authorities is mainly to iron out excessive fluctuations and ensure the orderly working of the market by mopping up surpluses and covering deficiencies which might produce otherwise unwanted self-aggravating effects on interest rates.

The money market obtains much of its funds from non-banking sources – insurance companies, mining finance houses, building societies and other near-banks. It is a highly competitive market. Commercial banks have to compete for outside deposits with discount houses and acceptance houses.

In addition to straight purchases and sales of bills and short Government securities, transactions often assume the form of repurchase. This form was applied especially to the sale of Land Bank bills by the Reserve Bank to discount houses when the authorities wanted to mop up excess liquidity.

CHAPTER THIRTY-NINE

The Rhodesian Money Market

(1) DEALINGS IN SALISBURY

BEFORE the war and during the early post-war period Rhodesia depended almost entirely on London for money market facilities. More recently, however, years before the declaration of independence, a money market developed in Salisbury. The newly formed Bank of Rhodesia greatly assisted in its development. The provisions of the Banking Act, 1959, concerning reserve requirements made it necessary for banks to equalise surpluses and deficiencies in the local money market.

Banks and finance houses to which the Act applied transferred to Salisbury substantial amounts of liquid resources which were formerly held in London. Their reserves employed in the London market declined sharply in the early 'sixties. A money market has been in existence in Salisbury since the middle 'fifties. Treasury bills have been issued since 1957. Two merchant banks were founded in 1956 and now there are discount houses and acceptance houses.

(2) DISCOUNT HOUSES

Although the discount houses were formed on the pattern of the London discount houses, their operations are controlled less strictly by the Central Bank. When they have to borrow on penalty rates they can do so for shorter periods than the minimum of seven days which applies in London. There is a call money market, depending largely but not exclusively on money supplies lent by commercial banks. Small but expanding markets developed in trade bills and later in bank acceptances. But the bulk of the turnover is in Treasury bills which are issued by tenders. They have a very active secondary market, more active than the secondary market of commercial bills.

Payments to and by the Government considerably influence interest rates in the money market. The Bank of Rhodesia engages in open market operations to equalise discrepancies between supply and demand, which might otherwise affect interest rates in an unwanted sense or to an unwanted extent.

There is also a small primary market in deposits to HP finance houses which accept deposits from banks as well as from non-banking sources.

As a result of the severance of links between Britain and Rhodesia the latter came to depend on her own financial resources. Being isolated from London, banks and other lenders and borrowers had to take in each others' washing. This stimulated the development of the money market the mechanism for which had already been in existence. The market had survived the dissolution of the Federation, because Southern Rhodesia had been its wealthiest and financially most sophisticated member. The absence of financial support from London, however, slowed down the expansion of the money market's resources, even though the resources of Johannesburg are at its disposal.

CHAPTER FORTY

The Future of Money Markets

(1) PROGRESS IS LIKELY TO CONTINUE

HAVING regard to the remarkable progress of money markets all over the world during the last decade or two, it seems reasonable to hope that, in the absence of a major war or a disastrous economic crisis, this progress will continue – though not necessarily at the same rate as it did during the 'fifties and 'sixties. There is indeed ample scope for progress even in the most advanced financial centres. Some of their parallel money markets are still at an early stage of their development. They have already added some valuable facilities to the monetary mechanism of the centres concerned, and there is a strong incentive for further improvement of those facilities. Nor can the emergence of some entirely new devices be ruled out. After all, twenty years ago some of the parallel markets which are in full operation today had not even been thought of. It seems conceivable for instance that the next decade or two might witness the emergence of secondary markets in Local Authorities deposits, finance house deposits and even in inter-company deposit receipts.

The rules of even some of the new markets which have been in full operation for years are still in a state of flux. Their practices have not become standardised to anything like the same extent as those of the well-established traditional markets. And even the latter are subject to changes, partly as a result of the impact of the new markets on them and partly as a result of institutional and background developments that might occur.

(2) SCOPE FOR STUDY

What is perhaps more important from the point of view of future progress, the broader implications of the recent changes in the money market mechanism are still largely *terra incognita*. There is a great deal to learn about them to enable the monetary authorities to adopt the right attitude in face of the changed and ever-changing situation. The need for investigation has at long last come to be realised as far as the Euro-dollar system is concerned, because by the major trends it caused during the late 'sixties it forced itself to the attention of economists, administrators, politicians and bankers. But very little actual progress has been made so far. Other recently created parallel markets too deserve much more attention from the point of view of their broader implications than they have been given.

(3) ONE-SIDED EXPERIENCE

The trouble is that all experience gained in these markets is rather one-sided. Although the trend of interest rates had its ups and downs the markets have been operating, during their brief existence, against a substantially unchanged background of national and international economies – a virtually uninterrupted process of creeping but escalating inflation. There has been no opportunity so far for ascertaining how the new mechanism would behave against a background of some major crisis – other than foreign exchange crises of which we had ample experience – or against a prolonged self-aggravating depression. It would be necessary to examine the system of an immense volume of un-secured credits under a wider variety of conditions before either economists or those in charge of monetary and economic policies could reach conclusions about how it operates in the long run and what could and should be done to ensure that it should operate satisfactorily.

Apart from the super-money markets of Britain, the United States and Canada and from the leading countries whose money markets could, if they made an effort, achieve a comparable advanced stage, there are now a number of developed countries which have moderately advanced money markets capable of further progress. Former British Dominions, having achieved political independence, have become less dependent on London for money market facilities. Should Britain join the Common Market they would have to become even more self-reliant for facilities of short-term lending and borrowing. Developing countries such as India, having made some progress in adapting their money market mechanism to their economic development, are likely to further improve their money market facilities.

(4) OUTLOOK FOR ADVANCED MARKETS

In all probability countries with modern and advanced financial systems such as the whole of Western Europe and Japan, South Africa, Hong Kong, Singapore, etc., are likely to step up their progress towards the achievement of much more advanced money markets. In particular their bill markets, which leave much to be desired if indeed they exist at all, have an ample scope for improvement. Considering that they have all made remarkable economic progress since their recovery from the effects of the war, and that they have highly developed banking systems and strong currencies, the requirements and possibilities for the expansion and diversification of their money market facilities are there, and it is only a question of time before much fuller use will come to be made of their potentialities in this sphere.

(5) TREND TOWARDS INTERNATIONAL INTEGRATION

In the absence of major setbacks through economic or political crises, the trend towards the international integration of local money markets as well as of foreign currency deposit markets is likely to continue. This need not necessarily mean a disappearance or even a drastic reduction of interest differentials between countries, given the prevailing differences in the relative degree of risk and in economic and monetary policies. But provided that exchange control will be mitigated in the long run, the extent to which interest differentials are due to differences between supply-demand relationship in various countries will become reduced. Lenders and borrowers of short-term funds will take advantage of interest differentials in so far as they do not feel the need for covering the exchange risk, or to the extent to which the premium or discount on the forward exchange does not wipe out the advantage of the interest differentials.

(6) POSSIBILITY OF SETBACKS

This process of integration would suffer a reverse as a result of major bank failures which would weaken mutual confidence that is a basic condition of an expansion of money market operations. The adoption of floating exchange rates too would mean a setback in the progress towards integrated money markets, because fluctuating exchange rates would inspire distrust and might lead to a reinforcement of exchange controls and credit controls, at the same time as making it difficult to secure adequate forward exchange facilities at reasonable cost. A major deflationary depression too would reverse the progress in the sphere of money markets, for a multitude of commercial failures would necessarily inspire distrust. So far the few isolated suspensions such as the Penn Central crisis in the United States, the Rolls-Royce and Upper Clyde Shipbuilders liquidation in Britain, or the Finsec suspension in Australia, have not produced any spectacular adverse effect, though they did affect some of the markets quite appreciably. But it would be idle to deny that the gigantic and growing volume of unsecured and non-self-liquidating credits in the various new money markets have not created a highly vulnerable situation.

It seems reasonable to assume, however, that, should the worse happen, the resulting setback in the money markets would be purely temporary, even though in case of really grave crises the world might experience a prolonged setback. The eventual gradual recovery from a slump would be accompanied by an all-round return of confidence and the new money markets would gradually resume their former activities. Since the banks have acquired the know-how of the operation of new money markets they would apply it once more as soon as background conditions would justify it. The parallel money markets would not have to be re-invented, any more than markets in acceptances and other pre-war money market instruments had to be re-invented after the recovery from the crises of the 'thirties and from the Second World War. Any disastrous experience suffered through the crises would merely result in their more prudent initial application after their revival, though, human nature being what it is, the lessons taught by the crises would be forgotten should the world experience another prolonged period without a major crisis.

(7) AN INTEGRATED EUROPEAN MARKET?

A question worth examining in dealing with the future of money markets is the prospects of an integrated European money market in the E.E.C. The separate money centres which exist now are bound to remain in existence. It is arguable that the plurality of financial centres with local money markets in the United States, in Germany or in Switzerland has not prevented the development and continuous existence of integrated local money markets. But we must bear in mind that those countries possess an integrated economic and political system, integrated to a degree which countries of the Common Market are most unlikely to achieve. Economic conditions, requirements and policies in the member countries are bound to remain less monolithic than in Federal Republics such as the United States, Germany or Switzerland. Even a complete removal of exchange control between them would fail to lead to a complete monetary integration. Clashes between their basic aims and their preferred methods of monetary policies – such as the one that occurred in 1970–1971 between the French policy of monetary stability and the German policy of monetary flexibility – are bound to occur unless complete economic and political integration is achieved and the Common Market comes to be governed by one super-national Government and one super-national Parliament. So long as this remains a Utopian dream there can be no truly integrated Western European money market.

(8) COMPETITION *v.* OFFICIAL INTERVENTION

It is an open question whether the progress of money markets will be against a background of greater freedom in unhampered competition or whether the authorities will deem it necessary to intervene with them more actively. At the time of writing there appears to be a growing trend developing in favour of official intervention in Euro-currency markets. Quite conceivably the system that would emerge from a grave crisis would be a more closely regulated system. This would mean that the advantages of more flexible money markets would be sacrificed for the sake of a higher degree of security. The formula under which we could get the best of both worlds is yet to be invented.

(9) PROGRESS OF BACKWARD MARKETS

It is to be hoped that progress will not be confined mainly to countries which already possess advanced money markets. There is much wider scope for progress in countries which have only just created, or are on the point of creating, a money market. Most of them made or will make a start by the creation of an efficient local call money market. Their money markets might progress by providing facilities for increasingly long inter-bank deposits, discount markets, markets in Government paper and other more sophisticated markets.

On the face of it such a progress will be detrimental to the interests of London and other well-established money markets, since the number of countries depending on their facilities in the absence of any facilities nearer home will decline. On the other hand, the superior facilities of advanced markets, and the wider choice of facilities they can offer to lenders and borrowers, will secure additional clients for them in spite of the progress of local money markets in the countries concerned – indeed largely because of it.

Why is it that in spite of the progress achieved by many over-seas money markets during the last two decades this has not prevented a noteworthy expansion of the London money market's activities? The explanation lies in the fact that the creation of a call money market or a Treasury bill market in a country which had possessed none of these facilities until recently tends to make many of their institutional or individual borrowers and lenders of liquid resources more money-market minded. It is true, many of them who had been employing their liquid resources in London or in New York might conceivably withdraw some of their short-term investments for re-inevstment in their local markets. But many others who had kept their resources in the form of bank deposits for lack of familiarity with money market facilities will come to realise the benefits of a wider choice of such facilities that are available abroad.

On balance the advanced money markets are likely to gain rather than lose as a result of the development of money markets in less advanced countries, at any rate until the latter will become just as advanced as London or New York are today. But that is a very long time ahead, and in the meantime the advanced mar-kets are liable to become even more advanced than they are at present.

Whatever the future may bring, there can be little doubt that the last two decades have prepared the ground for progress towards better money market facilities, for the benefit of the economies of all countries concerned. Given an adequate degree of caution, it is not outside the limits of possibility to make these benefits lasting.

A Selected Bibliography

WHILE the literature on traditional British and American money markets could fill a fair-sized library, the published material on the new markets in London and in New York is largely confined to brief references to them in revised editions of pre-war textbooks, to articles in quarterly magazines of banks, to newspapers and magazine articles, and to booklets by banks and brokers.

Similar sources are also available about overseas money markets, traditional and new. Central Banks in particular have produced a wealth of material on their respective money markets. To mention only a few, publications by the Federal Reserve Board and by several Federal Reserve Banks cover between them the American parallel money markets in great detail.

The Bank of Japan published several books on the Tokyo money market. Other Central Banks too have provided a great deal of information on their respective money markets in their quarterly or monthly reviews and in their annual reports. American and other banks, also have published detailed descriptions of the markets with which they are concerned, primarily for the benefit of their clients but also for the benefit of scholars in quest of factual evidence on the new markets.

Official reports, such as the evidence of the Radcliffe Report, and the reports of various other Commissions investigating prevailing conditions and suggesting improvements – such as, for instance, the *Rapport sur le marché monétaire et des conditions de crédit* by R. Marjolin, J. Sadrin and O. Wormser – contain much first-hand information on money markets by first-rate experts on the subject.

Some books on comparative banking go into some of the details of money markets, though they usually treat the subject from the point of view of its impact on banking. Among others *Commonwealth Banking Systems*, edited by W. F. Crick; *Comparative Banking*, edited by H. W. Auburn; *Monetary Policy and Central Banking in India*, edited by V. R. M. Desai and B. D. Ghomasgi; and *Banking in Western Europe*, edited by R. S. Sayers, are worth mentioning.

The problem of students of American and Canadian money

markets, like students of the London markets, is one of *embarras de richesse*. There is also ample material on the German money market, especially by Helmut Lipfert, author of *Der Geldmarkt, Der deutsche Private-Diskontmarkt* and *Internationale Devisen- und Geldhandel*. Also by Günter Schmid, *Der deutsch Bankengeldmarkt*, and *Wirtschaftslehre des Kreditwesens*, by W. Grill and H. Perczybski. *Mecanisme et politique monétaire* by A. Chaineau, and *Le système monétaire français* by J.-P. Gauller cover the Paris money market which is also dealt with very thoroughly by an American, Holger L. Engberg, in *French Money and Capital Markets and Monetary Management*.

The Swiss market is dealt with in Max Ilke's *Die Schwiez als internationale bank- und finanzplatz*. M. Scheitenhauer produced a fair-sized book on the small Austrian money market under the title *Geldmarkt und Notenbank in Österreich*.

The Australian money market is discussed by W. G. Dewald, *Short-term Money Market in Australia*, and the Reserve Bank of New Zealand produced a useful little volume, *Money and Banking in New Zealand*.

The list could be prolonged indefinitely. But all the same, there is ample scope for further investigation. While comparative banking is a well-established subject, a comparative study of money markets needs more attention than it has received so far.

Index